David James Burrell

God and the people and other sermons

David James Burrell

God and the people and other sermons

ISBN/EAN: 9783337266127

Printed in Europe, USA, Canada, Australia, Japan

Cover: Foto ©Lupo / pixelio.de

More available books at **www.hansebooks.com**

God and the People

GOD AND THE PEOPLE

And Other Sermons

BY

David James Burrell, D.D.
Pastor of the Collegiate Church at Fifth Avenue and 29th Street,
New York

NEW YORK
WILBUR B. KETCHAM
7 and 9 West Eighteenth Street

CONTENTS

	PAGE
GOD AND THE PEOPLE	7
THE LORD'S HORSES AND CHARIOTS	21
OFFENDED IN CHRIST	31
THE GREAT DAY	41
PETER'S FALL	52
HOW FELIX LOST HIS OPPORTUNITY	62
THE SECRET OF POWER	74
AMERICA FOR CHRIST	85
THE ETHICAL IMPERATIVE	96
DON'T WORRY	105
THE TWELVE	116
AT THE WATER GATE	127
AT THE THRESHOLD OF JOSEPH'S HOUSE	139
THE BREVITY OF LIFE	149
THE DELAYS OF PROVIDENCE	158
WHAT IS THAT TO THEE?	167
RHODA, THE GATEKEEPER	178
THE MARKS OF THE LORD JESUS	189
SILENCE IN HEAVEN	199
WHERE THE PATHS MEET, SHE STANDETH	209
WAS CHRIST A CHRISTIAN?	220

	PAGE
THE SOVEREIGNTY OF GOD	230
MINT, ANISE AND CUMMIN	240
THE FIRST EASTER SERMON	252
THE GREAT LAW OF CHRIST	264
THE LOGIC OF EVENTS	274
PETER'S SALUTATORY	287
THREE HUNDRED YEARS	297
THE FORBIDDEN FRUIT	310
AT THEIR WITS' END	320
INDIFFERENT GALLIO	330
THE BATTLE OF THE TWO WILLS	341

GOD AND THE PEOPLE.

"Let the people praise thee, O God; let all the people praise thee."—Psalm 67, 5.

In a bay window overlooking the Strand in London sat Thomas Carlyle, pen in hand and eyes upon the madding crowd. "There are in the world," he wrote, "about thirteen hundred millions—mostly fools." He was not far amiss; only he should have added, *Quorum pars magna fui*.

These are the People: Immortal men and women jostling one another along the busy ways; intent on getting together a little yellow dust, chasing butterflies and thistle-down, grasping at laurel wreaths; men and women "with the geometry of heaven in their brain and the unfathomable galaxies," born of God and bound for immortality, killing time, caviling at destiny, flinging opportunity to the left hand and high privilege to the right; their eyes hot with passion and brows scarred by the plowshare of vain chastisement; blind to yesterday and reckless of to-morrow, ever furnishing forth the wedding feast with the baked meats of the last funeral; wielding the lash or cringing under it; leading the rattling chariots to death, or following in chains; singers and dancers;

kings and potentates; misers with muckrakes, profligates scattering ill-gotten gains; the Upper Ten-thousand treading on the heels of the Submerged Tenth, and the Third Estate bearing the burdens of both; all sorts and conditions of men—reeling, staggering, jostling—"mostly fools"; fools who, "forever hastening to the grave, stoop downward as they run." And we, alas! among them.

Who cares? *God cares.* The philanthropist who leaves him out of the reckoning is an arch-witling. God knows the People, sees their Mardi-gras of folly, pities their sorrows, and contemplates an ultimate deliverance. The Problem of History is before us: he alone interprets the logic of events. What seems a topsy-turvy world to us is calm evolution to him. We are impatient for the consummation: "How long, O Lord!" But the eternal years are his.

There is said to be a focal point above us where earth's discords blend in harmony. The clang of the workshop and the confused noise of battle, hosannas, misereres, moans of the death-chamber and midnight carousals, children's prattle and kings' manifestoes— all combine in one harmonic chord. At that high center is God's throne. There is the viewpoint from which he surveys the procession of the ages and sends forth edicts that make for the final restitution of all things.

To leave him out of our social science is to run without a message; to undertake any reform without him is to ensure a fiasco. To profess God and then reduce him to a practical nonentity, as Law, or All-pervading Force, or A-Something-not-ourselves-that-maketh-for-righteousness, is to juggle with words.

"The Specter saith, 'I wait!'
And at the last it beckons, and they pass;
And still the red sands fall within the glass,
And still the hands around the dial sweep;
And still the water-clock doth drip and weep;
And that is all!"

Is that all? Nay, our God has eyes to see, a heart to pity and almighty arms to save. He cares for the People, for the surging multitude. Better still, he cares for every one. He calleth them by name. He numbereth the very hairs of their heads. And in this he is no respecter of persons. Purple and homespun are alike to him. A man's a man. The meanest Zulu kneeling to a wooden fetich is as precious in his sight as the Baron Rothschild. He notes the guinea, not the guinea's stamp. To this Husbandman at the threshing floor the adventitious conditions which separate us into castes, as rich and poor, plebs and aristocrats, are but chaff which the wind driveth away. All are God's children and his love is alike toward all.

Three facts are in evidence: *First, his Providence.* We lay stress upon the contrasts—rags and ermine, Murray Hill and Mulberry Bend, crutches and carriages, the plumed hearse and the dead cart—and leap to the conclusion, "God's ways are not equal." But we see only an insignificant arc of the great circle. And we forget the difficulties that confront the Ruler of a rebellious world. Colonel Ingersoll says that if he were governing the human race, he could improve on the present administration; but there is probably no other man who thinks so. The joint wisdom of our national Executive and both houses of Congress was overtaxed by the demands of a paltry camp of 25,000 soldiers at Montauk. But (not to speak of hypothetical myriads of other worlds) here are some sixteen hundred millions of malcontents ("mostly fools") in arms against the divine authority; each differing from his neighbor in character and disposition, and every one clamoring for his rights. All things considered, we may venture the opinion that the God of Providence does fairly well. There is an equable distribution of air, sunlight, and other necessities. When the state-secrets of the divine government are revealed, we shall probably discover that food and medicine were administered with absolute fairness, and accurately adjusted to individual need. And considering, further, the compensations of eternity—where the crooked shall be made straight and the rough places smooth—it behooves us to speak with modest reserve of the inequalities of Providence. The God of the People is making all things work together for the best of each and all.

The second fact in evidence is Grace. Over against all complaints as to the divine administration, its injustice or partiality, let us place this manifesto: "God so loved the world that he gave his only-begotten Son, that whosoever believeth in him should not perish but have everlasting life." Here is no discrimination; but universal amnesty, on the sole condition that the rebel shall lay down his arms.

The Man, in whom God inshrined himself for the making of these overtures, was one in homespun, an average man. He belonged to the Third Estate. This is an immensely significant fact in the consideration of all philanthropic or sociological problems. Holman Hunt represents the Carpenter of Nazareth in his shop, chips and shavings around his feet, the implements of his trade on the bench before him. There he stands in the very coign of vantage for the arbitration of all social and industrial controversies. He was distinctly a man of the people, knowing their needs and sympathizing with them.

So much as to his personality; What now of his teaching? At this point we appeal to the universal consensus. In the doctrines set forth by Jesus of Nazareth, finding their magnificent consummation in the Sermon on the Mount, we have the only known social solvent. Put those principles in practice and you reconcile the lofty and the lowly, the king and his subjects, capital and labor. Put them in practice and you cut the sinews of war and make an utter end of injustice. The Golden Rule and that alone can usher in the Truce of God.

Now turn from the teachings of Jesus to his Cross. Here is the great answer to all complaints against the divine equity. The Son of God was crucified on a hilltop, beside the thoroughfare, in presence of the multitude, with his hands outstretched. He was the people's Christ. He tasted death for every man. The benefits of his vicarious death are offered on terms within the reach of all. "Ho, every one that thirsteth, come ye to the waters, and he that hath no money; come ye, buy and eat; yea, come, buy wine and milk without money and without price." The words of his gospel are great words, "all," "every one," "whoever," "whosoever." Here surely is no respect of persons. The same terms are offered to

Nicodemus,—Doctor of Divinity and LL.D. by grace of the Sanhedrin,—and the penitent thief standing on the crumbling verge of the abyss. Rabbis and fishermen, knights and friendless outcasts, vestals and magdalens, gathered around his cross. The sublimest deed of self-sacrifice that earth or heaven ever gazed on was enacted there. It was the fitting climax and consummation of Christ's work for the people. There was never a moment in his ministry when he could not have relieved himself from all danger by identifying himself with the aristocratic party. The Jews, led by their phylacteried rabbis, wished him to dispense salvation to them alone. His answer was: "As Moses lifted up the serpent in the wilderness, even so must the Son of Man be lifted up, that whosoever believeth in him should not perish, but have eternal life." This "whosoever" was the shibboleth of his redemptive crusade. He had compassion on the multitudes, seeing them as sheep without a shepherd. The philosophers by the Ilissus had elaborated a system for the learned few; Jesus set forth a gospel plain and simple for wayfaring men. Wherefore "the people heard him," "the people pressed upon him," "the common people heard him gladly." His devotion to the welfare of the masses—"the unshod multitude"—provoked the wrath of the ecclesiastical gentry. It was they who sentenced him to death; and dying he "tasted death for every man."

The third fact in evidence is the Church. And here we approach more nearly the matter in hand. For the objection taken by non-Christian Sociologists to the gospel as a leavening force, is directed not against Christ but against his faithless Church.

What is the Church? Not a coterie of good people; but sinners all, distinguished from other sinners only by their acceptance of Christ. Not a company of truth-seekers; they are not seeking truth but profess to have found it in the revealed Word of God. Not an Ethical Society, casting about for a trustworthy code of morals; this also they profess to have found in the Decalogue, the Sermon on the Mount, and the exemplary Jesus, who alone of men lived up to the full measure of this moral law.

What then is the Church? *The great living organism through which God is working, by the power of his Spirit, for the deliverance of the world from sin.* Its business is to save men.

But where shall it begin? Its first concern, in the necessity of the case, is with the immortal soul. For what shall it profit a man if he gain the whole world and lose his endless life? Here is where a secular philanthropist fails—fails at the outset, utterly and lamentably. He magnifies an handbreadth of time beyond the measure of the interminable æons. He pleads for higher wages and sends the wage-earner out into eternity without a penny to his name. He insists on an antiseptic for typhoid germs, leaving undisturbed the mortal, miasmatic reek of sin. He puts a roof over a man's head for threescore years, and turns him forth at last a homeless tramp. The "rule of three" puts this altruist to an open shame, thus; as the flight of an eagle is to the incalculable sweep of eternity so is the work of a secular philanthropist to that of a wise fisher of men.

The Church begins at the beginning. It saves a

sinner from the record of a mislived past by pointing him to Christ who alone has power to forgive sin. Without this, no matter how you improve a man's outward conditions, his life is that of an unabsolved convict who "drags at each remove a lengthening chain." One of the current problems of legislation is the formulation of a wise and equitable bankrupt law, which shall cancel a hopeless indebtedness with no unnecessary wrong, rehabilitate a stripped and shivering insolvent and set him on his feet again, a man among busy men. There is a corresponding problem in the larger province of life. The sinner is an utter bankrupt. "Turning over a new leaf" will not help him. An effort to "brace up" is at once grotesque and pathetic. His life is hobbled with ball-and-chain; handicapped by hopeless insolvency. What will you do with him? The Church brings him to Christ; who says, "Arise and stand upon thy feet; thy sins be forgiven thee!"

At this point the Church stands alone as the great reformatory agency. But here her default begins. "This ought ye to have done and not to have left the other undone." What is that other? *All philanthropic service.* The Lord enjoined upon his followers the deliverance of the whole man. It is a difficult matter to consider soul and body apart; as Tristram Shandy says, "They are like a jerkin and its lining; if you rumple the one, you rumple the other." This the Church has too often forgotten. Her Master was ever mindful of it. He fed the five thousand while he preached to them. He healed disease while probing for the sin beneath it. He denounced the Pharisees not more for blocking the gateway of heaven than for devouring widows' houses. He preached a religion which touches life at every point in its circumference; a religion as free, all-pervasive and irrepressible as the atmosphere, which rests upon every portion of the body with an equable and invariable pressure.

Just here the Church should welcome all just criticisms from without. Faithful are the wounds of a friend. But let censure keep within the boundaries of truth. For when the worst is said, it still remains that the Church is the great Philanthropic Society of the ages. All other agencies for the betterment of society have been but as glowworms to a lighthouse. Notwithstanding the shortcomings of the Church, there is more of benevolent power in her little finger than in the loins of all secular bodies. In the Charities Directory of the Borough of Manhattan there are above twelve hundred institutions for the relief of diverse suffering, and of these all that depend upon non-religious support can be counted on the fingers of four men. "The world before Christ," says Luthardt, "was a world without love." Back of the fallible Church stands Christ, her faultless champion. He has been the historic Friend of humanity. We may accuse his people of manifold sins and shortcomings; but as for Christ himself, we bow the knee and cry, "Hosanna!" His gospel is the world's only hope. His Church, with all its faults, has come through the centuries like Milton's angel with the flaming torch, the morning following in its wake. Let us be fair. The Church is not what it should be, but by the grace of God it is what it is.

But O the unrealized possibilities, the latent energy, the lamentable waste! Let all men call these to the remembrance of the followers of Christ. Let them exhort us to give heed not only to spiritual want, but to all the ills that human flesh is heir to. It is recorded that when Christ came to a village the people, advised of his approach, brought their sick and laid them on couches along the way. He opened blind eyes, healed withered arms, bade the paralytic stand upon his feet; and he left the village rejoicing and making merry because he had passed through it.

The business of Christ's people is to follow him. We are reminded by those who make no profession of religion that we have not faithfully followed him into the dense centers of population, the haunts of misery and shame. The point is well taken; we must not resent it. "But what has the Church to do with the hygienic conditions of the slums?" Much every way. The only approach to a soul is through the atmosphere that environs it. In one of Dr. Guthrie's letters he tells of visiting on a winter's day a woman dying in an attic, on whom all his earnest appeals made no impression. At length he said, "My good woman, do you not realize that you are passing into eternity? Do you care nothing that you must in a few moments stand before the Judgment bar?" She shivered as she drew the scant covering of her bed about her, and said, "No more would you, Dr. Guthrie, if you were as cold as I am."

We are reminded, furthermore, that the Church has a duty to perform in the controversy as to Capital and Labor. It was not a churchman who wrote the "Song of the Shirt," but his words from without broke the spell of Christian apathy and revolutionized the wage-system of London :

> " O men with sisters dear,
> O men with mothers and wives,
> It is not linen you're wearing out,
> But human creatures' lives ! "

Nor was it a churchman who wrote,

> " O ye wha are so guid yoursel',
> Sae pious and sae holy,
> Who've naught to do but mark and tell
> Your neebors' fauts and folly ;—
> O gently scan your brother man,
> Still gentler sister woman ;
> Though they may gang a kennin wrang
> To step aside is human."

But Robert Burns's outburst made the ears of all Zion to tingle and shamed the unco guid into a larger charity.

We are called to account, also, for our comparative indifference to political reform. This world would be a better world to live in—our land a better country; our cities less like Sodom—had the followers of the Nazarene Prophet been true to his injunction, "Render unto Cæsar the things that are Cæsar's." Alas! they have too meekly acquiesced in the squatter's claim: "This is Satan's preserve; no trespassing." Welcome the day when from any quarter the shame and cowardice of this ecclesiastical inertia shall be exposed. Cry aloud, all secular philanthropists, cry aloud and spare not; lift up your voices like trumpets and show the Church her sin!

And what shall be said of the Temperance problem? In a land where church spires point toward heaven from every hilltop, and where twenty-seven millions of people profess the worship of the true God, we spend one thousand millions per annum for strong drink. And where is the adequate protest? Does the Church make it? Aye, as the chirp of a lone sparrow on a housetop against the whirlwind sweeping on! In this Borough of Manhattan there are six thousand dramshops; side by side they make a twenty-five mile thoroughfare of licensed man-traps. These are confessedly the breeding places of political corruption; and we clamor for Municipal Reform! There can be no municipal reform while we tolerate these belching mouths of hell. Let the ax be laid at the root of the tree. And let judgment begin at the house of God.

O, there is much to be done before the bride shall make herself ready for her marriage with the King's son. Let the taunt of "the lapsed masses" and "the unchurched multitude" ring in her ears unceasingly. Let altruists who decline to call themselves Christians, put her in perpetual remembrance of her shortcomings. She needs to come into a closer and more sympathetic contact with the People. She needs a wider door of welcome and as comfortable a pew for the fellow-craftsman of her Lord of Nazareth as for the man wearing the gold ring. Too often she permits the legend of St. Sebald—who warmed himself in an open piazza at a fire of icicles —to be realized in her vestibules. Her sacred hospitality must shelter the rich and poor alike, since the Lord is the Maker of them all.—She needs a broader sweep in all her charitable enterprises. Let the Priest and the Levite be admonished by the good Samaritan, that if they would win the gratitude and fellowship of the wounded traveler, they must no longer pass by on the other side. O men and women of the Christian Church, have ye forgotten the Master's word, "Go out into the highways and hedges and constrain them to come in"? Go! Christ said it long centuries ago: the world repeats it now. Ye have stood too long in your doorways beckoning and pulling your bell-ropes. Go up into the attics, down into the basements, out into the slums, away to the uttermost parts of the earth! Where is the lantern that your Lord carried on the dark mountains? Where is the quick, responsive heart that heeds the distant cry for help? The great commission is unfulfilled. At the threshold of the Twentieth Century we hear the cry of twelve hundred millions still unsaved, "No man careth for our souls!" Awake, O Zion; shake thyself from the dust and loose thyself from the bands of thy neck! Put on thy beautiful garments, O daughter of Jerusalem, and let all the people know that thou bringest good tidings of great joy!

One thing more. If those who are seeking by secular methods to regenerate society would make their philanthropic influence tell to the utmost, let them fall in with the Militant Church, like Hobab of Akiba, and *lend a hand*. The place to clean house is indoors. Guerrilla service is a poor makeshift for campaigning. If the Christian Church with all her faults is the greatest of social forces, the place of true reformers is within her fellowship. To spend one's energies in the mere betterment of the physical environment of the people is to undertake to boil the kettle from the top. The greatest of sociological problems, when all is said and done, is to regenerate the moral nature of humanity and bring it into harmony with the social order of the universe. God and immortality must come into the reckoning. Leigh Hunt was a poor philosopher. No man who fails to recognize the supreme claims of the All-Father can be written down as "one who loves his fellow men": for the brotherhood of man rests on the Fatherhood of God. Let us by all means make a heaven here below, but alas for us if we see not another, a larger and eternal heaven beyond. This is the vision revealed in the gospel of Christ. The prisoner of Chillon, doomed to a solitary despair, saw a rift in his dungeon wall. Dragging his chain, he clambered upward and looked through. There lay the green valley with the silver river gliding through and the blue heavens over all. As he gazed through tears, a bird began to sing—

> "A lovely bird with azure wings,
> And song that said a thousand things,
> And seemed to say them all to me."

Our world is populous with sorrowing souls; it is for us to lighten the pains of their imprisonment, but, best of all, to help them upward to the window that opens toward the eternal life. This is to bring them, despite all narrowness of circumstance, into the glorious liberty of the children of God.

THE LORD'S HORSES AND CHARIOTS.

"And Elisha prayed, and said, Lord, I pray thee, open his eyes, that he may see. And the Lord opened the eyes of the young man; and he saw: and, behold, the mountain was full of horses and chariots of fire."—II. Kings 6, 17.

The man at the front is not the only one who serves his country. Elisha the prophet would doubtless have cut a sorry figure in managing a catapult, or in handling a bow; but he turned his talents to splendid account as a spy. His gift of spiritual insight enabled him to see what was going on in the secret chambers of the king of Syria; and he rendered an invaluable service to Israel by disclosing his plans.

The matter being reported to Benhadad, he determined forthwith to make away with the meddling prophet. A wise decision;—but "first catch your hare." He was told that Elisha, in company with a young man from the School of the Prophets, had gone to Dothan; and straightway troops were sent to invest the place.

The next morning bright and early the young man arose and climbed the walls; perhaps, to see the glory of the sunrise or the fields glistening with dew. But what a sight was this? Syrians! Syrians on every side! Yonder was the pavilion of the Commander-in-chief, with the royal standard waving over it.

Sentinels were pacing to and fro. Little wonder the youth was dismayed. He called Elisha, saying, "Alas, master, what shall we do?" The prophet replied, calmly, "Be of good courage; they that be for us are more than they that be against us." What could he mean? Then he prayed, "O Lord, open the eyes of this young man that he may see!" And he saw, and, behold, the mountain was full of horses and chariots of fire.

It was a great day for that young man. He was beginning his postgraduate course. For there are some parts of a man's equipment which cannot be acquired in college or in the curriculum of professional schools. John Brown of Haddington said to one of his theological classes, "Young men, there are three things necessary to your success as ambassadors of Christ: one is grace, which the Lord stands ready to give you; the second is knowledge, which I have done my best to impart; but the third is common sense—and if you have not that, neither God nor man can help you." And there are other branches of learning, besides common sense, which can only be acquired by contact with the world and a practical acquaintance with men. Our youth at Dothan was learning some things of great value, things to ponder about and preach to the people in after days.

It must have dawned upon him at the outset that his eyes were not so good as he had supposed them to be. There is, indeed, an optic nerve that lies dormant until God touches and thrills it. In our natural state we are myopic and "cannot see afar off." Poor eyes of ours! We see "as in a glass darkly;" that is, by reflection. The atmosphere is hazy, the mirror is blurred, the image distorted. We reason from poor premises, and our conclusions are partial and inadequate. But one day the shadows will lift and we shall "see face to face and know even as we are known."

Meanwhile we do wisely to acknowledge the imperfection of our vision. "There are" as Hamlet said, "more things in heaven and earth than are dreamt of in our philosophy." We are bond slaves of the senses; refusing to believe in what lies beyond the reach of fleshly eyes and finger tips. Wherefore, "we know in part and we prophesy in part." The great world—the world of eternal realities and certitudes—is ever beyond us. But there is a better day coming, when we shall see with our Master's eyes; "when he shall appear we shall be like him; for we shall see him as he is."

The prayer of Elisha was heard. The eyes of the young student were opened and he caught a glimpse of things unseen and eternal. It marked a turning-point of his life. He could never again be the same man.

I. *He formed, that day, a new conception of God.* In the School of the Prophets he had devoted his particular attention to theology; that is the science of God. He had learned to define the Deity in such terms as are familiar to us: "God is a Spirit, infinite, eternal, and unchangeable in his being, wisdom, power, holiness, justice, goodness and truth." He had theorized about his attributes. He had estimated his stature in terms of arithmetic and measured his stately steppings with a span. He had speculated about him as an invisible and impalpable somewhat to be assumed as the convenient basis of a doctrinal system. But now he perceived that he was the living, all-pervading, immanent One. So Moses in the desert of Midian, seeing the bush burning and not consumed, said, "I will draw near and inspect this wonder." And, lo, a voice from the burning bush said, "Take off thy shoes from off thy feet, for the ground whereon thou standest is holy ground. I AM THAT I AM." It is a great moment for any man when he begins to apprehend God as a personal Factor in the affairs of nations and men.

The prophet and this youth were compassed about by their foes. It now became apparent that God had not forgotten them. He is indeed "a very present help in time of trouble," "a refuge from the storm, a shadow from the heat, when the blast of the terrible ones is as a storm against the wall." Here is sinking Peter; a helping hand is reached forth to him. Here is doubting Thomas; a hand pierced with the irrefutable logic of the atonement is stretched out to him, with the word, "Be not faithless, but believing!" Here is dying Stephen; amid a shower of stones, he beholds his Lord standing on the right hand of the Father, extending a hand of gracious welcome to him.

God wills that his people shall not fret nor worry; because he is always near by. "My foes compass me about like bees," sings David; "they are quenched as the fire of thorns; for in the name of the Lord I will destroy them!" He is recalling an incident of his boyhood, when he thoughtlessly molested the hive and the bees came swarming about him, buzzing, stinging; contemptibly small and irresistibly pestilent. So are the worries of life. They make our days melancholy and our nights sleepless. I know of no deliverance save in the thought of a present God. Our foolish fret and groundless fear are quenched as a fire of thorns when we realize that our Father knoweth and is mindful of us. Here is a great truth for common uses. In all Christ's teaching there is nothing more helpful than this: "Consider the lilies of the field, how they grow; they toil not, neither do they spin; and yet I say unto you that Solomon in all his glory was not arrayed like one of these. Are ye not of much more value than they?"

II. *The young man gained, moreover, on that memorable day, a new apprehension of History.* If you had asked him concerning the war then being waged, he would probably have told you that the parties immediately concerned were Jehoram and Benhadad. He had yet to learn that kings and potentates are but puppets in the hands of the Omnipotent.

> "He maketh kings to sit in sovereignty;
> He maketh subjects to their power obey;
> He pulleth down, he setteth up on high;
> He gives to that, from this he takes away:
> For what he will do, that he may.

God is ever present in the affairs of nations as of men. "The kings of the earth set themselves and the rulers take counsel together, saying, 'Let us break his bands asunder and cast his cords from us.' He that sitteth in the heavens shall laugh; the Lord shall have them in derision." What is history but the stately steppings of the Almighty along the ages? He is determining the outcome of every conflict with a view to his own glory in the setting up of his kingdom.

Pharaoh said, "I have the children of Israel shut up between the mountains and the sea." But God outwitted him, lifting the waters in crystal walls, that his people might go through dryshod.

Herod said, "If it be true that a new King is born in Bethlehem, I will speedily dispose of him." There was a voice of lamentation in Ramah, Rachel weeping for her children; but while Herod's men were bathing their swords in the blood of the innocents, the Christ-child was far away.

Philip of Spain determined to send an armada against the Protestant nations that should put a speedy quietus on their heresy. God said, "I will breathe on Philip's fleet." *Deus afflavit!* And lo, the great armada was scattered like driftwood on a hundred shores. Outwitted again!

The King of England led forth a magnificent army of cavaliers against the Covenanters. He looked over the brow of the hill and said, "Behold yon handful of Scots! They are on their knees. Up, brave men, and at them!" The cry was, "Ho for Cavaliers!" But the handful of Scots met them with a braver and calmer shout, "God with us!" And Edward's army was scattered like chaff before the wind. Thus God ever outwits the enemies of his people and maketh the wrath of men to praise him.

> "O, blest is he to whom is given
> The instinct that can tell
> That God is on the field, when He
> Is most invisible."

III. *The youth learned, also, in that day of revelation, that the world is larger than he had imagined.* Had he been asked the dimensions of the world, he would have said: "It is bounded on the north by Dan, on the south by Beersheba, on the east by the Euphrates, and on the west by the Great Sea." We are all living in our vicinage. We refuse to believe that there is anything beyond the crest of the hill. But, indeed, there is much beyond. There are nations stretching out earnest hands to us. The land of duty and responsibility lies largely past the Pillars of Hercules. We are little people because we choose to live in a little world.

And upward the outlook is larger still. Let us not shrink from accepting the doctrine of angels. The unseen world is infinitely more populous and nearer than we think. There is nothing irrational in the thought that invisible beings are all around us. The old poet, Hesiod, said: "Thrice ten thousand guardians of mortal men walk the broad, life-feeding earth. Enwrapped in air, they scan the good and evil deeds of men." Milton wrote:

" Millions of spiritual creatures walk the earth
Unseen, both when we wake and when we sleep."

Our youth, in the School of the Prophets, had doubtless read of Jacob's dream. He had questioned with his fellow students whether it was only a dream; or were these real angels passing up and down? To-day he understood. He saw beyond the overhanging bank of clouds the hierarchies of angels and archangels. Who shall number the Lord's host? It is like the sands of the seashore for multitude. Myriads on myriads! Armies on armies! The young man at Dothan saw merely a detachment of the vanguard;

but he began to realize that he was a living part of a great universe of rational beings, which includes angels and saints triumphant waiting at the throne of God.

IV. *And in the new light that dawned upon him, life seemed a more serious thing.* He had discussed at school the question of immortality *pro* and *con:* "If a man die, shall he live again?" Now he knew. Life is brief indeed; an handbreadth, a swift eagle hastening to its prey, a dream, a shadow, a tale that is told. "Out, out, brief candle; life's but a walking shadow!"

But what of the sequel? Life must be measured in terms of eternity. Otherwise it is not worth living. What we call life is but the opening chapter of an endless serial. It is the vestibule of an infinite temple; we climb the weary steps and reach the gates with panting breath, and knock; and an angel with shining face opens to us, saying, "I am he whom you have maligned as 'the King of Terrors.' Come in, and begin to live!"

Our present years are probationary to eternity. Herein lies their grandeur and solemnity. We are soon going to join the majority. We are destined to the incalculable possibilities of an endless future. What we are to be there depends upon what we make of ourselves here and now. As the tree falleth, so shall it lie.

In view of the revelations of that day at Dothan it is safe to say that the young student looked forward to the ministry with new plans and purposes. He had learned some things which cannot be gotten out of books. He could no longer think of himself as a prophet rendering a merely perfunctory service. When the saintly McCheyne lay dying, he opened his eyes and said, "I have looked into eternity! O, if I could come back now and preach! If I might but meet my people once again in the light of these revelations!" Ah, we should all be better preachers and better men if our eyes were opened to see things as they are.

O for open eyes! It was to this end that Christ visited the world. He came to show us God in a new light, as an ever present, ever living, ever potent One. He came to give us new conceptions of the world and the solemnities of life. He came to show us ourselves, so little in the sight of the Infinite and in comparison with the vast universe; and yet so great, having in our nostrils the divine breath, elect to be colaborers with God and destined to share his immortality. "How poor, how rich; how abject, how august; how complicate, how wonderful, is man! An heir of glory, a frail child of dust! A worm, a god!"

Let us make the prayer of Bartimeus, "O that I might receive my sight!" There was a world of life and beauty all around him, and he, blind beggar, had never seen it. "O that I might receive my sight!" Jesus heard him; and in an instant all was revealed; the sky above, the green meadows, the purple vineyards, the olive orchards. O the joy of seeing! But faith gets larger visions still, of God and immortality, of truth and goodness, of present duty and boundless vistas of influence. Why shall not our revelation come just now? Jesus of Nazareth passeth by. Make your prayer, "O that I might receive my sight!" Then, behold the King in his beauty; and stand ready at his word. "Say not, It is yet four months, and then cometh the harvest. Lift up your eyes and see; the fields are already white unto the harvest." Thrust in your sickle and reap! In view of all the solemnities and possibilities of life, here and hereafter, let us address ourselves to present responsibility. We live for eternity. Let us live for our Master, live to-day!

OFFENDED IN CHRIST.

"From that time many of his disciples went back, and walked no more with him."—John 6, 66.

The incident here referred to occurred on the day following the multiplication of the loaves. On the further shore of Gennessaret the Lord had been preaching to the multitudes. It was at the time of the Passover, and the road was thronged with pilgrims on their way to Jerusalem. Many turned aside to hear the great Preacher. The day closed with the miracle of the loaves. So deeply were the people impressed by the words and works of Jesus that they proposed to make him a king. "We are on our way to Jerusalem," they said, "where we shall meet a multitude from all parts of Jewry, thronging the streets and encamped on the hillsides. Why not employ the opportunity to deliver ourselves from the Roman yoke? Let us escort this Wonder-worker to Jerusalem, place him on the Davidic throne and raise the cry, 'God save the king!'" But Jesus knew their purpose and determined to thwart it; to this end he withdrew again into the mountain himself alone. Later, when he did not return, his disciples went down to the shore and embarked for Capernaum, while storm-clouds were gathering over the lake.

The next morning these pilgrims, resuming their journey, rounded the lake and came to Capernaum, and there they found Jesus. "Rabbi," they asked, "when camest thou hither?" He gave them no answer. The fact was that, as the night closed in and the tempest fell, he had seen from his mountain solitude the disciples toiling at the oars; and he had come to them walking on the sea. At his command the waves were stilled; and in the boat with his disciples he reached Capernaum before the pilgrims, who followed early in the morning.

He gave no heed to their inquiry, "When camest thou hither?" because he had somewhat to say more clearly to the point; namely, "Ye seek me not because ye perceived the deep significance of my miracles, but because ye did eat of the loaves and were filled." It was a merited rebuke and quite true; but indeed it was not a pleasant thing to say. The speaker was unmindful of that stringent rule of dialectics which requires him to win the confidence of his audience at the outset. How much wiser, apparently, was Paul's exordium on Mars' Hill: "Ye men of Athens, I perceive that ye are exceedingly devout." But Jesus was no word-juggler, no weaver of compliments; his introduction was an arrow speeding to the mark.

Then followed one of his most remarkable discourses, touching some of the deepest problems of the spiritual life; containing not a word of clever adulation, but much of profound, heart-searching truth. The further he proceeded, the more did he alienate his audience. "These are hard sayings," they murmured; "who can hear them?" One by one they dropped away, until he was left with a mere handful of the faithful. It was a stampede; and little wonder. Fair-weather Christians are ever offended by downright truth; and they are ever falling away, turning backward and following him no more.

It is a mistake to suppose that we can accept Jesus without approving his doctrine. No half-way approach will answer; no piecemeal approval can satisfy him. It is not enough to rhapsodize about his Sermon on the Mount; we must accept with equal heartiness his Sermon to the Pharisees, "Woe unto you, hypocrites; how can ye escape the damnation of hell!" It is not enough to approve his miracles of healing at Bethesda; we must consent, also, to the withering of the fig-tree. The parables of the Good Samaritan and the Prodigal Son, all sweetness and light, must be coupled with those of Dives and Lazarus and the Wheat and the Tares. The word of the Master, "He that believeth shall be saved" is no truer than its obverse, "He that believeth not shall be damned." His teaching must be accepted in its entirety, without demur or reservation. And this suggests why so many were and are still offended in him.

The first doctrine which gave offense to the multitudes on this occasion was that of Christ's Divinity. He said, "I am come down from heaven"; and "This is the will of the Father who sent me, that of those whom he hath given me, I should lose none but should raise them up at the last day." In this "coming down" and being "sent of the Father," we have a clear reference to his pre-existence. It is like a paraphrase of John's saying, "In the beginning was the Word, and the Word was with God, and the Word was God;

and the Word was made flesh and dwelt among us."

The people were perplexed and bewildered by this doctrine. "How is it that he saith, 'I came down from heaven'? Is not this Jesus, the son of Joseph the carpenter, whose mother and father we know?" There are many in our time also who are willing to believe that Jesus was an excellent man; that there was no guile in his heart, nor guile on his lips. Nay, they will go further; he was the very highest exemplification of manhood and truest character; the best of mortal men. Thus Renan, an avowed unbeliever, closes his biography of Jesus with the words, "Whatever may be the surprises of the future, Jesus will never be surpassed. His worship will grow young without ceasing; his legend will call forth tears without end; his sufferings will melt the noblest hearts; all ages will proclaim, that, among the sons of men, there is none born greater than Jesus." But this is not enough; by the stern necessity of logic, we must go further or turn back.

Others are willing to receive him as prophet—an ambassador with a message. They perceive how he touched the great problems of spiritual truth by which the philosophers of his time were perplexed and bewildered, cutting the Gordian knots. He set forth God and immortality, judgment and eternal glory, as an eye witness. He spoke "not as the scribes, but as one having authority." The Rabbis were amazed at his profundity; the common people heard him gladly. It is a proverb, "He spake as never man spake." All this may be admitted, and Christ rejected still. This is not enough. In common reason, we must go further or turn back.

The claims of Jesus were explicit. To the woman of Samaria who had spoken hopefully of the coming of the Messiah he answered, "I that speak unto thee am he." To Philip, who had said, "Show us the Father, and it sufficeth us," he replied, "Have I been so long time with you, and yet hast thou not known me, Philip? He that hath seen me hath seen the Father; how sayest thou then, Show us the Father? Believest thou not that I am in the Father and the Father in me?" To the young ruler who prostrated himself before him, crying, "Good Rabbi!" he made quick response, "Why callest me good? There is none good but one; that is God." In other words, he was either more or less than "Good Rabbi." There must be no half-way concession; it was Godhood or nothing for him. And when doubting Thomas, overwhelmed by the testimony of his piercéd hands, prostrated himself with the cry, "My Lord and my God!" he uttered no disclaimer. We have, therefore, no alternatives but these: we must either pronounce him a charlatan and an impostor, or else acquiesce in his tremendous claims and yield him homage as our Lord and God.

The second doctrine by which the people were offended that day was Justification by Faith. The sermon of Jesus turned on the similitude of bread suggested, no doubt, by the miracle of the loaves. He said, "I am the bread of life. Your fathers did eat manna in the wilderness and are dead. I am the living bread which came down from heaven, of which if a man eat he shall never die. And the bread that I will give is my flesh, which I will give for the life of the world."

The meaning is plain: he presents himself *as their Saviour from sin*. Of all that multitude of pilgrims there was not one who was insensible of guilt, or who did not desire to be delivered from it. Else why had they journeyed from afar to partake of the paschal lamb? The figure is most expressive; bread is "the staff of life." So is Jesus, to an immortal soul, the way, the truth, the life.

And here, furthermore, is a suggestion of *the plan of salvation, salvation by the cross*. "The bread which I will give is my flesh." This bread must be broken; it is broken on Calvary. He was wounded for our transgressions and bruised for our iniquities, that by his stripes we might be healed. He took upon himself the burden of our sins, and bore them on his mighty heart until it broke. He suffered death that we might live through him.

And further, it suggests *the condition on which a soul receives the benefit of the great redemption:* "He that believeth shall be saved." Faith is acceptance. It is not the lamb on the altar, but the blood sprinkled on the door posts, that averts the sword of the destroying angel. It is not bread on the table that satisfies our hunger, but bread eaten and assimilated, so that it becomes bone, sinew, brain, our very selves. Wherefore he said, "Except ye eat the flesh and drink the blood of the Son of Man, ye have no life in you."

This is the hardest of all the hard sayings of Jesus; it is "the offense of the cross." A thousand excuses are given for rejecting Christ, but back of them all is a natural repugnance to free grace. Our pride revolts at a salvation "without money and without price." It were easier for men to undertake a pilgrimage to

Mecca or the Ganges than to consent to be saved *gratis*. Yet this is the gospel plan. "The Jews require a sign, and the Greeks seek after wisdom; but we preach Christ crucified, to the Jews a stumblingblock, and to the Greeks foolishness; but to them that are saved, Christ the power and the wisdom of God."

The third of the hard sayings of Jesus, by which the multitude were repelled, was the doctrine of the Kingdom. He said, when they murmured, "Doth this offend you? What and if ye shall see the Son of Man ascending up where he was before?"—that is, to reassume the glory which he had with the Father before the world was. There he sits to-day, "expecting until his enemies shall be made his footstool." He superintends from that high place the setting up of his kingdom by the deliverance of the world from sin.

It was perhaps too much to expect that the people would receive this truth. The contrast was too great. There he stood; a man in homespun, the carpenter's son, a man of the people. Some of his hearers, perhaps, had seen him in his shop mending the plows and furniture of the village folk. And he claimed to be the heir-apparent of the heavenly throne! They had been willing in their enthusiasm to bestow upon him the Judæan crown; but that was nothing to him. A mere bauble! He awaited a crown of stars; and the kings of the earth should bring their glory and honor to him.—It was indeed a hard saying; who could hear it?

But there is no such reason for rejecting the doctrine of the Kingdom now. We have the testimony of history. This Jesus of Nazareth has come down through the centuries, a most majestic Figure, with a light shining from his face that has long since penetrated the regions lying in darkness and the shadow of death. He has marked out with his scepter the ever-enlarging boundaries of the mystic circle which we call "Christendom." At his approach the doors of the benighted nations have opened to the proclamation of the evangel. The logic of events adds new force to the argument with each succeeding day. The conquest of the Soudan, the rending asunder of China, the partition of Africa are mere episodes along the march. Thoughtful men and women, can ye not discern the signs of the times? Who is this that cometh from Edom with garments dyed in blood? From the distant hills where the banner of the cross waves over an ever-victorious host, returns the answer, "I that speak in righteousness, mighty to save!"

The visible token of Christ's kingdom is his Church. Who shall explain the Church? Here is the great miracle of the ages. See the little group emerging from the upper chamber, "a feeble folk" like the conies, a group of humble fishermen and toiling men. The wrath of kings and potentates goes forth against them; "Let us whet our swords and kindle the fagots; we will exterminate them!" But past the fagot-fire and ax and gallows tree, on they come along the centuries; thousands, tens of thousands, millions now; and still the royal standard onward goes. To-day there is a great multitude whom no man can number in goodly fellowship; the air is resonant everywhere with their chorus, "All hail the power of Jesus' name!"

And the progress of the past is a foregleam of the apocalypse. The prophecy of the Kingdom draws near its fulfillment. Jesus shall surely reign from the river unto the ends of the earth. And the sorrow is that men, busy amid the sordid affairs of life, are blind to the rising of this "house magnifical." They go about their small affairs, getting together a little yellow dust, chasing butterflies and grasping after laurel wreaths, oblivious of the fact that the Omnipotent has made bare his arm, and that multitudes of earnest men are laboring together with him for the betterment of the world in the setting up of this kingdom of truth and righteousness. They live for things that perish, spend their money for that which is not bread, die of soul hunger; and the world pronounces them successful. The most brilliant life, unmindful of the Kingdom, is stupendous waste. On many a tombstone of king, statesman, millionaire, let this be written: *Here lies one whose life was a failure. He amassed wealth, found pleasure, was crowned with honor; but dying, he went out into eternity a pauper before God.*

The man who undertakes to reason against the logic of events has a hopeless task before him. The words of Jesus with reference to his own ultimate triumph, are indeed an hard saying when set over against the personality of the carpenter's son; but it is impossible to resist them when we lift our eyes on what he has wrought in the progress of the centuries. As Alexander the Great was advancing through the Orient, he asked of a provincial governor the privilege of passing through his territory. The answer was, "I will call my counselors and deliberate." The great conqueror retorted: "You may deliberate, but I shall be marching on." A man may reject Christ, may refuse to receive his doctrines or admit his claims. This however is certain: with or without him, the Lord of righteousness will pursue his triumphal course among the nations and children of men.

It is written that when the people heard these sayings of Jesus, "many of them turned back, and walked with him no more." There they go! Away from Christ; offended by his frankness; all needing him and dying for want of him. There they go; their backs upon the noonday, their faces toward the night. *Will ye also go with them?*

A little group still gathered about Jesus. He asked them, "Will ye also go away?" And Peter answered, "Lord, to whom shall we go? Thou hast the words of eternal life; and we have believed and are sure that thou art the Holy One of God." To whom, indeed, can we go? Is there any other who can satisfy us with spiritual truth? Alas! none. This Jesus alone has the words of eternal life; and blessed are they that are not offended in him.

THE GREAT DAY.

"He hath appointed a day, in the which he will judge the world in righteousness."—Acts 17, 31.

It is the Apostle Paul who makes this announcement. The "ugly little Jew," as Renan calls him, was a wonderful preacher. He had made such an impression upon the people of Athens in his disputations in synagogue and market-place that he was brought up to Areopagus for a better hearing. It was an historic pulpit; here Socrates had made his apology, and Demosthenes had uttered "breathing thoughts in burning words." Paul was equal to the occasion. His text was the inscription upon an altar in the market-place, "To the unknown God." In his discourse he showed himself a master of dialectics. In rounded periods he set forth the nature and attributes of the invisible God. He drew upon his familiarity with Greek literature for an apt quotation,—"We are also his offspring." The audience that sat upon the stone steps below him listened with respectful interest until he ventured to speak of the Judgment: "He hath appointed a day in which he will judge the world in righteousness by that man whom he hath ordained; whereof he hath given assurance unto all men, in that he hath raised him from the dead." At this point the sermon was interrupted by derisive outcries and the assembly was broken up.

Why is it that we are so averse to a frank consideration of this theme? We are like children frightened in the dark. "What fools we mortals be!" Horace Smith said, "If a general collection were taken to head off the Judgment, the great Jehovah would get all our gold and the world would go begging forever." The congregation asks for pleasant platitudes, and the preacher shrinks from declaring the whole counsel of God. Yet our faces are turned toward the Judgment, and the issues of eternity are there. Let us, like men, confront it.

As to final retribution there is a universal consensus. The heart of the race trembles with "a certain fearful looking-for of judgment." The words of Longfellow,

> "The mills of God grind slowly,
>   But they grind exceeding small;
> Though with patience he stands waiting
>   With exactness grinds he all."

were transcribed from the German, and previously from an Oriental couplet running back beyond the memory of man:

> "God's mills grind slow,
>   But they grind woe."

It stands to reason that the present order of things cannot be final. We are living in a topsy-turvy world. There is little of justice or equity in human relations. The wicked man prospers, makes merry all his life on the profits of evil deeds, is followed to the tomb by an imposing procession, and transmits his name to posterity in a carven catalogue of virtues. The righteous meanwhile lives from hand to mouth and dies with none so poor to do him reverence. Dives arrayed in purple and fine linen fares sumptuously every day; while virtuous Lazarus, sitting at his gate, begs for the crumbs that fall from his table. Is there, then, no justice? A Scotch woman came to her pastor complaining of poverty, "There are so many mouths and so little bread." He comforted her with the assurance that the gracious God who sends mouths sends loaves as well. "Aye, minister," she answered, "but whiles it happens he sends the mouths to ane hoose and the loaves to anither." It was a fair statement of the present order. What shall we conclude, then? *There must be a final adjustment.* If there is a God in heaven, he must level down and level up and balance the books. As Anne of Austria said to Richelieu, "God is a sure Paymaster; it may not be to-day, nor to-morrow; but presently, my Lord Cardinal, he will administer justice betwixt thee and me."

The teaching of the Scripture as to this matter is very clear. Its response to the universal intuition and reason is Yea and Amen. "God hath appointed a day in which he will judge the world." Now it is called the Day of Reckoning, in which the Master requires his servants to give an account of the talents entrusted to them. Now it is the Day of Ingathering, when the Husbandman gathers the wheat into his garners and casts the tares into the fire. And now it is the Marriage Day, when the wise pass in to mingle in the merrymaking of the Bridegroom's house, while the foolish stand without, knocking and crying vainly, "Lord, Lord, open unto us!" But always it is the Great Day. It is the day toward which all the solemn hopes and purposes of the present life are tending, and out of which proceed the momentous possibilities of eternity.

The Scriptures speak, with reference to the general Judgment, in terms of oriental imagery. Indeed, all great spiritual truths are conveyed in parables. We are but children, and God must stoop to kindergarten methods if he would instruct us. Yet there are little people who overlook the stupendous truth in their eagerness to pick flaws in the metaphor. They ask, "Is the adjudication to be held within a solar day?" "And will it be ushered in, do you mean, with the blowing of a ram's horn?" These are the cheeseparers of scholarship—mere triflers, who turn their microscopes upon the jot and tittle, while heedless of the revelation that glows and lightens around them. They waste their privilege, like Charles II, who busied himself in sticking pins through moths and butterflies, while Dutch William and his fleet were sailing up the Thames to capture his crown.

Let us address ourselves to the solemn truth. The drama of destiny is before us. We shall best arrive at a proper apprehension of the Judgment if we view it through the metaphors of Scripture. What, then, are the accessories of that day?

I. *The Trumpet.* What does it mean? Resurrection. "For, behold, I show you a mystery; we shall all be changed, in a moment, in the twinkling of an eye, at the last trump: for the trumpet shall sound, and the dead shall be raised." It is the reveillé of the sleeping multitude; to some like a Tyrolean wake-song, to others a tocsin of doom. "The earth and the sea shall give up their dead." The dust of those who sleep in all graveyards—dust from the unknown mountain paths, dust from the coral crypts of mid-ocean—all shall reassemble and come forth to judgment. Adam and Eve will be there; the antediluvians, patriarchs and prophets; Pilate and the rabbis of the Sanhedrin, the noble army of martyrs; saints and sinners of all ages; our soldiers who fell in the trenches before Santiago—all there; *and you and I among them.*

But how can these things be? The earth is a vast cemetery. The very dust that blows along our streets is dust of the dead. Nevertheless with God all things are possible; nothing is too hard for him. Shall he who originally created man by a fiat be unable to restore his ashes, though scattered to the winds? In A. D. 117, in the persecution under Marcus Aurelius, a long procession of Christian martyrs was brought to the stake. When the holocaust was over, the emperor caused their ashes to be thrown on the waters of the Rhone, which would carry them to the sea, saying, "Let us see if the God of the Christians can restore these to life!" But who art thou that opposest thyself to the Almighty? Thou dost err, not knowing the power of God. At the sound of the trumpet all shall awake and stand before him.

II. *The Throne;* the great white throne. What does it mean? The rounding-up of history. This is the vision that Daniel saw in a vision upon his bed: the winds of heaven strove upon the sea, and four great beasts came up, diverse one from another; a lion with eagle's wings, a bear with a carcass between its jaws, a winged leopard, and a nondescript, terrible and strong exceedingly, with iron teeth and monstrous feet of power.   These were the great powers—Babylonia, Medo-Persia, Macedonia and Rome.   One by one they vanished, and a throne was set in heaven, and one came like unto the Son of Man, to whom was given dominion and glory and a kingdom, that all people should serve him.   This is the parable of history.   Its consummation is the great white throne. Look to your eyes!

> " The head that once was crowned with thorns
> Is crowned with glory now."

The Princess Wilhelmina of Holland was recently enthroned with demonstrations of almost unparalleled splendor. But how paltry are such earthly coronations in comparison with that of the glorified Son of Man! He shall take his place upon the throne as Judge of nations and of every one of the children of men.

> Great God, what do I see and hear?
> The end of things created;
> The Judge of all mankind appear
> On clouds of glory seated.
> The trumpet sounds, the graves restore
> The dead whom they contained before!
> Prepare, my soul, to meet him.

III. *The Books*. The books shall be opened as the basis of the final adjudication. What are they?

(1)   The Book of Life. This is the roster of saints. It is called, " The Lamb's Book of Life," because it contains those only who are washed in his blood. The gate of heaven bears the legend: "There shall in

no wise enter here anything that defileth, neither whatsoever worketh abomination or maketh a lie; but they which are written in the Lamb's Book of Life." Here is the momentous question: *Is my name written there?*

(2) The Book of Remembrance. This was written before the Lord for them that feared him and thought upon his name (Mal. 3, 16). Our words and actions and very thoughts are recorded here. We live before the all-seeing Eye and speak as into a phonograph which treasures all for the final reckoning. And when the scroll shall be unrolled before us, our memories shall affirm the record: "Thou didst it," or "Thou didst it not."

(3) The Book of Judgment. This is the Lord's Ledger, in which all balances are drawn. By this his vindication shall be made clear as the noon-day. In view of its revelations the lost and saved alike shall exclaim, "The judgments of the Lord are true and righteous altogether!" In the light of this final clearance it will be seen that God makes no mistakes and that the strange providences of the earthly life were in full accord with equity. In the pages of this Book of Judgment there is one deed which will shine resplendent above all, to wit, the acceptance of redemption in the blood of Jesus Christ. For faith in his gospel is the only saving work; as it is written, "This is the work of God that ye believe on him whom he hath sent."

Luther relates, in one of his letters, that the great adversary came to him in a dream, saying, "I have looked into the Book of Judgment and have seen the black record of thy sins." As the accuser enumerated them, the dreamer was overwhelmed with despair. Then he looked to God in prayer and answered, "I, too, have gazed into the Book of Judgment, and, as thou sayest, my sins are all recorded there; but I saw one entry to my credit which thou hast overlooked; namely, 'The blood of Jesus Christ cleanseth this man from all sin.'"

IV. *And then, Separation.* The fisher draws his net to shore, saving the good and casting the worthless back into the sea. The vinedresser with his pruning knife enters the vineyard, sparing the living branches and cutting away the worthless for the flames. The shepherd with his crook divides the sheep from the goats—the sheep on the right side and the goats on the left. There are but two sides; there is no middle ground. To these the Lord says, "Come, ye blessed!" and the gates of heaven open before them. To those, "Depart, I never knew you!" There they go to "their own place." Where that place is, it matters not; we know it is afar from God. The outer darkness is exile from him. No more to behold His face; no more to hear the message of grace—this is fire unquenchable. We speak of lost souls; but indeed the sorrow is not that the soul itself is lost, but that it has lost God.

V. *And this disposition of things is final.* We hear in certain quarters of a "larger hope," by which is meant the possibility of restoration after death. This "larger hope" is not in the Book. We find there "*aiones ton aionon,*" which all the torturing of eager scholars cannot twist into aught but "forever and ever." And there is the "great gulf fixed;" fixed and bridgeless forever. There too is the crystallization of character at the dead line: "He that is unjust, let him be unjust still; he that is filthy, let him be filthy still; he that is holy, let him be holy still; and he that is righteous, let him be righteous still." The eternal punishment of the incorrigibly wicked is not because of divine ordinance, but on account of the inevitable fixity of character. The twelve gates of heaven shall never be shut; but souls that dwell in the outer darkness, having wasted their probation and stereotyped their characters in habitual sin, must be forever indisposed to enter in; since, in truth, heaven would to them be more painful than hell. Thus neither in Scripture nor in reason is there room for the "larger hope." Be not deceived; whatsoever a man soweth, that shall he also reap. In the place where the tree falleth, there shall it be.

What then? Our great duty is Preparation. The King of Persia called his grand vizier and courtiers, and asked of them, "What condition in life is most to be deplored?" One answered, "A friendless old age"; another, "Poverty"; still another, "To be bedridden in hopeless pain." But the grand vizier said, "It is to pass through life unmindful of the future, and suddenly to be called unprepared before the judgment-seat of God."

A wise preparation for eternity must be twofold. On the one hand, *pardon of sin*. No man who has refused redemption in Christ can stand with the redeemed in the Great Day. One thing can never enter the Kingdom of Heaven; to wit, an unforgiven sin. All who have traveled among the petty states of Continental Europe will remember the vexations attendant on the search for contraband goods. No man can cross the border line that separates between time and eternity and enter Canaan with an unforgiven sin. But why should he? Behold the Christ uplifted and the piercéd hands stretched out! Hearken to the voice of mercy: "Come now, let us reason together, saith the Lord; though your sins be as scarlet, they shall be as white as snow; though they be red like crimson, they shall be as wool." My friends, how shall we escape if we neglect so great salvation, so free, so plain, so glorious? And what excuse can a man make if he appear without this garment at the marriage of the King's Son?

And then *a holy and consistent life.* This is impossible until we have "done the first works." No man can serve God with the record of the mislived past pursuing him. It is like a prisoner's ball and chain. Get rid of it by faith in Jesus Christ; and then proceed to live. Live as becometh those who have gratefully aceepted the heavenly grace. Follow close in the footsteps of Jesus, whose ye are and whom ye serve. Do your duty every hour of every day and fear not!

In 1780 a strange darkness overspread New England; it is known in history as "The Dark Day." The Legislature of Connecticut was in session at Hartford and the members were seized with panic, thinking that the Judgment was at hand. The president of the assembly said, "Gentlemen, if this is not the Great Day we are foolishly alarmed; if it is, we cannot be better found than in the discharge of duty. I ask, therefore, that candles may be lighted and brought in." Such is the wise method of life. If we have committed our salvation to Christ, and consecrated our lives to him, let us borrow no trouble, give way to no apprehension, but attend to present duty *and watch.* Aye, ever watch; for we know not at what hour the Son of Man cometh. Let your door be on the latch; let your lamps be trimmed and burning. It may be that he shall come at evening, or at the cock-crow, or in the morning; and blessed are those servants whom the Lord, when he cometh, shall find watching.

PETER'S FALL.

"And when he thought thereon, he wept."—Mark 14, 72.

On the night when Jesus was apprehended in the garden, there was a panic among his friends; they all forsook him and fled. Peter following afar off came to the High Priest's palace, entered and stood by the fire in the open court. The maid at the wicket looking intently at him said, "Thou also wast with Jesus." He replied, "I know not what thou sayest." Presently one asked, "Art not thou one of his disciples?" He denied, saying, "I am not." And later still one of the company, a friend of Malchus whom Peter had wounded in the garden, said, "Of a truth this fellow also was with him." Then he began to curse and to swear, lapsing into the billingsgate of his earlier life, protesting vehemently, "I know not the man!"

All four of the Evangelists relate this incident, but in different ways. Matthew, the publican, gives us a matter-of-fact statement, as passionless as an official tax-list. Luke, the beloved physician, enters somewhat more into particulars, as if making a diagnosis of the case; he alone mentions the intentness with which the damsel peered into Peter's face; he alone says, "The Lord turned and looked upon Peter." John, the apostle of charity and Peter's friend, relates the occurrence as briefly as possible, omitting its most harrowing details and making no mention whatever of the profanity. But Mark, who was Peter's personal companion and probably wrote under his immediate dictation, recounts all. His account is in the nature of an autographical confession; its frankness reminds us of what Cromwell said to the court painter; "Portray me," said he, "scars and all."

It is a sad story, and we search in vain for extenuating circumstances. Bring it before any jury of tried men and true, and their verdict would be "Guilty," without a recommendation to mercy. The case is aggravated by the fact that Peter had probably a deeper insight than any of his companions into the personality of Jesus; it was he who had witnessed the good confession, "Thou art the Christ, the son of the living God." He was one of the chosen three who were received into the inner place of the Lord's confidence. He had been with Jesus on the Mount of Transfiguration; had seen the homespun garments of the Nazarene flutter aside, revealing his royal purple. Still further, Christ had admonished him: "Satan hath desired to have thee that he might sift thee as wheat; but I have prayed for thee that thy faith fail not." In view of such considerations it would appear that the offense could scarcely have been worse. He had been forewarned, should have been forearmed, and knew that Christ was praying for him.

How, then, did it happen? The inquiry is important; since we are all exposed to similar temptation and liable to deny our Lord. Happy is the Christian who has never said, by word or action, "I know him not."

I. The fall of Peter was primarily due to thoughtlessness. He was an impulsive man. We call him "blundering Peter." On that memorable night when Jesus girt himself with a towel and, with basin in hand, went about to wash his disciples' feet, he came to Peter and, lo! a mutiny. "Thou shalt never wash my feet!" he cried. "If I wash thee not," said Jesus, "thou hast no part with me." Then, without an instant's hesitation, he sped from one blunder to another, exclaiming, "Lord, not my feet only, but my hands and my head also." Thus, after his custom, he spoke first and thought afterward. But, alas! we who live in glass houses should be slow to throw stones at him.

Here is our common fault. We invest our funds in losing ventures for want of thought. We vote the wrong ticket on election day for want of thought. We alienate our friends, give way to ill temper at home and trouble the neighborhood, for want of thought. We fall into evil habits and indulge ourselves until they bind us as with adamantine chains, for want of thought. We run with the multitude to do evil, waste our best privileges and golden opportunities, and reject the overtures of divine mercy, for want of thought. The blast of the judgment trumpet startles us in the midst of a heedless career and we stand before the great assize with no answer to the long indictment but this, "I did not think." It is a child's excuse. O men and women made in God's likeness and hastening to eternity, it is our business to think. Here are three words for the guidance of earnest people in the face of duty and responsibility, *Stop and think!* For indeed an ounce of prevention is always worth a pound of cure.

II. Self-confidence also had much to do with Peter's fall. Just before the crucifixion Jesus had said to his disciples, "All ye shall be offended because of me this night; for it is written, 'I will smite the shepherd and the sheep shall be scattered.'" But Peter said, "Though all men shall be offended because of thee, yet will I never be offended." And when Jesus continued, "Verily I say unto thee that this night before the cock crow thou shalt deny me thrice," he protested the more vehemently, "Though I should die with thee, yet will I not deny thee!"

> "Beware of Peter's word,
> Nor confidently say,
> 'I never will deny my Lord,'
> But, 'Grant I never may.'"

A few years ago it was my privilege to welcome into the fellowship of the church a young man who had been plucked as a brand from the burning. He was a rough diamond like Peter, and very confident in his own strength. "Do you think," I asked, "that you will be able to hold out?" His answer might have been Peter's own; "I assure you that whenever I set out to accomplish anything I get there with both feet." It is safe to say that his subsequent experience has taught him humility and the need of dependence on divine help. "Let him that thinketh he standeth take heed lest he fall."

He is a wise man who knows his own limitations; who knows also the craft and power of his adversary;

and who knows above all the sustaining grace of God. Pride goeth before a fall. I will look unto the hills from whence cometh my help! "We wrestle not against flesh and blood, but against principalities and powers and world-rulers of darkness." Blessed is the man who confronts temptation as David went to meet the Philistine champion, saying, "Thou comest to me with sword and spear but I come to thee in the name of the Lord of hosts!" Our strength is in a sense of utter dependence. Let our prayer be, "O Lord, hold thou me up."

III. It should be observed, furthermore, that Peter's temptation found him at the ebb tide of devotion. It may be that his sensibilities were dulled by previous days and nights of anxiety and foreboding. In any case the record sadly says, "He followed Jesus afar off." He could hear in the distance the outcries of the rabble who were leading his Lord to judgment, could see their flaming torches; and he went skulking in the rear.

The word of the Master is, "If any man will come after me, let him deny himself, take up his cross and follow me." So, then, it is one thing to come after him, and another to follow him. How shall we follow him? As a sheep follows a shepherd? Aye; but the silly sheep nibbling by the way may lag behind and be lost; and the shepherd must needs go out and seek until he find it. As a child follows its mother? Aye; but the child plucking flowers and chasing butterflies may awake to sudden fright and bewilderment, and the mother must go seeking after it. Nay, rather, let us follow Christ as a tourist follows his guide along the Alpine heights; roped fast to him, safe in his guide's safety, falling only when he falls. If we are given over to doubts, if we lack assurance, if we are averse to duty, if we find ourselves disheartened, if the fine edge of our devotion is dulled, it is because we have severed the vital bond. Come closer, friend, and follow in his steps. Enter into such sympathetic union with him that, like Roland Hill, you may say:

"So close is my friendship with Jesus, I find,
He can't go to heaven and leave me behind."

IV. And while we are inquiring the causes of Peter's fall, we must not omit his evil companionship. He stood in the open court with the soldiers; it was a chill night and they had kindled a fire; "and he sat with the servants and warmed himself by the fire."

A Scotch woman commenting on this incident said quaintly, "He had nae business among the flunkeys." It is not possible, however, to avoid association with the enemies of Christ. We must mingle with them more or less closely on the street, in business life, in society and everywhere. But one thing is possible; that is, to avoid warming ourselves at their fire. "Be not thou partaker of their evil deeds." We must be in the world; but we need not be of it.

John was as near to the enemies of Jesus as was Peter that night. He was in the judgment hall with scribes and soldiers all about him; but, fortunately for John, he was wholly out of sympathy with them: his heart was with the prisoner at the bar. Not so Peter; he was with the enemies of Christ and desired to be accounted one of them. Evil associations corrupt good morals as well as good manners. We cannot help our environment always, but by divine help we can keep ourselves above it.

In my judgment, the most unworthy piece of statuary in our city,—a city distinguished for its public exhibit of ignoble art,—is that of William E. Dodge in Herald Square. This statue is unspeakably awkward and feeble. Not so its original. He was a robust and erect man. Being in attendance at a banquet at Fortress Monroe where wine was served, he dared to be singular in turning down his glass. He resigned his membership in the Union League because it provided a bar for the sale of intoxicating drinks. He withdrew from directorship in three railroads because they insisted on running Sunday trains. Here was a man connected with almost all the great enterprises of our metropolis. He could not avoid his association with irreligious people; but he declined to warm his hands at their fire. We should do likewise. "Be ye not conformed to this world, but be ye transformed by the renewing of your mind, that ye may prove what is that good and perfect and acceptable will of God."

V. But back of all Peter's faults was arrant cowardice. He fell before the pointed finger of a maidservant. O the poltroon, put to rout by a pointed finger! Had it been a leveled spear, he might have braved it; for, indeed, no weapon is fiercer than ridicule. We blanch and tremble before it.

We are not in a position to deal hardly with this man. There are joints in every harness. In the stress of temptation we all need to "screw our courage to the sticking place." Napoleon, whom the terrors of the fiercest battle-field could not move, was smitten with dismay by the sound of a mouse nibbling in the wall. I recently asked a non-commissioned officer of the Rough Riders if he was sensible of fear in the assault on San Juan. He replied, "I can't speak for others; but as for myself I was scared stiff. We threw ourselves down under a tempest of leaden hail, and just then I saw the colored troops sweeping past singing a camp-meeting hymn. I heard one of them, as a shell burst overhead, cry, 'No use, Mister Shell, no use! We's gwine to reach de top!' Then I heard the command, 'Forward!' And the next I knew I was standing by the blockhouse with a colored man on either side of me." It is thus that victories are won. O, for the inspiration of the battle's heat! O, for a clear vision of the white plume of our Henry of Navarre! O, for a fear-dispelling hope of triumph!

The story of Peter does not end with his downfall. There is a glorious sequel. No sooner had he uttered the fateful words of denial than the cock crew; and never did chanticleer carry such a message to the heart of man. Then Peter lifting up his eyes, saw Jesus yonder in the judgment hall; and the Lord turned and looked upon him. It was a look of reproach and infinite tenderness of love. And he "went out and wept bitterly." Then came three days of shame and self-reproach. He wandered alone in his bitter sorrow. At night he awoke from troubled dreams to hear himself saying, "I never knew him!" At length one came saying, "The Master is dead; come to the upper-room and weep with us." But he could not. "Leave me to my shame," he said.

Then another said, "Jesus is risen and hath sent a message to thee." But the nightmare of his sin was still upon him.

One morning in the twilight he was with his companions in the fishing boat, when a lone figure was seen walking on the shore. They whispered among themselves, "It is the Lord." Peter could not wait. In a passion of repentant love he threw off his fisher's coat and sprang into the water; and a moment later he stood dripping before his Lord. "Simon, son of Jonas [alas, his old name!], lovest thou me?" "Yea, Lord, thou knowest that I love thee." And again, "Simon, son of Jonas, lovest thou me?" "Yea, Lord, thou knowest that I love thee." Then a third time, "Simon, son of Jonas, lovest thou me?" And Peter said, "Lord, thou knowest all things—my sin, my shame, my remorse, my penitence—and thou knowest that I love thee!" Thus he was restored to the apostolate. And from that time he never blushed to own his Lord. He earned his knighthood as the "man of rock." He stood before kings, met persecution with a courageous front, became a familiar acquaintance of scourge and prison damp, braved the terrors and weariness of missionary toil, and at length went through the gates of Rome to martyrdom. A moment later as he entered on his heavenly reward, we may believe that to the gracious word of welcome he replied, "Now, Lord, thou knowest that I love thee!"

But, perhaps, friend, you have no interest in this narrative. Ah, happy man! Have you never fallen from grace? Have you never been silent when the name of the Master was blasphemed? Have you cast no reproach upon the character of Jesus by inconsistent walk and conversation? Have you had no occasion to chide yourself for base ingratitude? Alas! how have we all denied and grieved him by conformity to the fashions of a wicked world, by neglect of duty, by indulgence in sin! Let us return to our first love. Let the past suffice for lukewarmness and cowardice and worldliness. Let us come close to our Master, follow in his steps, be true to our conviction and faithful unto death; that so we may receive the crown of life. If we have sinned as Peter sinned, let us make quite sure that we have repented as he did; and that we may meet our Lord with his avowal at the last, "Thou knowest that I love thee!"

HOW FELIX LOST HIS OPPORTUNITY.

"And as he reasoned of righteousness, temperance, and judgment to come, Felix trembled, and answered, Go thy way for this time; when I have a convenient season, I will call for thee."—Acts. 24, 25.

The man trembled, and well he might. He desired entertainment, but not such as was here provided for him. He was a worn-out epicure who, if we may trust the chronicles, had swung around the circle of pleasure and surfeited his soul. A happy thought now occurred to him. He had among his prisoners a follower of the crucified Nazarene who was famed for logic and eloquence; him would Felix summon to display his powers in the judgment hall. So Paul was brought and required to speak "concerning the faith in Christ."

What should he say? He was a man of mean presence, dim-eyed, stoop-shouldered and loaded with chains. On the one hand Caution whispered to him, "Take heed how you offend this magistrate;" on the other, Conscience said, "Quit you like a man!" Caution said, "Curry favor with him by a little harmless flattery;" Conscience whispered, "No fear nor favor now! Deliver your message as an ambassador of Christ. Bring this libertine to his knees; make him cringe before God!"

Then Paul began to speak. His sermon was under

three heads: First, *righteousness*. And as Felix listened he must have seemed to hear voices from above crying, "Holy, holy, holy!" and another from within, "Thou art a guilty man!" Second, *temperance;* rather, continence. Here the man changed color; for his shameless vices were matter of common fame. He looked into the face of Drusilla, the third of his unlawful queens, and tried to smile. And the preacher, heedless of his confusion went right on. Third, *judgment to come*. Then the eyes of Felix fell and his courage failed him. The scene was like that in Belshazzar's palace when an unseen hand wrote, *Mene, Tekel, Upharsin* along the wall. And still the preacher went mercilessly on. He "reasoned" of these verities; there was no ranting or fierce objurgation; but logic glowing and irresistible. And Felix moved uneasily; his color changed; he trembled.

Now is his opportunity. The truth has smitten to his heart, to his conscience, to the marrow of his bones. What will he do? He opens his lips. Will he echo the words of the Philippian jailer, "What shall I do to be saved?" Will he beat upon his guilty breast, like the publican, crying, "God be merciful to me a sinner"? If so, there is mercy on the instant for him. He is not far from the kingdom of God. Oh, if he will but summon his resolution now; if he will but "screw his courage to the sticking point"! God is so ready to forgive. The gates of a better life are open to Felix; and the world may yet revere him as a just and gracious man. The supreme moment is at hand. What shall be its issue? Life or death? He speaks: "Go thy way for this time; when I have a convenient season, I will call for thee."

"To each man's life there comes a time supreme,
  One day, one night, one morning or one noon,
  One freighted hour, one moment opportune,
 One rift through which sublime fulfilments gleam,
 One space when fate goes tiding with the stream,
  One Once in balance twixt Too Late, Too Soon,
  And ready for the passing instant's boon
 To tip in favor of uncertain beam.
 Ah, happy he who, knowing how to wait,
  Knows also how to watch and work, and stand
   On Life's broad deck alert, and at the prow
 To seize the passing moment, big with fate,
  From opportunity's extended hand,
   When the great clock of destiny strikes NOW!"

The story of Felix was written for our admonition. God grant that like an arrow it may smite between the joints of some man's harness here. It is a portentous thing for an hour of opportunity to come and go. Yours is at hand. What will you do with it? Let us inquire the reasons for the default of Felix at this juncture; for it is probable that his excuses and subterfuges were such as are common among us.

I. He would have said, "I wish to know more about this new religion. One must not be precipitate in a matter of such consequence. I will send for this prisoner again and make further investigation."

Observe how he deceived himself. He knew enough, and he knew that he knew enough, for the purpose in hand. It was not necessary that he should be a philosopher or acquainted with the deep problems of theology in order to accept Christ as his deliverer from sin. A man need not be a botanist, like Linnæus, to detect the perfume of the lily or see God's name on its white vesture. He need not be an expert in astronomy, like Kepler or Galileo, to feel the deep lesson of the starry dome: "When I consider the heavens the work of thy fingers, what is man that thou art mindful of him?"

The essential facts of religion are very clear; as it is written, "An highway shall be there and a way; the wayfaring men, though fools, shall not err therein." Felix knew sin; felt it in his heart and conscience; was aware that retribution must follow it. He knew that he was bound to die, and after death the judgment. He knew that Jesus had died upon the cross, bearing the world's sin; and he had heard the statement, "He that believeth hath everlasting life." Thus he was as familiar as we are with these essential facts of the Christian religion. All that God asks of any man is that he shall bring his life up to the full measure of his light.

II. As a further reason for the postponement of his decision, Felix would probably have said that he must first relieve his mind of distracting cares. The office of procurator was no sinecure. It was no easy matter to look after the interests of the turbulent Jews. A considerable correspondence must be carried on with Rome. Felix was indeed an exceedingly busy man. He must clear his docket of pending cases before he could give serious attention to religion.

There are many busy people who thus delude themselves. The cares of this world crowd religion to the wall. Clerks and capitalists, professional men and handicraftsmen, all plead alike the pressure of business. A child asked her mother, "Are you going to heaven?" "Yes, my dear, I hope so."—"Then, Mamma, I must be going too; else it will be very, very lonely for you."—"But why, dear? Your father will be there."—"No, Mamma," she replied, "he can't possibly leave the store." It was a juvenile paraphrase of the Tares and Wheat.

We are naturally so averse to a just consideration of the claims of religion that we ask but a very little subterfuge. The folly of Æsop's Simpleton, who stood by the flowing brook, saying, "If this flows on it must empty itself, and I shall go over dry-shod" is obvious. Why are we so slow to perceive the infinitely greater folly of one who postpones the serious business of eternity until the world shall give him respite for it? No business can be so important as the reconciliation of the soul with an offended God; all else can wait. The world gives no man leisure for consideration of the great verities. Business never lets up.

III. It is probable, also, that the heart of Felix was set upon the further accumulation of wealth. His office was very lucrative. The farmers of his province were required to pay tribute on every sheaf of wheat and basket of olives. The taxation of those days was an elaborate system of blackmail; not so far reaching, perhaps, as that which prevails on Manhattan Island, but still immensely profitable to this procurator. No doubt he hoped that, in a little while, he should have acquired sufficient to warrant his retirement; when he might perhaps endow some institution of learning or benevolence, and then at his leisure make his peace with God.

The sophism is apparent,—yet multitudes are excusing themselves in this manner for rejecting Christ. To all such he himself has this to say: "*The ground of a certain rich man brought forth plentifully; and he thought within himself saying: What shall I do; because I have no room where to bestow my fruits? And he said, This will I do; I will pull down my barns and build greater, and there will I bestow all my fruits and my goods; and I will say to my soul, Soul, thou hast much goods laid up for many years, take thine ease, eat, drink and be merry. But God said unto him, Thou fool! this night thy soul shall be required of thee; then whose shall those things be which thou hast provided?"* An eviction! An eviction without postponement or appeal. A just eviction, too; since the tenant had misused his trust. *"So is he that layeth up treasure for himself and is not rich toward God."*

IV. Felix, if candid, would probably have confessed that he wished to enjoy the pleasures of the world a little longer. He had a magnificent palace, with luxurious facilities for enjoying life. To his mind religion was a melancholy affair, to be considered by those who were burdened with age or alarmed by the ominous pangs of disease. He would surely repent before he died. His decision was by no means a refusal, merely a postponement.

His reasoning was plausible but false. For religion is not melancholy. At God's right hand are pleasures forevermore. No moment in human life is so ecstatic as that in which a man realizes his deliverance from sin: "O happy day that fixed my choice on thee, my Saviour and my God!" There are seasons in the trysting-place when we sit at the king's table and feast on fat things and wine upon the lees. And beyond all words is the sweet anticipation of eternity: "Eye hath not seen, nor ear heard, neither have entered into the heart of man the things which God hath prepared for them that love him." What are earth's revels when compared with these?

> "For pleasures are like poppies spread:
> You pluck the flower, the bloom is shed."

It is said that workmen who mine for copper in Cornwall under the sea, can always hear the roll of the ocean above them; but there are times when the raging tempest drives them in terror from their tasks. Thus do the ungodly make merry within sound of the trumpet blast of judgment. They dare not stop to think. O! to sell heaven for such passing joy is a fool's bargain. It was the wisest of men who said, "of laughter It is mad, and of mirth What doeth it?"

V. The hope of political promotion was doubtless a further consideration to the mind of Felix. He was ambitious. He had been an efficient magistrate as magistrates went in those days. His unpopularity with the Jews was greatly in his favor at Rome. Who knew but he might yet be Emperor? Stranger things had happened. But a confession of Jesus of Nazareth would certainly ruin his prospects; it would offend his influential friends. So, though his duty seemed clear, he could not undertake to do it just now.

Can we afford to put off the great decision for such considerations? "What shall it profit a man, if he gain the whole world and lose his own soul?" A pleasure yacht was sailing off the coast of Nova Scotia, when an iceberg was sighted. It was suggested that, since the day was fair and the sea quiet, the passengers might disembark upon it. It was a hazardous enterprise; but they succeeded in climbing the sides of the crystal mass, and remained there until sunset. No sooner were they safe aboard, however, than the iceberg, as if by magic, fell asunder and dissolved. Awestruck they saw its domes and pinnacles, crimsoned by the setting sun, disappear like the fabric of a vision and leave not a wrack behind. So will pass away the glory of this world; its thrones and dynasties, its honors and emoluments, all vanish with life's setting sun.

One thing only endures; to wit, Character. All other ambitions are vain and frivolous when compared with the living of a holy and useful life. Scepters will fall and royal purple will shine no more than beggars' rags. He is the wise man, therefore, whose ambition is to win character, to wield influence and to make life tell.

VI. But back of all the excuses which Felix made to his own conscience was one which he would not have avowed: namely, his love of sin. By his side sat Drusilla, a famous beauty and a conspicuous figure in the gallantries of the time, though but eighteen years old. She had been the wife of Azizus the king of Emesa, from whom the solicitations of Felix had won her. He cringed and trembled now beneath the unanswerable logic of Paul; but, alas! he gazed at Drusilla; and he could not give her up!

Let us be honest with ourselves. Back of all our subterfuges lies our devotion to sin. It is this that prompts the rejection of Christ. Probe deep enough and you will surely find some darling sin. You may hate yourself for loving sin; and still you love it. You fondle it like a tiger's cub; knowing full well that presently it will taste blood and get the better of you. The sin that smiles most sweetly on us is our master; it lays an ever stronger hold upon us with the passing days. And for this we are "condemned already." We do not wait for judgment; sentence has been passed upon us. As Manton says, "Whoso delayeth his repentance, leaveth his soul in pawn to the evil one, saying in effect, 'Here, Satan, keep my soul; if I fetch it not again by such a day, 'tis thine forever.'"

The dangers of delay under such circumstances are manifest. (1) Death may come in an hour when we think not. (2) Or, if not this, then habit may fasten itself upon us beyond all deliverance; for conscience is like a blacksmith's arm, which in his apprenticeship shrank from the heat and quivered with pain; but now he bares it to the shoulder and unshrinking thrusts it into a shower of sparks. (3) Or—more fatal danger still—the Spirit may cease to strive with us. God is patient, but he will not be mocked. His word is plain: "My Spirit shall not always strive with men."

VII. There is one reason for delay which Felix could not urge; to wit, that he wanted more feeling. He "trembled." The iron had gone into his soul.

You say: "I do not feel a vivid conviction of sin. I can stand at Calvary and hear the dropping of blood and shed no tear. I do not turn pale at thought of the Judgment day." Ah but, friend, there was a time when you did. There was a time, years ago, when a sermon like this would have deeply moved you; when you lay awake at night fearful lest the daybreak should find you unprepared at the great assize. It cost you a struggle to resist, in those days. You were almost persuaded; now you are indifferent. You lie down to sleep with no fear or scruple. What does this mean? Have you grieved God's Spirit? Have you quenched the vital spark? Not yet; else you would not be listening to these words. You are still on mercy's ground; but, I pray you, do not trifle now.

And indeed this is not a matter of feeling but of duty. When you are reminded of an honest debt, you do not plead want of feeling. You know that it behooves you to meet your obligation; and you meet it like an honest man.

Are you awaiting a convenient season? When will it be? To-morrow? Nay, that were to offer a Spanish plea, *Mañana!* Yet the Spaniards know their own infirmity, for they have a proverb, "The road of By-and-By leads to the house of Never." To-morrow, my friend, is God's; to-day is yours. "To-day if ye will hear his voice, harden not your hearts." This is the day of salvation.—Or are you thinking that the convenient season will be the hour of death? Surely not that. God can save, indeed, *in articulo mortis;* but the man who reckons on this takes fearful chances. "A dying thief was saved, so that none might despair; but only one, so that none might ever presume."

Of all excuses this is surely the basest and most cowardly. To think of raking one's field and flinging the riddlings at the altar! To calculate calmly on saving out the wheat of life and then casting the worthless chaff before the heavenly throne! To burn one's candle to the socket and then at the last to fling the snuff into the face of God!

No, friend, your one convenient season is just now. No future hour has any place in the economy of salvation. All God's promises center in this moment, for you. The Orientals tell of a man who watched a thousand years sleeplessly before the gates of Paradise in hope that they might open to admit him; then for a moment he dozed and awoke to find that the gates had opened and shut. It is a parable of opportunity. You stand just now before the open gates. I present to you the gospel of forgiveness and eternal life. All the glories of a blessed eternity are yours for the taking, just now. The pierced hands of the Saviour are stretched out; if you will but signify your acceptance of his overtures, he stands ready to say, "Thy sins be forgiven thee."

So far as we know, the impression made upon the mind of Felix wholly passed away. He remained two years in the palace at Cæsarea and was then deposed for malversation of office. Meanwhile he had many opportunities of seeing his distinguished prisoner and hearing further of the religion of Christ; but we are left to believe that he never trembled again when he heard him. So this man passes from view, a victim of the Fabian policy. His inaction was his ruin. You stand where he stood on that momentous day, when Paul preached to him of righteousness, temperance, and judgment to come. What will you do?

I have passed along the street late in the afternoon and seen the people streaming from the theatre doors. They had witnessed a tragedy or a melodrama, and had probably been moved to tears. Out of the artificial passion they now returned to the world; and conversed as cheerfully as if heart-breaking dramas were unknown. Their impressions had vanished like a dream. In like manner you will be going from this presence in a few moments. Shall it be to the old life of habitual sin and indifference, or to the higher life of salvation in Christ? It is for you to say. *Ab hoc momento pendet æternitas.* The issues of the endless future may depend upon this hour. Here is the offer of life; will you receive it? Here is the line that separates between sin and pardon; one step will cross it. Like Felix you open your lips to speak: What is it you say? "Not now"? or, "I will"?

THE SECRET OF POWER.

"Tell me, I pray thee, wherein thy great strength lieth."—Judges 16, 6.

There are no accidents in history. Coincidences are providences. The Weaver sits at the loom casting the shuttle to and fro, weaving in the sun and shadow, and making all things work together in the beauty of the seamless robe wherewith he purposes to clothe himself when the last thread is cut. Time and eternity are warp and woof. Causes and events are made to blend as complementary colors. There are no chances; times and men come together by divine predetermination. The clock strikes, and the hero answers, "Here am I."

The Church is enveloped in darkness. God wants a man; and the monk of Wittenberg, unbinding his rosary, sets forth to nail his Theses on the chapel door.—The tocsin of Saint Bartholomew's appeals to heaven. God wants a man; and afar in the Netherlands a silent champion girds himself for the occasion.—Over-populated Europe needs more room; who shall find it? The Santa Maria sets sail for the far Indies and the man of destiny stands at her prow gazing into the misty West. Thus we observe an unvarying law of demand and supply; and God presides over all.

Now to the circumstances of our context. The glory had departed from Israel. Fires were kindled everywhere on the high places in honor of Baal. Up from the southern plains came the Philistines in their rattling war chariots, devastating the fields, plundering the villages; and there was no resistance. The banners of God's people were in the dust. The Ark of the Covenant was in the hands of the enemy. Was there no eye to pity, no arm to save? Had God forgotten to be gracious?

At this juncture, in the house of Manoah at Zorah, a child was born in whom centered a peculiar interest. He was the child of prophecy. His name, Samson, "the sunlike," is an intimation of a joyous parental welcome: it suggests also the benediction of the infinite Source of light and power.

I. *The Secret of Power.* The mission of Samson had been indicated in the annunciation of his birth; to wit, "he should begin to deliver Israel out of the hand of the Philistines." This was the reason of his life. There is no life without a reason; though many, failing to discover this, live and die unreasonably. Our power is measured by our loyalty to God's purpose concerning us.

The lad was set apart at birth as a Nazirite. The Nazirites were persons who regarded themselves as divinely called to special tasks and shaped their habits of life accordingly. They were pledged to self-abnegation, the putting down of every personal feeling and ambition. They abstained from the fruit of the vine, not merely as it came foaming from the winepress or sparkled in the cup, but in every form "from the husk to the kernel." They were bound to observe the Levitical law with the utmost scrupulosity; they must refrain from kissing the lips of a dead mother for fear of ceremonial defilement, and from mourning at her grave lest they should compromise their vow. The badge of this austere brotherhood was their unshorn hair, which hung over their shoulders in seven braided locks.

The physical strength of Samson was a supernatural gift. His sturdy limbs, broad shoulders and muscles like twisted cord, were a special endowment for his work. In his youth he met a lion in the way and rent its jaws asunder as if it had been a kid. This was but an earnest of larger deeds of prowess; as when he should meet the enemy at Ramath-Lehi and single-handed smite them hip and thigh; then shout a rude alliterative battle-song: "Asses on asses! Masses on masses! Heaps upon heaps! A thousand men!" Or, as when he should lift the gates of Gaza from their hinges and carry them off in grim derision to a neighboring hilltop, laughing back, "See how bars and bolts restrain me!" All this while his locks were unshorn, his duty remembered, his vow at the center of his heart.

But his endowment was more than physical; as it is written, "The Spirit of the Lord strove with him." Here is the true enduement of power; God helps those who are mindful of their duty. In the home at Zorah the growing lad was reminded by his mother of the angelic annunciation: "My son, be faithful to the task which the Lord hath ordained for thee." He sat upon his father's knee and heard of Jephthah's expeditions among the villages from Aroer to Minnith. The eyes of the youth flashed fire, the moving of a great purpose was within him; he longed for the opportunity to show himself a man.

Let the terms of his appointment be noted; he was not to deliver Israel out of the hand of the Philistines, only "to begin to deliver Israel." The man was fitted by nature and training for this work. He was, indeed, in many points a semi-barbarian. In him we observe a strange mingling of weakness and strength; of questionable valor and still more questionable virtue. But he was the man for the time; and preëminently the man for his task. He was to enkindle strife, like John Brown of Osawatomie. He was to open the ranks of the enemy like Arnold Winkelried, at mortal peril to himself. This required a willful, passionate, capricious nature. He must provoke the enemy to deeds of insufferable violence, and then with a tocsin cry of revenge awaken the sleeping courage of Israel. I see him on the way down to Eshtaol, trespassing on the fields, embroiling the people in strife, sowing dragon's teeth which were to germinate and develop better men than he.

A strong man is ever a man with a mission and loyal to it. Saul of Tarsus was an inquisitor up to the hour when the great light shone upon him. Then, realizing that his occupation was gone, as one who could not live without a definite work, he straightway required of his new Master, "What wilt thou have me to do?" All servants of Christ are appointed to special tasks. Alas for the Christian who gives to the sordid world the energies which should be consecrated to the Kingdom of God! He lives like an eagle tethered to its stake; its wings drooping, its eyes blinking at the sun. O Christian, find thy work and address thyself to it! Rend thy chain and let the divineness within thee mount aloft to kindle its eyes at the full midday beam!

II. *The Loss of Power.* The fall of a mighty soul into moral debility is usually through a process of gradual decline. The sun is eclipsed not by the instant veiling of its brightness; an arc of twilight creeps over its verge and, encroaching more and more, brings on at last a very blackness of darkness. So is the enfeeblement of a strong man.

It began in Samson's case with certain journeys down to Timnath. He saw there a woman of the daughters of the Philistines and was captured by her fair face. His temptation came in at Eye-gate. In vain did his parents remonstate, "Is there never a woman among the daughters of thy brethren?" It was enough for Samson that he fancied her. "Get her for me," he cried; "she pleaseth me well." As time passed, the serious business of life was forgotten. The beguilements of the fair Philistine were woven about him like the bands of Gulliver in Lilliput. It is always perilous to trifle with sin. We find in the district messenger-boy an inexhaustible source of pleasantry. He is sent upon an errand posthaste. As he turns the corner the bell of a fire-engine arrests his steps. A little further on, a group of lads are tossing jack-stones; and our youthful ambassador, agape with interest, hands in pockets, lingers to look on. And meanwhile his message waits. Who are we however that we should make merry at the lad's expense? Are we not also sent on an ambassage, and a vastly more important one? Has not the word been clearly spoken, "Go ye; declare the Evangel!"

Does not the King's business require haste? Yet we stand in Vanity Fair, charmed with sweet music and the glint of tinkling feet; or, mayhap, we mingle with the self-seeking multitude and lose ourselves in sordid cares. And our message, meanwhile? Behold, the world lieth in darkness and the shadow of death, still waiting for it.

The story of Samson's fall is full of warning. He laid his head in the lap of the temptress and rose up shorn of his manly strength. Not all at once, however. Observe how he played with the mystic symbol of his calling. "Tell me," said Delilah, "wherein thy great strength lieth, and wherewith thou mightest be bound to afflict thee."

And Samson said, "If they bind me with seven green withes, then shall I be weak as another man."

He slept and was bound with the green withes; and she cried, "The Philistines be upon thee!" Then he awoke and brake the withes as tow that is scorched in the fire.

And the temptress said, "Behold, thou hast mocked me. Tell me, I pray thee, wherewith thou mightest be bound."

"If I be bound with new ropes that never were used, then shall I be weak and be as another man."

He slept again and was bound with new ropes. "The Philistines be upon thee!" she cried. And he brake the ropes like a thread from his arms.

And she said, more persuasively still, "Thou hast mocked and deceived me: tell me now wherewith thou mightest be bound."

He approached perilously near his great secret as

he answered, "If thou weavest my seven braids with the web."

And again he slept; and his locks were woven in the loom. Then she cried, "The Philistines be upon thee!" and he awoke and, laughing, walked away with the beam and the web.

And she poutingly urged: "How canst thou say, I love thee? Thy heart is not with me. Thou hast mocked me thrice and hast not told me wherein thy great strength lieth." Thus she pressed him daily with her words until his soul was grievously vexed.

Then he told her all: "If I be shaven, my strength will go from me." Once more he slept and the lords of the Philistines were in waiting. His locks were shorn and his strength went from him. Again the cry, "The Philistines be upon thee!"

And he awoke and said, "I will go out as at other times and shake myself." And he wist not that *the Lord was departed from him!*

He wist not. Aye, there is the sorrow of it. The most insidious diseases are those which give no pain. Their victims in the midst of business or pleasure swoon and are gone. So does a sin indulged creep, like an ambushed assassin, nearer and nearer to the center of life. Habit is like an adder warmed in the bosom: it need smite but once. O that God would enable some of us to look backward and perceive our unconscious loss of influence. Has the fine edge of your moral sense worn off? Is your conscience, once as sensitive as the palm of an infant's hand, now seared as with a hot iron? These are ominous signs of spiritual declension. We started out at the beginning of our Christian life with a determination to be strong. We coquetted with sin and, behold, we are weak like other men.

III. *The Recovery of Power*. Blessed be God, all is not lost! The man who has forgotten his vow, forsworn his duty, and denied his Lord, shall yet have an opportunity of grace. "Return unto me, saith the Lord, and I will have mercy upon you."

In the prison house of Gaza sits the champion of Israel; a captive, grinding like a woman at the mill. His eyes are out. He sits in open view: that the people may make sport of him. The fair women of Philistia pass by and deride him; but he sees them not. Temptation enters no more at Eye-gate. In his enforced solitude he remembers. He recalls the prophecy of his birth: "He shall begin to deliver Israel out of the hand of the Philistines." He bemoans his wasted strength, his squandered privilege. He is alone in the surging crowd; alone with God. His consecration vow is before his blind eyes in letters of fire. O that he might prove himself a Nazirite again before he dies! His enemies have not perceived that his locks are growing again. They grow as he renews his vow. His affliction is not in vain; he remembers the riddle he once gave to his enemies; "Out of the eater is come forth meat, and out of the strong is come forth sweetness." Thus in the secret place of his repentant heart he renews his fealty to God.

The closing scene is pathetic beyond words. The festival of Dagon is at hand. The Philistines are gathering to offer a great sacrifice to their god. The blind giant of Israel is brought to the temple where the assembling multitude may behold him. He bears their mockery in silence; and the Spirit of God moves within him. His heart is no longer with the past; in that fierce hour he renews his consecration. He will yet, with God's help, "begin to deliver Israel out of the hand of the Philistines." He hears the footfall and murmur of thousands gathering in the temple. The galleries are full. His hour of triumph has come. He stretches forth his hands, feeling for the great pillars. The muscles of his iron frame are tense and swollen. He lifts his scarred face with its eyeless sockets toward heaven. His lips move; he is making his last prayer, "O God, avenge me!" There is a trembling of the pillars, a momentary hush, then cries of the fear-stricken and the dying, as with a crash the temple falls, burying in its ruins the blind captive and his persecutors. And from the silence of that ruin forevermore may be heard a voice, "Return from thy backslidings, O Israel, and I will restore thee! Return and I will return unto thee!"

In the eleventh of Hebrews, the inspired roll-call of heroes, it is written that Samson was "by faith made strong out of weakness." Faith is the vital bond of our union with God! It holds us fast to duty; it bring us back from wandering, makes all things possible to us. We are never strong until we are weak, because then the power of God rests upon us.

Here is our lesson: No man is without a "calling." Each has his "vocation" in the kingdom of Christ. And the secret of a successful life is in the concentration of energy on one's mission. There is a world of wisdom in the Cottar's words:

"An' O be sure to fear the Lord alway,
  An' mind your duty duly morn an' night!
Lest in temptation's path ye gang astray,
  Implore his counsel an' assisting might.
They never seek in vain who seek the Lord aright."

It has been said that while a tallow candle cannot be thrown through the wall of a tent, it can be shot through an oaken plank. The reason is easy to see. Here is a concentration of power. The man who lives according to the divine purpose makes a sure success of life. No arrow is wasted that speeds toward the mark.

A young Englishman, fifty years ago or thereabouts, was moved to carry the gospel to Terra del Fuego. The divine call was clear. This was his appointed task; he must accomplish it. He spent his limited fortune in fitting out an expedition; only to be repulsed by the natives and driven back a penniless, unsuccessful but still resolute man. He urged his plea upon the churches and sailed again. He was now permitted to land; he pitched his tent among the people and prepared for work. His companions died and he was driven again by the superstitious natives to the shelter of his boat. At length in the shadow of a torn sail he lay dying. Not a soul had been given for his hire. Was his life wasted, then? In his last moments he wrote these words, to be found long afterwards: "My little boat is a very Bethel to my soul. Asleep or awake, I am happier than tongue can tell. I am starving, yet I neither hunger nor thirst. I feed on hidden manna and drink at the King's well. I am not disappointed; for I remember this: 'One soweth and another reapeth.'" A failure?

A wasted life? Nay; let the thousands of converts, who go each year, in that far away country, to water with their tears the grave of Allen Gardiner pass their verdict upon it. No life is futile whose strength is spent in pursuance of a divine call.

Let the past suffice us for the squandering of power. God calls us to return from the dissipations of Vanity Fair to our appointed work. Let us hear and heed forevermore this "high calling" of God. Our place is among the athletes who stand at the crimson line. Let us so run that we may obtain the crown. "This one thing I do; forgetting those things which are behind, and reaching forth unto those things which are before, I press toward the mark for the prize of the high calling of God in Christ Jesus." This one thing I do! This one thing I do!

AMERICA FOR CHRIST.

"If ye shall diligently keep all these commandments which I command you, to do them, to love the Lord your God, to walk in all his ways, and to cleave unto him; then will the Lord drive out all these nations from before you, and ye shall possess greater nations and mightier than yourselves. Every place whereon the soles of your feet shall tread shall be yours; from the wilderness and Lebanon, from the river Euphrates even unto the uttermost sea shall your coast be."—Deut. 11, 22-25.

In the Dark Ages of ancient history, when truth and righteousness seemed in danger of perishing from the earth, it pleased God to select a people who should keep the oracles and hand down the Messianic secret to coming times. In furtherance of his plan a little strip of territory on the eastern shore of the Mediterranean was set apart for the habitation of this people. It was singularly well adapted to this purpose, being separated by almost impassable barriers from the surrounding country. It was bounded on the south by the Arabian desert, on the north by the Lebanon range, on the west by the Great Sea and on the east by the trans-Jordanic cliffs. Thus the Israelites were set apart as a hermit nation. At the same time they were in closest touch with the world's enterprise. The caravan routes which connected the three great centers of civilization, to wit, Egypt on the south, Assyria on the east and Greece on the northwest, crossed each other just here. So the land of Israel, while protected by its seclusion from the contaminating influences of paganism, was peculiarly fitted to be the depositary and radiating center of the religion of the true God.

In the Dark Ages of more recent history, when the world was threatened with a universal prevalence of wrong and error, it pleased God to set apart for the remnant of his oppressed people a barbaric region in the distant West. At this point we observe a striking coincidence. Our country is not unlike Palestine, in the seclusion afforded by its impassable sea walls; while it lies precisely at the focal point of universal commerce. Is this an indication that God would have us foster our power for the ultimate benefit of the race? A French artist conceived the thought of a colossal image of "Liberty Enlightening the World." He accomplished his task, and the question arose, Where shall the statue be placed? By the banks of the Seine? In sight of the July Column, which commemorates the horrors of the Bastile? In sight of the Garden of the Tuileries and the Palace of the Louvre, where the Commune vented its wrath? In sight of the Arc de Triomphe and the golden dome of the Invalides, under which rest the ashes of Napoleon the Scourge? Nay, not there! The place chosen is at the portals of the western continent. There stands the colossal figure, uplifting a lighted torch, more eloquent of great achievement than even its illustrious maker imagined. It is not Liberty but the Evangel enlightening the nations of the Earth.

The Lord Jesus wants our country; we read this in the romantic story of its discovery and settlement. It is an open question who discovered America. Was it the Phœnicians, who, as Strabo says, effected a landing about 400 B.C. on the mysterious Island of Atlantis in the Western Sea? In any case, they made no settlement, better things being in store for our continent than that the fires of Baal and Astarte, the furies of ancient Israel, should be kindled on its altars. Shall we then accord the honors of discovery to Eric the Red who, about 1000 A.D., landed on our northern coasts? He also was unable to effect a settlement. His hardy Norsemen were driven away, the very elements conspiring against the gods of Walhalla, and the hammer of Thor. Was Columbus then the real discoverer of America? On October 7, 1492, the Santa Maria was making straight for the coasts of Florida, when a flock of paroquets, heading to the southwest, crossed her bows. The course of the vessel was changed accordingly and her crew disembarked on the Bahamas. So, God be praised! the civilization of Spain based on the religion of Rome was averted. The belt of power in the Western hemisphere was reserved for a better race and purer religion.

In 1609 a truce was signed between Holland and Spain; and the liberated energies of the Dutch Protestants sought a new outlet. The Half Moon sailed,—Hendrik Hudson, skipper,—and a trading and trapping post was established on Manhattan Island. A little later the Pilgrims,—who being exiled from their native country had made a protracted sojourn in Holland, coming into close contact with her spirit of ecclesiastical and civil freedom,—set forth in the Mayflower and in due time landed at Plymouth. These were the people, the Chosen

People, for whom God had reserved the Western World and whom he had prepared to occupy it.

> What sought they thus afar?
> Bright jewels of the mine,
> The wealth of seas, the spoils of war?
> They sought a faith's pure shrine.
> Aye, call it holy ground,
> The ground whereon they trod ;
> They left unstained what there they found,
> Freedom to worship God !

The Lord Jesus wants our country for himself; we read it in the strange record of our territorial expansion. The Thirteen Colonies, as originally banded together for mutual protection and defense under the Declaration of Independence, represented about eight hundred thousand square miles of territory; but they had no outlook toward the West, no southern seaboard and no commercial right in the Mississippi, the great waterway of the continent.

The first step toward an important enlargement was in the Louisiana Purchase, which was effected by Jefferson in 1803. This gave us the Mississippi River and doubled the national area. The purchase could not have been made but for the financial straits of Napoleon. In closing the bargain he said, "I have strengthened the power of a nation which, as a maritime rival, shall yet humble the pride of older nations beyond the sea." In 1845 Texas was annexed. This was done under the leadership of Calhoun and for the extension of slavery. It is not an easy matter to defend it.

In 1846 the Northwestern Territory, previously held by England and America jointly, passed into our hands. The story of the Oregon Trail, the encroachments of the Hudson Bay Company, the controversy of the frontiersmen with the watchword, "Fifty-four-forty or fight!" are matters of common fame. In all our history there is no more interesting episode than the ride of the missionary, Marcus Whitman, from Walla Walla to Santa Fé, three months over the mountains, through falling snow and wintry blasts, and thence to Washington; where President Tyler was persuaded to negotiate a compromise with the British Government, by which our Northwestern boundary was fixed at the forty-ninth parallel.

In 1848, largely through the enterprise of Fremont, "the Pathfinder," we secured our possessions on the Pacific Coast. The less said about this and other results of the Mexican War the better for our national honor; since these acquisitions were made according to the "good old plan, that he may take who has the power, and he may keep who can."

In 1867 Alaska was purchased from Russia; adding six hundred thousand square miles. At the time, the wisdom of this purchase was seriously questioned; but the vast development of Alaskan treasure has abundantly vindicated it.

We thus find ourselves in possession of a territory of three and one-half millions of square miles; and are just now facing the question of a further addition. We do not want Cuba, Porto Rico or the Philippines; but the question is, Can we avoid taking them under our care? We are in a dilemma. On the one hand we dare not restore them to the tender mercies of Spain; on the other we cannot leave them as a bone of contention among the great powers of Europe.

We are in the position of a Christian man whom I knew. He had a family and responsibilities to the full measure of his resources. One day a friendless waif appeared at his door asking to be taken in. There was the problem of the cruse and the barrel; but the waif stood hollow-cheeked and shivering at the threshold; there was nothing to be done but to adopt him. God save us, as a nation, from the pride of conquest; but may he make us willing to assume any responsibility whatsoever in the interest of broad civilization and humanity, which he may impose upon us.

The Lord Jesus wants our country; it looks like manifest destiny; we read it in the startling development of our national power. This power centers in the Christian Church as really as the Tabernacle stood in the midst of the Jewish camp.

It is affirmed on statistical authority that there are twenty-seven millions of religious people in our country! What a suggestion of power and responsibility! For "power to the last atom is responsibility."

One of the surprises of our recent history is the discovery that we are the richest nation on earth. Our wealth is estimated at not less than fifty thousand millions. Ponder that for a moment in view of the responsibilities which it involves. Who hold this treasure? Much the larger part of it is in the hands of the twenty-seven millions of religious people. They represent the thrifty, cultured and prosperous class. And what are they doing with this treasure? Has the Church increased her influence commensurately with her wealth? Nobody thinks so.

An eminent cardinal was once walking arm in arm with a barefoot friar: he looked on his ruby ring, his purple robe, his splendid mansion, the gilded dome of his cathedral, and proudly said, "The time has passed, brother, when the Church must say as Peter and John did, 'Silver and gold have I none.'" "Aye," replied his barefoot comrade, "and mayhap, my lord cardinal, the time has passed when she can say to paralytics, as Peter and John did, 'In the name of Jesus Christ of Nazareth, rise up and walk!'"

We have recently discovered, also, to our amazement, that we are among the great military nations. We have, indeed, no standing army or fleet worth mentioning; but we have what is better, an indefinite reserve. Pompey said, "I can stamp my foot and summon an army." We have proven that a word from Washington can call an irresistible host from the farm and workshop and marshal them on the high places of the field. We have demonstrated that by the subsidizing of our merchant marine and mere pleasure craft we can improvise a fleet stronger than the Spanish Armada. But, better than all, we have shown the world that war can be waged in the interest of peace. The dominating influence in our recent conflict was the gospel of the humanities. Over our armies and fleets waved the banner of the Prince of Peace.

Yet another of our surprises is this: our forebodings with reference to immigration have been vain. It has been supposed that the inpouring of heterogeneous peoples might involve us in anarchy or revolution. We were afraid our hopper was receiving more than the mill could grind into a wholesome grist. In fact, however, there is no more homogeneous nation than our own. And we have no better citizens than those who have come to us from among the oppressed regions of the earth. This is a fact for God's people to contemplate. It is as when the people came to Pentecost; "Parthians, Medes and Elamites and dwellers in Mesopotamia, strangers of Rome, Jews and proselytes, Cretes and Arabians." What shall be done with them? Ours is indeed the pentecostal nation. Let us lift the prayer that God's Spirit may rest upon these multitudes in cloven tongues as of fire, that they may be filled with the influence of the gospel of Christ; that so, as the Passover pilgrims of old carried back the Evangel to their homes, these also may be radiating influences of the gospel of Christ.

The Lord Jesus wants our country for himself; in the light of that statement we may read our denominational responsibility. The Reformed Church is the oldest evangelical body in America, having been organized on Manhattan Island not earlier than 1614, and not later than 1628 when Domine Michaëlius was installed as minister of Saint Nicholas Church. The fact that we are one of the smaller denominations is due measurably to our own default, and particularly to the fact that the Dutch people were in possession of this island only for a period of about fifty years, being crowded aside by the English occupation in 1664, since when they have not been a segregated factor in our national life.

We are proud of our honorable history, but danger lies that way. We cannot turn the wheels with the waters gone by. Forgetting the past, let us reach out toward the things which are before. We are told the Spaniards have carried away the bones of Columbus from Havana. They are welcome to them. A living dog is better than a dead lion. Let the Dons dwell among the tombs. God give us the living genius of enterprise! Let us cherish all the honorable memories, but remember that honor lies in consecration to present duty and future usefulness.

Our church is peculiarly adapted to present needs by reason of its historic loyalty to truth. It has stood like a rock amid the tempestuous swirl of controversy. It has been loyal to the faith once delivered to the saints, loyal to the historic landmarks of doctrine, loyal to the revealed Word. It is written that our Lord, having compassion on the hungry multitudes, asked his disciples, "How many loaves have ye?" They answered, "There is a lad here who has five in a basket." These he took and, breaking them, said to his disciples, "Give ye them to eat." This is not to suggest that other denominations have not been as loyal and conservative as our own. But the time has come for every lad with a basket to add his contribution for the feeding of the multitudes with living bread.

O for the baptism of fire on our venerable church! Conservatism is an honor; but inertia is a shame. The Moravians tell of a missionary ship that sailed for Greenland a hundred years ago and was never heard of. She was caught somewhere among the ice-floes and failed to reach her destination. God save us from the guilt of arrested power; from falling short of the work ordained for us!

He wants men; men and women dedicated to his work. "Say not, It is yet four months and then cometh the harvest. Lift up your eyes and see: the fields are already white. Pray ye the Lord of the harvest that he would send forth laborers into his harvest." The flaming cross is on the hills. Where are the consecrated youth who shall respond? Where are the mothers, Hannahs in Israel, who shall bring their children to the sanctuary and consecrate them to the Lord?

He wants money also. Yours? No, not a penny of it! If you have money that you can call your own, keep it. If, however, you have any of the Lord's money entrusted to your stewardship, then give him his own. Now is the time for Christian men and women to recognize their stewardship. *Bis dat qui cito dat.* The curse of our Christian civilization is unconsecrated wealth in Christian hands. The Scriptural word "covetousness" is *pleonexia*, which might be liberally rendered, "I will have more!" The sorrow of the situation is that the Church controls our national wealth and grips it as with a clenched fist.

Let no follower of Christ suppose that he discharges his responsibility by promising to remember the missionary boards in his will. A man was recently caught in one of our leading homes in the very act of burglary. With his arms full of silver and jewels he started to run, but was obliged to drop everything in order to escape. So does many a wealthy man who professes to be a follower of Christ; he keeps his treasure as his own, until the grim specter of Death pursues him; then perforce he drops the plunder: and men gather around it, saying, "Let us now read his Last Will and Testament."

But what the Lord wants above all is personal consecration. Such appeals as this would be quite needless, if we could but realize that we are not our own but are bought with a price, even the precious blood of Jesus as of a lamb without blemish and without spot. But, alas! we withhold ourselves so that he cannot reach or use us. A traveler in the East relates that, being suspicious of his Bedouin guards, he bought of his dragoman a musket for personal protection. At the first opportunity he tried the weapon, only to find that it would not go. He picked the flint; he primed it with powder in the pan; all in vain. At length he opened it at the breech and discovered that the wily Arab had rammed home a solid wad before pouring in the powder; so that the fire could not get through. Such is the effect of cherished sin or worldliness in a Christian life. It presents an impassable barrier to the influence of the Holy Spirit. The heavenly fire cannot penetrate it.

The Lord Jesus wants our country for himself and he wants his people to deliver it to him. He is waiting for us to lay it before his feet. We as individual Christians and as a denomination have tarried long enough. The immigrant ships are coming in; they will not wait. The line of population moves toward the west at the startling rate of thirty miles a year; it will not wait. We have tarried in camp too long. The pillar of cloud is lifting from the tabernacle; it moves onward! Shall we fall in with the cavalcade of Israel and go forward? Shall we make our influence felt in the Conquest of America for Christ?

THE ETHICAL IMPERATIVE.

"At even my wife died, and I did in the morning as I was commanded."—Ezekiel 24, 18.

The soul of Ezekiel burned with a passion of holy zeal. He lived at a critical time in the history of Israel. Truth and knowledge had perished from the way: the nation had gone into its dotage and must be taught in object lessons. This was Ezekiel's task. On one occasion he stood before the multitude with a tile on which was a rude sketch of the Holy City. Laying it on the ground, he cast up a mount and raised fortifications against it. This needed no explanation. Again he appeared with a chain in hand saying, "Thus saith the Lord, I will do unto the people after their way, and according to their deserts will I judge them." And again, he cut off his hair in the presence of the multitude, divided it into three portions, reserving a meager lock which he bound in the border of his skirts: and when the people asked, "What meaneth this?" he replied, "Sword, famine and captivity. But a remnant shall be saved." Thus he was the kindergartner of the prophets. His work was to admonish the recreant nation of approaching disaster, and to this mission he gave himself with an utter abandon of consecration. His attitude was fearless; his words were relentless as fate; but the soul within him was overwhelmed with pity. The severest duty put upon him is recorded in our context: "And the Lord said, I will take away from thee the desire of thine eyes with a stroke; yet thou shalt make no mourning for the dead." The character of the man is set forth in the sequel: "And at even my wife died, and I did in the morning as I was commanded." He made no outward sign of sorrow, uttered no moan, shed no tear; but, with covered head and sandaled feet, addressed himself to the business in hand. Thus, to Israel he taught the imperativeness of duty.

The same important truth was inculcated by our Lord when certain men came to him and expressed a desire to follow him. The first was an impulsive aspirant, who said, "Lord, I will follow thee whithersoever thou goest!" To him Jesus replied, "The foxes have holes and the birds of the air have nests, but the Son of Man hath not where to lay his head." The next was a dilatory candidate, who said, "Lord, I will follow thee; but suffer me first to go and bury my father." To him reply was made, "Let the dead bury their dead; go thou and preach the kingdom of God." The last was a double-minded man, who said, "Lord, I will follow thee; but let me first go and say farewell to my dear ones," and this was the stern rejoinder, "No man having put his hand to the plow and looking back, is fit for the kingdom of God." In other words the call to duty takes precedence of all.

I. *But What Is Duty?* Let the etymology of the word define it: Duty is debt; that is, the thing due. Due to whom? To God.

This repellent view of the matter is modified by the fact that the debt referred to is a debt of love. Duty is "love in action." If once I realize that all I have is of providence and grace—the breath in my nostrils, the bread on my table, kinship and friendship, remission of sin and the hope of heaven,—my service takes the form of the recognition of an honest debt, and the pleasure of my life will be to pay it. Service is still service, yet not servile but filial; for "the love of Christ constraineth" me. This was in the mind of Wordsworth when he wrote his apostrophe to duty:

> "Stern Lawgiver! Yet thou dost wear
>   The Godhead's most benignant grace;
> Nor know I anything so fair
>   As the smile upon thy face."

II. *Here Is the Highest Motive of Life.* A man is at his best when discharging his duty; that is, meeting his obligation to the good God who created and redeemed him. The possible motives of life are only three:—

(1) *Self-gratification.* The world's trinity is livelihood, pleasure and honor. He who pursues these enters into fellowship with the lower orders of life. An ambitious man is fellow to the lion that roars and ravages in order to be King of Beasts. The pleasure-seeker is fellow to the cheerful dog that moves from the chill of the creeping shadow and ever follows the sun. And he who devotes himself to a livelihood or "getting on in the world," is fellow to the horse that bears his burden or walks the weary treadmill for an evening meal of oats.

(2) *Altruism.* God forbid that aught should be said against the doing of kindly deeds; for "though I speak with the tongues of men and of angels and have not charity, I am become as sounding brass and a tinkling cymbal." Yet kindness, in the usual acceptation of the word, is by no means the greatest thing in the world. Everybody knows how poor "Posty" in "Auld Lang Syne" ended his shiftless life by leaping into the water to save Mrs. Macfadyen's child; wherefore the author sent him to heaven straight. But why? It was a splendid act, indeed; but is any life so barren as to have no noble impulses? In fact, such deeds are humane but not distinctly human; that is, they do not differentiate us from the lower orders. The dam cares for her litter. The hen shelters her brood under her wings when the hawk hovers in the air. I have seen a wild goose circle about for hours after its mate had been slain. No, we must look higher than this for the quality that separates man from all beneath and makes him akin with God.

(3) *Duty.* Here we are at our best, because the law of our being controls us. A stone for falling, a flame for rising, a bird for the air and a fish for water; such is their nature. By the same token, a man for duty. In this he stands alone and singular. Of all living things he alone was made in the divine likeness; he alone has God's breath in his nostrils; he alone can "think God's thoughts after him"; he alone is burdened with moral responsibility, and he alone has power to distinguish betwixt the worse and better reason. Joseph Cook says: "If you please, sum up the globes as so much silver and the suns as so much

gold and cast the hosts of heaven as diamonds on a necklace into one scale, and if there is not there any part of the word Ought—if Ought is absent from the one scale and present in the other—up will go your scale laden with the universe as a crackling paper scroll is carried aloft in a conflagration ascending toward the stars. God is in the word Ought; and therefore it outweighs all but God."

In the life of Duty, then, a man is at his noblest. Here he is meeting the obligations of his nature; feeling his way back to his original estate, working out the possibilities of his destiny. Here he becomes a participant of the divine life.

> "'What shall I do to be forever known?'
>   'Thy duty ever!'
> 'This did full many who yet sleep all unknown.'
>   'Oh, never, never!
> Thinkst thou, perchance, that they remain unknown
>   Whom thou knowst not?
> By angel trumps in heaven their praise is blown,
>   Divine their lot.'"

III. *There is No Absolution from the Behest of Duty.* It is aside from my present purpose to point out the spheres of personal obligation. Nor is this necessary. The farmer who owns a thousand acres in Dakota needs no fences nor landmarks to enable him to distinguish his own field. A place is reserved in the divine economy for every man. The life of a shirker is a vast default. There is a portion of the temple wall unbuilt as yet; my friend, it awaits you. There is a shop where the tools lie unused on the bench; the door is open for you. There is a corner of the field untilled and overgrown with weeds; yours is the call to sow there and reap and garner for God. Alas for us! we know our duty and we do it not!

And what vain excuses we offer; in what mean subterfuges we hide ourselves. "I want more light on the matter." Nay; rather, as Shaftesbury said to Locke, "You know too much; the want is not of knowledge but of will." God asks only that you shall live up to the measure of your light. Or do you say, "The obligation does not appeal to me"? that is, you want more feeling. But moods are for poets and lovers, not for plain servants like us. Duty is not a matter of sentiment, but of common honesty and common sense. Or, possibly, you are too preoccupied, and waiting for leisure. Alas! the gift of a man's leisure is an affront to God. He asks no crippled lamb, but the firstlings of your flock. He wants not your superflux, but you.

In some cases the default is due to discouragement. You set out bravely once, and failed. You ploughed, sowed, harrowed, and reaped not. So the disciples by the lake shore were resting on their oars in the early morning when Jesus came and said, "Launch out into the deep and let down your nets for a draught." One answered, "We have toiled all the night and taken nothing; nevertheless, at thy word we will let down the net." And when they had done so, they enclosed a great multitude of fishes. The word is for you, my disheartened friend. Launch out, take heart, strive again. You are responsible only for the effort: God for the results. Do your best, and he will be with you.

There are others who under the shock of sudden grief or calamity have been stunned into a moral paralysis. I knew a devoted servant of Christ who, smitten thus, resigned his positions of church usefulness saying, "I have no heart for anything but to be alone and weep." The word of Ezekiel is for such: "At even my wife died; and in the morning I did as I was commanded." Our sorrows, however deep and overwhelming, are relatively of slight moment in the economy of the eternal life. They are "light" at the heaviest, and "but for a moment" at the longest.

A few evenings since, a poor woman of the town came into a concert hall on the Bowery while a dance was in progress, sat down at a table, leaned her face in her hands and died. The intrusion of the King of Terrors caused but a momentary hush. The woman was carried out and laid upon the pavement; then on went the dance. What is pain or trouble, what death itself, in our busy world? The breaking of a heart, the wreck of a fortune, the toppling of a throne,—these are but ripples raised by the wind on the surface of an irresistible tide. Whatever happens, the world rolls on. Duty is clamorous, even at the gateway of God's Acre. We walk among our trials bewildered, as in a dream, but the world is larger than many graves and life than many heartaches. These are but for a moment, duty is forever. Let the man who sits mourning under the juniper tree heed the voice of reproof, "What doest thou here?" The work undone, the wall unbuilt, the field untilled, the vintage untrodden, are calling us. The test of religion is to heed that imperious voice. Profession is but lip service; work tells. There is no piety but applied piety.

Vows are but vagrant zephyrs; it is wind on the wires of the æolian harp, in the bellows of the organ, on the keys of the flute, that makes the music of life.

IV. *Here too is the Secret of Happiness.* Shirking is misery. The contented man is he who lives above circumstance, who realizes that there is no subterfuge from responsibility, who recognizes the imperativeness of duty.

The two great men of the Reformation were Luther and Erasmus. The latter, while preëminent for learning, was the victim of an incurable melancholia. The reason is not far to seek; it was he who said, "I am resolved to do my duty—as far as circumstances will permit." The life of Luther, on the other hand, was like a murmuring brook or a singing lark. And again the reason is not far to seek; it was he who said, "Though there were as many devils at Worms as there are tiles upon the housetops, yet would I go there at the behest of duty."

It may be that, at the outset, duty is akin to drudgery; but drudgery loses its grim visage on closer acquaintance. An apple as it leaves the blossom turns its thought and spends its energies on growing big, heedless meanwhile of a puckery sourness and bitterness within; but presently, having attained its necessary growth, it turns its attention to the making of succulent juices. Then, observing its rosy flush and sweetness, we say, "The apple is ripe." So it is with a consecrated life; the beauty of holiness is the result of a calm and normal expenditure of energy in the rigid discharge of duty day by day. The trudging pilgrim gains strength as he moves on, leaning on divine strength as on a staff and resting on a good conscience as on a soft pillow, until at length he catches sight of the glistening domes and pinnacles of the heavenly city. In that supreme moment the past is forgotten in the renewal of strength. Like David, he "runs in the way of God's commandment" and finishes his course with joy. Alas for one who knowing his duty refuses or neglects to perform it: but O the blessednesses of the man who honors his conscience by the way and hears his Lord's approval at the last, "Well done, good servant!"

Our Lord is our Exemplar. Duty was his watchword. There was one great duty which he owed to himself as God. He had come into the world under a vow to accomplish the deliverance of men. Calvary was the goal toward which he "set his face steadfastly." All his life was a journey to the cross. At length he came to Gethsemane; there his enemies found him. As they drew near with staves and lanterns, he said "Ye seek Jesus of Nazareth; I am he." There was never a moment of swerving from his task. As a sheep before her shearers is dumb so he opened not his mouth. Three mortal hours on Golgatha he drank the cup of the world's guilt to its bitterest dregs; then, crying, "It is finished!" he yielded up the ghost. His was the path of duty. Take up your burden, friend, and follow him. Lay down no conditions, make no compromises, offer no excuses. Duty is ultimate. When conscience speaks, the last word is spoken. Meet your obligation as Christ met his; and count it your highest joy to meet him at the last, saying, "I have finished the work which thou gavest me to do."

DON'T WORRY.

"Take therefore no thought."—Matt. 6, 34.

The word "thought" is an archaism; its precise meaning is *anxious thought*. Luke gives us the paraphrase, "Neither be ye of doubtful mind." The figure is that of a ship in the offing rolling to and fro. Our religion should hold us steady; as an anchor to the soul, sure and steadfast, taking hold of that which is within the veil.

What a world this would be if there were no fret, no worry, no anxiety! We Americans are often reminded that this is our besetting sin. We are ever in a feverish haste. Our eyes are restless, brows wrinkled, nerves aquiver. We go through life like a train at full speed, stopping only to take water for more steam, to cool off hot boxes, or for repairs after an accident. It is little wonder that we break down or prematurely wear out. Our national maladies are insomnia and nervous debility. But Americans are not the only feverish folk; the fault pertains to the whole race. Thackeray says, "When I was a boy, I wanted taffy; it cost a shilling and I hadn't one. Now I am a man; I have a shilling, but I don't want any taffy." It is safe to say, however, that he was still longing after the unattainable; in boyhood it was taffy; later on, it was fame.

Our Lord suggests a remedy. "Come with me into the fields," he says, "and observe how God cares for the world. Consider the lilies how they grow; they toil not, neither do they spin. And yet I say unto you that even Solomon in all his glory was not arrayed like one of these. How much more shall he clothe you, O ye of little faith?" So let us stop awhile and allow the axles to cool while we sing:

> "Father, whate'er of earthly bliss
> Thy sov'reign will denies,
> Accepted at thy throne of grace,
> Let this petition rise:—
> Give me a calm, a thankful heart,
> From every murmur free;
> The blessings of thy grace impart,
> And make me live to thee."

Our Lord, in advising against all anxious thought, offers no encouragement to improvidence. On the contrary, the Scriptures constantly enjoin a wise foresight and preparation for future need. "Go to the ant, thou sluggard; consider her ways and be wise." Our Lord, having fed the multitude, said to his disciples, "Gather up the fragments that remain, that nothing be lost." It is every man's duty to lay by for a rainy day. Be prepared for contingencies. Insure your house; it may burn down. Insure your life; there is no telling when you may die. Above all, get ready for eternity. If your sins are not forgiven, it is the part of wisdom to attend to that matter here and now. If your accounts are unbalanced, balance them at once. To-day is yours, to-morrow is God's. He is a prudent man who is so guarded against all future possibilities that he can say, as Paul did when he heard the footfall of the executioner near his door, "I am now ready to be offered; the time of my departure is at hand. I have fought a good fight, I have finished my course, I have kept the faith; henceforth there is laid up for me a crown of righteousness which the Lord the righteous judge will give me in that day."

This is the lesson of the lilies. True, they do not toil; yet they are busy all the while. They take no anxious thought; yet they are ever preparing for the morrow. They fulfil the law of their being, assimilating air and sunshine and the fructifying elements of the soil, making ready thus to bloom in their season. They fold their leaves when the storm draws near, bow their heads meekly and wait until the clouds roll by. They work but do not worry. They are busy but never anxious. Here is the gist of the matter. Let us also abide in our places and rest in God.

The word is, Take no anxious thought. About what? About anything. Worry is the great hindrance to success. He is a good workman who whistles at his bench. I have seen an old negro woman in the South carrying a burden on her head that would have bent me double. The secret was a perfect poise. He who gets his burden just over his head, just above his conscience, just in the zenith of his heart—that is, in the precise line of spiritual gravity—will have no difficulty in bearing it. Our religion should be our strength. This was Paul's meaning when he said, "Be anxious for nothing, but in everything by prayer and supplication with thanksgiving let your requests be made known unto God."

Let us cover the case. The common grounds of

worry are seven. And in all these our anxiety is groundless if we really believe in God.

(1) Let us begin at the bottom: "*Why take ye thought for Food and Raiment?*" Here is the universal occasion of worry. All honest people are striving for a livelihood. The men and women whom we meet, moving their lips as they hurry along the streets, are muttering, "Food and raiment." This is "the care of this world," which our Lord likened to weeds that choke the word. They vex, entangle, hamper the plough; trip us up along the garden paths, crowd out better things and kill the fragrance and fruitfulness of life. It is, indeed, the business of every man to earn a livelihood; but, if we are in the kingdom of Christ, we must needs believe that, with a proper attention to industry and thrift, this will be provided for us. The argument of Christ just here is fourfold. *First*, God remembers all. *Second*, If he is mindful of birds and flowers, how much more shall he care for you? *Third*, It is useless to worry; for "which of you by taking thought can add one cubit to the measure of his life?" And *fourth*, such anxiety is unchristian; "for after all these things do the Gentiles seek." We are in the kingdom; wherefore it devolves upon us to seek first the kingdom of God and his righteousness, with confidence that all lower and material necessities shall be added unto us.

(2) Much of our worry is about *Things that Cannot be Helped;* such as irretrievable losses, incurable maladies, thorns in the flesh. The Stoics would say, "What can't be cured must be endured." But there is better comfort in our Christian philosophy. Take this: "**All** things work together for good to them

that love God;" or this: "Our light affliction, which is but for a moment, worketh for us a far more exceeding and eternal weight of glory;" or this: "Trust in the Lord and do good; so shalt thou dwell in the land, and verily thou shalt be fed."

God makes no mistakes. If we are groaning under some remediless trouble, he means that we shall let patience have her perfect work. A caged bird gains nothing by breaking its wings against the bars. Bide a wee and dinna weary. God knows all and he means all for the best. Luther says, "If thou hast a sorrow beyond thy healing, one thing thou knowest: God can give thee a sweet physical herb called *patientia* that will sustain thee." In answer to Paul's prayer for deliverance came the word, "My grace is sufficient for thee."

(3) And then, as to the *Things that Never Happen*. How grievously we suffer in anticipation of troubles that come not! We watch the gathering clouds and are sure that our plans for to-morrow will come to naught. We are alarmed by an ominous flush on our children's faces. We are apprehensive lest our over-eager creditors or our tardy debtors shall land us in bankruptcy. We are sure the coming election will go wrong. Thus we borrow trouble on trouble, forgetting what the Lord said: Sufficient unto the day is the evil thereof.

> "For human bodies are sic fools,
> For a' their colleges and schools,
> That when nae real ills perplex them,
> They mak' enow themsels to vex them."

I wonder how Adam felt when he saw the first sunset. All day he rejoiced in the benignant light:

but now the great luminary sank nearer and nearer toward the west, the birds betook themselves to their perches, the twilight deepened into darkness, and silence was over all. No doubt he bade a sorrowful farewell to the vanishing orb of light. But with the next morning it rose in the east again, coming forth like a bridegroom from his chamber. So a kind Providence is ever putting us to shame in the dawn of bright mornings. Life has enough of real sorrow; why shall we anticipate the future? Let us hope for the best, and have faith in God.

(4) But surely we have reason to be anxious with reference to our *Personal Salvation?* Not at all. The way is perfectly clear. If we receive the Scriptures, there **is** one thing to do: "He that believeth in the Lord Jesus Christ shall be saved." To believe is to accept Christ as our Saviour from sin. And then, "There is therefore now no more condemnation to them that are in Christ Jesus." We have done our part and he will assuredly do his. There is nothing to gain by worrying about it. If we are ever in doubt, the reasonable thing to do is to get upon our knees and renew our surrender. And so again and again, as often as need be. "But can I hold out?" No, indeed, you cannot. The question is not as to whether you can hold out, but whether God can. It is his grip, not ours, that secures us. His word is, "Ye have not chosen me, but I have chosen you"; and further, "No man shall pluck you out of my hand." It is better to look up than to look in; for our help cometh from the hills. I am not at all sure that I shall be able to stand: but "I know him in whom I have believed, and am persuaded that he is

able to keep that which I have committed unto him against that day."

(5) We are deeply concerned and anxious furthermore, as to our *Progress in the Christian Life*. Are we growing duly in grace and in the knowledge of the truth? This, also, is God's affair if we are wholly committed to him. The question is not of growth primarily, but of life. A marble statue cannot grow because the vital principle is not within it. A branch cut from the vine withers because the life current no longer flows through it. Life necessitates growth. We do not grow by trying to grow, but simply by growing in pursuance of law. A true Christian is a better man with each succeeding day, though he may not be aware of it. The very fact that he laments his shortcoming and feels an increasing desire for larger measures of spiritual power and wisdom, is proof of it. He who busies himself in the Master's work, need not fret about the deepening of his spiritual life. His path must be as the shining light that shineth brighter and brighter unto the perfect day.

The life principle is faith, which unites us with Christ. Faith has been likened to the gastric fluid, a wonderful solvent which separates and dissolves our food so that the body can appropriate and assimilate it. All our food is thus put under contribution to feed the blood and sinew and bone and marrow, and to further the development of the whole man. In like manner faith makes pain and pleasure, bereavement and joy, success and disappointment, work together for our good. These are the spiritual diet which God prepares for us; but they "profit us nothing," as Paul says of the word, unless they be "mixed with faith" in us.

(6) Still further, we wish and wonder and worry as to *the Results of our Labor*. A faithful Christian said recently, "I have been a teacher in the Sabbath School for thirty years; and I do not know that I have ever brought a single soul to Christ." The prayer of Moses finds an echo in the heart of many a devoted servant, "O Lord, establish thou the work of our hands upon us; yea, the work of our hands establish thou it!"

But pause and reflect. We are mere underlings. The work is God's. Paul may plant and Apollos may water, but God giveth the increase. Our responsibility ceases with the discharge of duty. He sends some into his field as ploughmen to break up the fallow ground; like Adoniram Judson who labored for years with no apparent fruit. He sends others into the field to scatter the seed-wheat; like Rutherford who toiled long at Anworth and bemoaned his ill success. He sends others with sickle in hand to reap and gather into the garner; like Whitfield and Moody to whom a multitude of souls are given for their hire. But here is his definite assurance, "He that soweth and he that reapeth shall rejoice together." Meanwhile, let us have no undue solicitude, but rejoice in this: "My word shall not return unto me void, but it shall accomplish that which I please and prosper in the thing whereto I sent it."

The woman of Samaria after her conversation with Jesus left her water-pot at the well, and hastening into the city said to her friends and neighbors, "Come, see a man that told me all things that ever I did. Is not this the Messiah?" This was her particular work; and, having performed it, she is heard of no more. Time passed; and Philip the Evangelist came to Samaria and sowed the gospel there. A great revival followed: but just as the harvest grew yellow under his hand, Philip in turn was sent away; the angel of the Lord saying, "Arise and go toward the desert." It must have been a grievous disappointment to him; but he arose and went. Then came Peter and John with sickle in hand and reaped the harvest. Theirs was the great honor among men; but in heaven the unnamed woman, the evangelist and the two apostles rejoice together.

Let all faithful workers be of good cheer. No labor is for naught, no prayer is unanswered, no holy purpose is wasted. Many a farmer who scatters the grain in June dies before September. But what matters it? All alike are serving the glory of God. And here is our comfort: "He that goeth forth and weepeth, bearing precious seed, shall *doubtless* come again with rejoicing, bringing his sheaves with him."

(7) Our last anxiety is with reference to the *Conversion of the World.* I recently attended a humanitarian Congress where frequent expression was given to the thought that Society is going to the bad. For even a secular socialist to entertain that view, is suggestive of a most lamentable color blindness. But blue glasses are not for Christians. "Let those refuse to sing who never knew our God." The melancholy view of human affairs which prevails in some quarters may be due in part to a disorder of the physical functions, and in part to the overturning of personal schemes. We are like a colony of crickets

who, when a ploughshare goes through the hill, begin with one accord to chirp that the world is coming to an end. But God reigns and everything is going right. We may vanish from the earth, and our plans for social betterment may go with us; but the world will roll on. The word of our Master is full of encouragement: "All power is given unto me in heaven and on earth; go ye therefore and evangelize; and lo, I am with you alway even unto the end of the present order of things."

We have covered the entire ground; and what is our conclusion? Let us alway and under all circumstances take God at his word. He sees the end from the beginning, and we can trust him. In the court of the prison sat Jeremiah bathed in tears. Jerusalem was besieged by the Babylonian army and the Lord had declared that its inhabitants were to be carried into captivity. Just then the word came to Jeremiah, "Buy the field that is at Anathoth." This was the very field on which the Babylonians had pitched their camp. It was to be sold under foreclosure and would "go for a song;" for, under the circumstances, who in Israel would be so bold as to purchase it? But the prophet had faith, blind faith; and taking God at his word, he bought the field at Anathoth, and "weighed out the money even seventeen shekels of silver." Then when the purchase was consummated, the word of the Lord came again to Jeremiah, saying, "Houses and fields and vineyards shall be possessed again in this land." And events proved the wisdom of the investment. O what outlays of time and energy we should be constantly making in the spiritual province, if we could implicitly and unreservedly believe in God! We note the conquests and encroachments of passing errors and wonder what the end will be: but the time will surely come when the ground now occupied by the enemy shall be in possession of the church of God.

In this confidence let us live by the day. A day at a time is enough. The year has been likened to a desk with three hundred and sixty-five drawers, each containing a letter of instructions for a single day. To open them all in over-eagerness and to confront all future duties and responsibilities at once, is to court perplexity and embarrassment. "The day present," as Tyndale translates, "hath ever enough of its own trouble." Let us in the morning open our instructions for the day. Let us do this on our knees and, rising with strong faith, go forth to meet our duties. *Trust and rest;* here is the secret of a happy life. And the great word of comfort is this: "As thy day, so shall thy strength be."

THE TWELVE.

"And he ordained twelve, that they should be with him, and that he might send them forth to preach and have power to heal sicknesses and cast out devils."—Mark 3, 14-15.

A newborn child has need of special care. The Church at the outset must be safeguarded and fostered by means that would be quite unnecessary in its maturity. For this reason the Twelve were endued with extraordinary powers. They are sometimes spoken of as "a Cabinet"; but this is as far as possible from the truth, since they had no advisory power, nor executive either apart from their Chief. Their function was transmission, they being the channels through which the Lord was to communicate himself to succeeding ages.

The marks of their holy office were three: *First*, they were to "be with him"; that is, in constant attendance upon him. Since they were to be his biographers, they must be able to speak with authority as to his character and manner of life. *Second*, they were to preach; that is, to declare the evangel. This included the stereotyping of that evangel in Scripture. The New Testament was wholly written by the apostles; for which particular duty they were endowed with infallibility; they "wrote as they were moved by the Holy Spirit." *Third*, they received the *charismata*, that is, spiritual gifts for the working of miracles.

At the time of the ordaining of the Twelve, the followers of Jesus were a feeble folk like the conies. It was necessary that the new enterprise should be sustained and fostered in an extraordinary manner. But as the strength and numbers of the Church increased, her symbols of faith and practice being finished, and her Oracles sealed, the Day of Pentecost being "fully come" and the common gifts of the Spirit conferred on all, the special provision might be dispensed with. A scaffolding may be necessary in the rearing of the elevation of a temple, but as the walls rise the temporary supports are removed. That which is no longer important would better be taken out of the way.

In the organization and personnel of this Duodecemvirate there are striking evidences of divine wisdom. It was a curiously constituted body. Some of its peculiarities are most interesting and profitably suggestive:—

1. To begin with, *the number Twelve*. In this the mystics discovered an important symbolism; to wit, as three is the number of the holy Trinity and four the number of universality, so their product marks the Duodecemvirate who in the name of the Trinity should go forth to the conquest of the world. This is interesting but wholy fanciful.

The number was probably suggested by the twelve sons of Jacob. An emphasis is thus put upon the fact that Judaism and Christianity are not two religions but one. There is one God. There is one Bible covering all history from the protevangel to Malachi, and from the advent to the announcement of the strong angel, "Time shall be no more."

There is one cross throwing its radiance backward over all prophecy and forward into all history; giving significance to every lamb slain on the ancient altars and providing the only hope of deliverance from sin. There is one religion also and one only, covering the Old Economy and the New. Christianity is not a new system, but the consummate fruit and flower of Judaism with its rites and symbols all centering in Christ. It was meet and proper, therefore, that our Lord, in organizing his Church, should ordain the twelve apostles to stand side by side with the twelve sons of Israel for the propagation of the religion of the one true God.

2. The question occurs, *Why were there no Women among them?* The reason is not far to seek. It was certainly not because our Lord would suggest any disparity of the sexes. There is a difference, however, to ignore which would be to set oneself athwart the law of nature. The work to which the apostles were called was one of peculiar hardship; it was distinctly a work for men.

The "new woman," though clamoring for a conspicuous place in public life, was eloquently silent when volunteers were recently wanted for our war with Spain. Her part in that conflict was important, indeed, in ministering to the sick and wounded, but not amid the confused noise of battle on the high places of the field. In like manner the Lord had need of woman's ministry, but not among those who were to mingle in the tumult of the early propaganda, exposed to the publicity of the madding crowd and braving dangers oft by land and sea. The duties of the apostolate were of such a character that it is no reflection on womanhood when we say that men were better fitted to discharge them.

3. *Why were not Celibates exclusively chosen to this holy office?* Had that been done, our friends of the Romish Church would have been spared a great perplexity; but indeed it would have been contrary to the divine economy. It is God who setteth the solitary in families; and his well-beloved Son put a perpetual sanction on wedlock in attending the marriage supper at Cana. We cannot say with absolute certainty how many of the twelve were married, but there is no question whatever as to Peter, who is claimed as the original Pope (Mark 1, 30). This fact is referred to by the Apostle Paul, in asserting his right to marry a sister in the Lord (1 Cor. 9, 5). The doctrine of a celibate clergy is unsparingly denounced in Paul's letter to the young pastor of the Corinthian church, where he warns him against certain seducing spirits who are "forbidding to marry;" such teaching he characterizes as "a doctrine of devils" (1 Tim. 4, 3). The consistent teaching of all Scripture is that wedlock is "honorable in all."

4. Let it be observed that *the apostles were all Men of the People.* There was not an aristocrat among them, nor a beggar, though there is room as well for beggars as for millionaires in the church. Christ himself was a carpenter. In the immediate circle of his followers there were several fishermen. Philip is reputed to have been a charioteer. All belonged to "the Third Estate." Wealth is, indeed, no bar to the fellowship of Christ, nor is poverty; but alas for the church made up of the indolent rich or of the indolent poor! The Church is mainly recruited from

among the bourgeoisie, the men of brain-craft and handicraft, the producers.

Time was when labor was held in disrepute; the gospel in its calm influence along the centuries has glorified it.

We hear it rumored in some quarters that the Church has lost its grip on the laboring classes. This is as far as possible from being true. Too many, indeed, are still alienated from the Church and from Christ their fellow-craftsman. But an ever-increasing number is being won year by year. The conquests of the propaganda are chiefly among this class. The efforts of the Church are most welcome and successful here; and the ultimate winning of the Third Estate is destined to usher in the Golden Age.

5. *The Twelve were all Unlettered men.* It would have been an easy matter for Christ to gather an apostolate from among the rabbis and philosophers. The Sanhedrin was ever willing to endorse his claims and purposes, would he but comply with their terms. But Nicodemus was not chosen; the young lawyer, a professor of Biblical exegesis, was not chosen; the Scribes and Pharisees, so far from being chosen, were repulsed in severest terms.

The world had had enough of rabbinical wisdom and philosophy, enough of wire-drawing and hair-splitting. The people were weary of theological controversy. The truths that were essential to life and that must needs be proclaimed for the world's deliverance, were of the simplest character. Sin and salvation; love Godward and manward; these were fundamental and these were within the comprehension of all. There would presently be a place for

Paul and ultimately for Augustine and Calvin; but what the world needed at this juncture was a deliverance from subtle dogmatics and apologetics and a clear statement of rudimental truth. This was Christ's meaning when he took a little child upon his knee and said, "Verily, verily, I say unto you, except ye become as this little child, ye shall in no wise enter the kingdom of God."

6. *They were all Townsmen ;* not a farmer nor a shepherd among them. The announcement of the incarnation came to shepherds while watching their flocks and to magi watching the stars. But the men needed for the organization of the Church were not dreamers and anchorites, but such as were familiar with earnest life. It is the city that gives knowledge of human nature. "As iron sharpeneth iron, so a man sharpeneth the countenance of his friend." Not dreamers of dreams and seers of visions, not diffident husbandmen, not introspective anchorites were needed at the organization of the Church, but rather men of affairs accustomed to busy life and fearing not the faces of their fellow men.

7. *They were as Unlike as possible.* A man of rock, two sons of thunder, a doubter, a guileless Israelite; each had his characteristics, and each was fitted to the place ordained for him. We may find here a suggestion as to rational Church-union. There are those who would blot out all the distinctions between the denominations and set up a rigid uniformity in thought and method. But "fences make good neighbors." There was never a time since the beginning of the Christian era when the various bodies of believers were more clearly differentiated in their peculiar

tenets or more cordially united in the fellowship of service than now. God be praised that they can thus agree to differ and keep the peace! The twelve apostles, so diverse in temperament and character, were still united and harmonious in their consecration to Christ. Not uniformity but harmonious action is what we need. "In essentials unity, in non-essentials diversity, in all things charity" is the watchword that should unite us.

8. *They were Alike in their Conviction and Confession of Sin.* There was not a "saint" among them. They were men of like passions and infirmities with ourselves. Had Jesus desired an apostolate of perfect beings, he must have chosen from among the angels. All of the apostles were imperfect and some had glaring faults. If Peter could speak for himself to-day he would say, "Take me out of your Calendar of Saints; I am the man who denied my Lord." And Thomas would say, "Take me also out of your Calendar; I am the man who doubted his power over death." And the Twelve with one accord would say, "We were not Saints, but sinners all, sinners saved by grace." We are drawn nearer to these men by this consideration; and furthermore, it emphasizes the sweet lesson of charity. It minimizes self and magnifies Christ; it makes the grateful song of Wesley ours:

"I'm a poor sinner and nothing at all,
But Jesus Christ is my all in all."

9. *And there was One Hypocrite among them.* Jesus knew Judas; he said of him, "He hath a devil"; nevertheless he chose him. It is as if Kaiser Wilhelm were to select an arch-anarchist to be his Chancellor of the Exchequer. Was this to teach us that a man

may mingle in the sweetest Christian fellowship and still be an enemy of truth? "Anear the kirk, afar frae God." A name on a church roster or a high place of ecclesiastical preferment is no proof of vital godliness. The Lord knoweth his own. The tares and the wheat must grow together until the harvest. "A man may cry, 'Church, Church,' with no more piety than other people." Let us not conclude, however, that to be overtaken in a glaring fault or exposed to public shame is proof positive of hypocrisy. Who am I, or who are you, to pass judgment in this matter? The Lord looketh on the heart. "Let him that thinketh he standeth, take heed lest he fall." One betrayed Christ, another denied him, all forsook him. It behooves us, in view of these things and of Christ's admonition, to ask with all earnestness, "Lord, is it I?"

10. *Not a few of the Twelve were Nobodies;* that is, there is little or no record of them. Let us not infer, however, that they accomplished nothing. God keeps the chronicles. He knows how many churches they founded, how many sermons they preached, how many miracles they wrought, how many sinners they brought to him. Our standards of success and greatness are illusory. The makers of history have not been the conspicuous leaders whose names are writ large on the monuments. We have much to say of Cromwell and the Silent William and Coligny; but it is the tramp, tramp, tramp of the rank and file—the Puritans, the Beggars of Holland, the Huguenots— men who lived unknown and died unhonored and unsung—that has marked the advancement of the centuries. Here are names without a record, as Seth

and Enos and Jared and Mahalaleel. And here are records without names: as of the little maid in Naaman's palace, the little lad with the basket of loaves, the man who brought the beast of burden to Jesus for his triumphal entry, the soldier who quenched his fever thirst on the cross. God knows about them. "The Master praises; what are men?" Let us be willing to serve God in obscurity if need be. He that seeth in secret shall reward us openly. The names of the faithful, though unrecorded in earth's annals, are written on the palms of his hands.

11. *All the Twelve were Martyrs.* The only one in question is John; and tradition says that he was dragged by his gray hairs through the streets of Ephesus and cast into the arena "to be ground as God's fine wheat by the teeth of lions."

> They climbed the steep ascent to heaven,
> 'Mid peril, toil, and pain;
> O God, to us may grace be given
> To follow in their train!

Here is a lesson for these piping times of peace. The story of the apostles, who faced the gleaming ax for Jesus' sake, puts us to shame. There is no room for a coward in the goodly fellowship. Why should we "be carried to the skies on flowery beds of ease?" The danger of martyrdom has passed; and, alas! we shrink before a pointed finger. Let us be ready to endure hardness as good soldiers of Christ. His word is, "If any man will come after me, let him deny himself, take up his cross and follow me."

12. *The Apostles had No Successors.* There was no occasion for any to succeed them. The infant Church,

during the century which elapsed before the death of John the Evangelist, had grown to such maturity in strength and influence, that it could be left safely to the protecting care of God's common Providence. He who kindles a fire on his hearthstone must select the proper sort of tinder and arrange it carefully; then kneel and blow gently on the kindling spark; but after a while he rises to his feet, knowing that with proper oversight the fire will burn of itself. Thus Christ fostered the early Church; but presently came Pentecost; and thenceforth the air was full of oxygen to feed the flame.

I am not disposed, however, to controvert the claim of those who insist on "the Apostolic Succession." We stand open to conviction; and it should be an easy matter to convince us. All that is necessary in order to establish the apostolic lineage and authority of these brethren is that they should show themselves to be possessed of the three apostolic signs; to wit, *First*, They must have lived and walked with Jesus in the flesh, listened to his words, beheld his miracles, and witnessed his resurrection (Acts 1, 21, 22). *Second*, They must be infallible in the communication of spiritual truth. The twelve wrote Scripture; so far as we are aware, no one of their alleged successors has ever added a single page. Indeed, there is only one man living to-day who claims infallibility in these premises; and some of us have doubts of even him. *Third*, They must have power to work miracles. There are some who profess to heal the sick by laying on of hands; but at the best they cannot claim an unvarying success, nor do they attribute their therapeutic power to any aposto lic *charismata*. There is apparently less of healing virtue in the entire College of Cardinals than in Peter's shadow or John's handkerchief.

In addition to the Apostolate, the Lord appointed "other seventy also" to go forth among the villages and preach his gospel. In addition also to these seventy he made every one of his followers an agent of the propaganda. He breathed on them all, men, women and children, saying, "Receive ye the Holy Ghost"; adding, "As the Father hath sent me into the world, so send I you." Thus, in a broad and blessed sense, all are apostles, being "sent ones."

In the mind of Jesus there was a magnificent purpose; no less than the setting up of his kingdom on earth and the deliverance of the race from sin. A place in that great purpose is assigned to the humblest of his people. The man who hears not or heeds not such appointment makes a failure of life. On the back of Holman Hunt's picture of "The Light of the World" — representing the King, thorn-crowned, lantern in hand, standing without the door, knocking—is the artist's autograph in these words: "Lord, pass me not by!" But, indeed, the Lord passes by no man who is willing to receive him. He calls us to a large salvation, which means not merely redemption, but election to the high privilege of service. He sends us every one to carry on the work which he began and his apostles furthered in the laying of the foundations of the Church. If we follow in his steps, pursue his work, devote ourselves to the winning of souls and the building of his kingdom here and now, we shall pass in through the apostolic gate at last and receive his commendation, "Well done, good servant, enter thou into the joy of thy Lord!"

AT THE WATER-GATE.

"And all the people gathered themselves together as one man into the street that was before the Water-gate."—Nehemiah 8, 1.

In the year 604 B.C. the city of Jerusalem fell into the hands of Nebuchadnezzar and was presently reduced to utter ruin and desolation. The inhabitants were carried away in successive deportations to Babylon, where they "hung their harps on the willows and wept when they remembered Zion." In 536 B.C. a proclamation was issued by Cyrus authorizing the return of a colony under Zerubbabel to rebuild the temple and restore the sacred rites. In 479 B.C.—fifty-seven years later—Ezra the scribe returned with another company; he devoted himself particularly to the reformation of morals. It was very clear that there could be no permanent improvement until the people should renew their loyalty to the Scriptures, which were the symbol of both their political and their religious life.

To the help of Ezra came, after ten years, Nehemiah, the cup-bearer of Artaxerxes. As governor of the province, he was instructed to address himself to civil affairs and particularly to the rebuilding of the walls. He was an astute politician as well as a devout man. He conferred with Ezra, who said, "We must get back to the Constitution of the Theocracy."—"But where is that Constitution?" asked Nehemiah.— "In the Scriptures," was the reply, "which have long been a dead letter among the people."—"Where are those Scriptures?"—"The copy which was preserved in the Ark of the Covenant was carried away to Babylon and lost. I have been engaged, during the ten years since my return, in getting them together. The scroll is now complete; and I suggest that the people be assembled to hear it."

In pursuance of this suggestion, a Constitutional Assembly was convened on the first of the seventh month, 444 B.C. It was in the great public square of Ophel, before the Water-gate. Not less than fifty thousand men, women and children came together there. It was a stirring scene. For the first time in a century, the walls being now completed and the gates in place, the inhabitants of the city might assemble thus in security. Their purpose was to hear the Scriptures. A platform had been reared, on which Ezra, with thirteen priests and as many Levites took their place. This platform is called "a pulpit"; but it was distinctly not what we understand by the pulpit. It did not enclose the ministers or separate them from the people.

Our pulpit took its rise in those ages of spiritual declension when the truth was minimized and "holy orders" were invested with an unseemly authority. The priest climbed by a winding stairway to his place on a pillar, far above the congregation; a place beseeming one who, as Dryden says, "swelled to counsel kings and govern kingdoms." A railing must needs be there for protection; and within this enclosure stood the superior being, like an angel leaning from a balcony. In the dawning light of the Reformation this platform was gradually lowered to the level of the people, with only so much of elevation as was needed for the convenience of being seen and heard. But, alas! the fence remained and still remains; and this is the pulpit. I say it is an archaism, a traditional impertinence, and a vast inconvenience. There is no reason for it, in Scripture or in common sense. The preacher is not a being apart from or above his fellows, but a man among men.

I. *"And Ezra opened the book in the sight of all the people; and when he opened it, all the people stood up."* There were no listless or indifferent ones; but at the opening of the scroll, all as one man assumed an attitude of attention and reverence. Why? What was this scroll that so impressed them? It was the Pentateuch, the long-neglected Book of the Law. It was those Five Books of Moses which, in many quarters to-day, are treated with scant courtesy. It was Genesis, Exodus, Leviticus, Numbers and Deuteronomy—the same Deuteronomy which some of our sapient critics have discovered to be a forgery!

They say we are living in an age of Bible study. It is probably true that there never was a time when the Scriptures were viewed with such severe scrutiny by scholars devout and otherwise. There is reason to suspect, however, that among average Christians there is much neglect of Holy Writ. We are informed by scientists that the germs of many contagious diseases are circulated in the dust blowing along our streets. The dust that lies on our unused Bibles is the occasion of much of the spiritual infirmity of our times; in it are the germs of doubt and skepticism and infidelity. No man can live an earnest Christian life except as he is loyal to the word of God.

It must be said, furthermore, that not all the scholars who devote themselves assiduously to the study of the Scriptures, show a due regard for its divine character. There are many who openly and flagrantly dishonor it; not merely by sneering at considerable portions, but by reducing it for critical use to the level of other books. The position assumed in some of our theological seminaries is this: In order to a judicial investigation and critical study of the Scriptures, you must put aside all preconception of its sacred character and regard it precisely as you would an uninspired writing. This is a most unreasonable and pernicious sophism.

It may do for outsiders to view revelation in this manner; but surely not for Christians who have solemnly accepted the Book as an infallible rule of faith and practice, and who stand pledged to the proposition that the Scriptures were prepared "by holy men who wrote as they were moved by the Holy Ghost." It is impossible for these to waive the doctrine of inspiration. Nor is it necessary. A man need not put aside his loyalty as an American citizen in order to an impartial study of the principles of the Constitution. The son of Lord Tennyson was not required to disavow his filial love when he undertook to write a just biography of his father. A juryman is not asked to dispossess his mind of preconceptions as to dishonesty before he can pass judgment on a prisoner at the bar. If the contention of the destructive critics is just, we are driven to this preposterous conclusion: that we as Christians must not presume to view judicially the life and character of Jesus Christ, unless we previously lay aside all our love and devotion to him.

In justice to our religion, in fulfillment of our espousal vows, we are bound to regard the Scripture as a book by itself, solitary and alone, given by inspiration as the unveiling of the divine mind. "Do you mean to assert, then, that Christianity is the religion of a book?" Aye; why not? "But we thought it was the religion of Christ." So it is; the religion of Christ as he is portrayed in the Book. We speak of our Republic as a Constitutional Government,—that is, a government resting on a written symbol. Is it not, then, the republic of Washington and Madison, of Jefferson and Hamilton, of Franklin and Adams? Aye; but only as they have recorded and perpetuated their political convictions in the Constitution. And by common consent the perpetuity of our nation depends upon our loyalty to that compendium of political truth. In like manner the Bible, as the reflex of the divine mind, is the very life of Christianity; and, as such, it stands apart from and infinitely superior to all other books.

In the desert of Midian there were many acacia bushes, and Moses might have smitten any with his shepherd's crook. But one day he saw a bush aflame and not consumed. He said, "I will now turn aside and see this great sight." But a voice came from the bush saying, "Draw not nigh hither: put off thy shoes from off thy feet; for the place whereon thou standest is holy ground. I am the Lord thy God!" Then Moses hid his face and was afraid to look. In like manner the world is full of books; but there is one which we approach with reverence, because it has fed bonfires through all the ages and is not yet consumed; and a voice proceeds from it saying, "I am the Lord thy God!"

The conspicuous sin of our time is irreverence toward the sacred Word. We take all manner of liberties with it. We draw upon it for riddles and pleasantries. *Procul, procul abeste, profani!* Hands off the Ark! For it is written, "Thou hast magnified thy word above all thy name!"

Ministers of righteousness, stand up at the unfolding of the scroll! Put away your penknives and veil your faces. God speaks from his oracles; let all the earth keep silence before him.

Men and women of Christ, bow your faces at the opening of the Book! Speak with caution. Who are we that we should put our quarter-ounce of pedantry against omniscience? The wisdom of man is as ephemeral as the breath of his nostrils. The heavens shall be rolled up as a scroll and the earth shall be consumed as with fervent heat; but the word of the Lord endureth forever!

II. "*So they read in the book distinctly, and gave the sense, and caused them to understand the reading.*" At this point "the people were in their place;" this probably means that they sat down. But why should they sit down? Because there is a clear difference between God's word and a preacher's exposition. One is authoritative and inerrant; the other is an opinion, true or false as the case may be. A wise minister does not expect his people to receive his interpretation of Scripture as final; he asks only that they give due attention to his statement as the result of careful study and investigation, and then put it to the test, weighing, judging, proving all things and holding fast that which is good. My friend, let no man take your crown. Think for yourself; let no man, preacher or otherwise, do your thinking for you. Make the word of the Lord your court of last appeal; and be able to give to every man a reason for the faith that is in you.

An important part of the work of Ezra, with his scribes and Levites in the great assembly, was the translation of the sacred writings into the Aramaic tongue. For the people in their long captivity had almost or quite forgotten the Hebrew.* God be praised for Wyclif who, at peril of his life, translated the Scriptures into the English tongue, saying, "If God please, I will cause that every ploughman and every apprentice shall be able to read the divine oracles for himself." God be praised that the meanest of the Stuarts was moved to give us the King James Version. It is rumored that the Romish Church is about to retranslate the Vulgate for a more general circulation among the people. Who shall estimate the possibilities of such an enterprise? We have had enough of cabalistic prayers and scriptures. Paul wisely wrote to the Corinthians, "I would rather speak five words with the understanding than a thousand words in an unknown tongue."

Then came the Exposition of the Word. The scribes and Levites "gave the sense and caused the people to understand." This was preaching. The

---

* The language of Jesus in his preaching was the Aramaic; as in the words, Ephphatha; Talitha cumi; Eloi, Eloi, lama sabachthani.

only true preaching is expository. Not that a text is necessary; this being purely conventional. Nor is it always best to analyze a particular paragraph and treat it *seriatim*. But true preaching is ever a setting forth of those great principles which are enshrined with quickening power in Holy Writ. It is to state them "distinctly," to "give the sense," to "cause the people to understand," and to apply those principles to the common affairs of life. This is what the people want; not vocal gymnastics nor oratorical pyrotechnics; and certainly not a treatment of current problems without reference to divine truth. The word *sermo* means "a thrust." A sermon is a clear, effective thrust with the sword of the Spirit which is the word of God.

We are not unfrequently told that the pulpit of our time "has lost power." It is doubtless true that some pulpits have done so; but ministers of the gospel who hold themselves to the declaration of the inerrant Word are not complaining of a lack of hearers. The pulpit as an institution is and must ever be the greatest power in the world. "The Pulpit *versus* the Press" is not an open question. We do not underestimate the power of the Press for good or evil; but on what basis will you compare them? The ratio in the last reduction is that of a penny whistle to a roll of thunder. The press is the purveyor of news in politics, in society, in international affairs. We want the news, the secular news, from the remotest corners of the earth; but the Good News of salvation we must have or die. So long as sin runs through the veins of the race; so long as the universal heart throbs to the question, "What shall I do to be saved?"; so long as men have splendid dreams of character and influence and eternal life; so long must the power of the pulpit be supreme. The telegraph wires are laden and vibrant with messages; but there is no message like this which comes from the heavenly throne, the news that God so loved the world that he gave his only-begotten Son to suffer and die for it.

III. *As to the Results of that great Assembly.* For events like lives must be measured by their fruits. "If any man be a hearer of the word and not a doer, he is like unto a man beholding his natural face in a glass; for he beholdeth himself, and goeth his way, and straightway forgetteth what manner of man he was. But whoso looketh into the perfect law of liberty and continueth therein, he being not a forgetful hearer, but a doer of the work, this man shall be blessed in his deed."

It is recorded that, as the reading and exposition of the Scriptures proceeded, the people answered, "Amen, Amen, with lifting up their hands." They saw themselves reflected in the Law. They knew the law was holy, just and good; they knew that they had broken it. An old man and his wife once sat down to read. Presently he said, "Wife, if these things are true, we are all wrong." As they read further she said, "Husband, if these things are true, we are lost." They still read on; until they were moved to say, "If these things are true, we are saved!" There is no more striking evidence of the divinity of the book than in the quick response which mind, conscience and heart make to it.

"And all the people wept." It was an affecting

sight; the great assembly moved to passionate tears, as a wheat field bowing in the wind. But why weep? No doubt on the outskirts of the assembly there were some who curled their lips in scorn at the reading of the Mosaic Cosmogony, the Flood, the Destruction of the Cities of the Plain, the Giving of the Law, the Pillar of Fire, the Blood streaming from the brazen Altar. These were mere fables to their minds; for there were overwise people in those days as now. But life had gone wrong with the multitude, and they were moved by the very opening words of the scroll, "In the beginning God!" They saw their own experience in the sorrow of the antediluvians. They shook and trembled with the multitude who gathered around Sinai. They feared with their fathers on the Passover night, with the blood on the lintels of the doors and the angel of destruction passing over. They bowed their faces to the earth around the flaming altar and beneath the pillar of cloud. They were in no mood to speculate on the jot and tittle of moral or doctrinal distinctions now; they were as sinners in the hands of an angry God.

But more, they "worshiped the Lord" and renewed their covenant with him. It was a time for reconsecration. They determined that day to abandon their inconsistent manner of life, to give up usury and extortion, to observe the holy convocation. This was a Revival indeed. It was a return to pure and undefiled religion.

And Nehemiah said to the people, "Go your way, eat the fat and drink the sweet, and send portions unto them for whom nothing is prepared; for this day is holy unto the Lord; neither be ye sorry, for the joy of the Lord is your strength." Why should they not rejoice? They had indeed been smitten to the heart by a clear perception of their sins; but they had also seen at the altar a foregleam of the cross, and they knew that God stood ready to forgive their sin. Then came the Feast of Tabernacles. Up and down the streets of Jerusalem went the multitude waving lulab branches and singing, "O that men would praise the Lord for his goodness and his wonderful works to the children of men!"

Let us return to our Bibles, dear friends, if we would know the joy of the Lord. We cannot too soon assume a loving, reverent and responsive attitude to his Scriptures. Dear Book! In the darkness of sin, thou hast been our dayspring from on high. In sorrow thou hast given us the garment of praise for the spirit of heaviness. In trial thou hast lightened our burdens. Thou hast been our sun by day, our moon and stars by night; and in the valley of death thou wilt be a rod and a staff to comfort us. Thou art a well in the Valley of Baca, from which we drink up strength along the way. Thou art deep as the sea; sharp as a two-edged sword even to the dividing asunder of soul and spirit; fierce as a consuming fire to those who reject or revile thee; soothing as balm of Gilead to the wounded soul.

To the Law and the Testimony, O people of Christ! Have you been absorbed in selfish cares and pleasures? Take down the Book and prayerfully read it. Have you been mourning, "Dear Lord, and shall we ever live at this poor dying rate"? Open the Book, and observe how God waits to be gracious. See how the face of Jesus looks out upon you from every page;

how his love is written everywhere between the lines. Hear his word of invitation, and let your soul respond "Amen."

It is said that when the war of Holland with Spain was over, the people of Haarlem, reduced to starvation by a protracted siege, assembled to hear the proclamation of peace. The oldest man in the city had been appointed to read it. His eyes were dim; his voice was tremulous. The people strained their ears to hear; they watched the moving of his lips; whatever else they missed, one thing was clear; the day of peace had come! So in our perusal of the blessed Book, we come upon much that is difficult to understand. How could it be otherwise, since it came from the infinite Mind? But this is plain as the sun at noon: God loves the world and has given his only-begotten Son to die for our salvation. In the pages of the Book we behold a picture of ourselves and thereat we weep. We behold God, and seeing him, we weep; for he is just and righteous altogether. And we behold the cross, his overture of peace to sinners; and thereat we cease to weep. The joy of the Lord becomes our strength. We make merry as in the Feast of Tabernacles, because his goodness is great toward us.

AT THE THRESHOLD OF JOSEPH'S HOUSE

"And when they were come into the house, they saw—."—Matt. 2, 11.

The tetrarch of Judea was much disturbed. He had hardened himself against the memories of a mis-lived past. He could laugh at the specters that shook their fingers at him in the night-watches. But what he could not endure was the thought of losing his crown. The air was filled with rumors of a coming king. The Jews had long been expectant. Virgil had sung his Ninth Eclogue, predicting the approach of One who should usher in the Golden Age. The same thought was prominent in the contemporary drama of the Greeks. And on all hands there was a substantial agreement, mentioned by Tacitus, Suetonius and Josephus, that this Messiah was to be born among the Jews.

The arrival of the Magi at Jerusalem threw the naturally suspicious Herod into a paroxysm of jealous fear. They had gone from door to door asking, "Where is he that is born King of the Jews?" The rabbis, subservient to the tetrarch's will, came together in haste. "Tell me," he demanded, "where this King of Israel should be born?" The prophecy of Micah was recalled: "And thou, Bethlehem Ephratah, though thou be little among the thousands of

Judah, yet out of thee shall he come forth that is to be ruler in Israel; whose goings forth have been from of old, from everlasting." Thereupon the Magians were sent for. "Go to Bethlehem," said Herod, "and search diligently for the young child; and when ye have found him, bring me word again, that I also may come and worship him." As they passed through the gates, the star that had previously guided them reappeared, and they rejoiced with exceeding joy.

It must have been toward morning when they entered Bethlehem, still asking, "Where is he that is born King of the Jews?" They were directed to the house of Joseph. And now they are standing at the threshold; but let them pause before they lift the latch, and let us pause with them; for within that door is the greatest of mysteries,—the Incarnation. Let not mortals rush in where angels fear to tread The Ark of the Covenant was a symbol of that truth, God manifest in flesh. Over it the cherubim stood in reverent attitude, with downcast eyes; as it is written, "which things the angels desire to look into."

I. Let us remark of these Magi before they enter, that *they believed in God.* They were Zoroastrians, worshiping the sun as a visible symbol of the true God. They were astronomers also; versed in theological lore as set forth in the music of the spheres.

> "What though in solemn silence all
> Move round this dark terrestrial ball?
> What though no real voice nor sound
> Amid those radiant orbs be found?
> In reason's ear they all rejoice
> And utter forth a glorious voice,
> Forever singing as they shine,
> 'The hand that made us is Divine.'"

It has been written, "An undevout astronomer is mad"; and the same may be asserted of any rational being who denies the existence of God. Theism is an intellectual necessity. If one were to account for the speed of a locomotive by saying, "The wheels are doing it," you would naturally ask, "But what is back of the wheels?" If he should reply, "The steam is moving them," you would still ask, "But what is back of the steam?" And your reason would not rest until it found the engineer. If you were to observe from a hilltop the skilful maneuvers of a battle, the marchings and countermarchings, the infantry in line, the cavalry speeding over the hills to reenforce them, the artillery placing their guns in every coign of vantage, the suggestion that this was automatic would provoke a smile. You would sweep the valley with your field-glass until you found the commander-in-chief before his tent directing all. We are on a world that speeds along its orbit with a thousand times the rapidity of the Empire State Express, aud it needs no argument to prove a hand at the throttle. We are in the thick of the conflict of current events; and it needs no argument to prove a directing Providence. A profession of atheism is proof presumptive of an ill-balanced or unsettled mind. "The fool hath said in his heart, There is no God."

II. But these Magians not merely believed in God; *they wished to see him.* They inquired for "the King of the Jews," indeed; but there was a profound significance in the phrase. It was a proverb, "Salvation is of the Jews." The expectation was that God would, from among his chosen people, make bare his arm for deliverance. This was "The Hope of Israel," and the world sympathized with it. "The King of the Jews," was, therefore, a Messianic title; as were "Immanuel" and "Son of God." There is a sense in which all, being created in the divine image, are sons of God; but this Messiah was to be the "only-begotten." All the coins that were issued under the dominion of Cæsar bore his image and superscription; but that image was impressed in a peculiar manner on his son. In his veins flowed the royal blood; he was heir apparent to the throne. It had been prophesied that God would manifest himself in like manner in the last days: "For unto us a child is born, unto us a Son is given: and the government shall be upon his shoulder: and his name shall be called Wonderful, Counsellor, The Mighty God, The Everlasting Father, The Prince of Peace;" also, "A virgin shall conceive and bear a son and shall call his name, Immanuel; that is, *God with us.*"

It was to see Messiah—not another Ahab or Manasseh—that the Magians came so far. Their apprehension of the great truth was probably dim as compared with ours; but the star gave it emphasis. It was a singular star; going before them in the heavens and beckoning. Here surely was "a heavenly conjunction" in a higher sense than scientists understand it. All the potentates of the earth could not kindle such an omen in the skies. It was as if God himself were saying, "Follow! Follow! I have somewhat to show you."

To see God is the desire of all earnest men. "Show us the Father and it sufficeth us." The eldest of the patriarchs has left a pathetic story of this quest: "O that I knew where I might find him, that I might come even to his seat. I would order my cause before him, and fill my mouth with arguments. Behold, I go forward, but he is not there; and backward, but I cannot perceive him: on the left hand, where he doth work, but I cannot behold him; he hideth himself on the right hand, that I cannot see him."

In pursuance of this longing for a visible God the children of Israel made them the golden calf. It is so hard to worship the Incomprehensible Essence. Perhaps a philosopher may grasp it; but the multitudes still go asking, "Where is he?"

III. The Magi, standing at Joseph's door, *have come to the right place to find God.* If there is a God, as all believe, and if he is our Father, he will surely manifest himself in some way. But how? The hope of Moses, in his prayer "Show me thy glory," was that the veil might be withdrawn before his fleshly eyes. That, however, is impossible; for no man can see God and live. The light of all the orbs floating in space, concentrated into one fierce sunburst, could not equal the dazzling brightness of his face. The prayer of Moses was heard; he hid himself in the cleft of the rock and God passed by; there was the rustling of a moving garment, a momentary shadow; and that was all.

We search for God in nature; and the result is the Pantheon. There are gods from hill and valley; nymphs, dryads, nereids, deifications of nature in every form. Men worship the sun, the scarabæus, great Moloch with his fiery arms, a lizard, a crocodile, an onion. O the lamentable depths to which the race has fallen in its desire to find or make a suitable symbol of the invisible God!

We search for him in philosophy with no better result. The orientals ended their researches in a deification of the universe; that is, All things are God. The Occidentals arrived at Pantheism; that is, God is all things. These ultimates were equally false and equally true. Thales professed to have discovered in Water the potency of life. Xenophanes proclaimed that nothing could be more divine than Thought. Plato anticipated the investigations of modern scientists who declare that the Ultimate is all-pervading Law or Force. The Stoics were agnostics, giving up the quest in despair; saying, like Fichte, "We know nothing, not even that we know nothing."

Shall we then evolve God from our inner consciousness? The utmost that a man can do in this direction is to project himself in large dimensions on the skies, a Brocken of the Alps. As there are many men of many minds the result must be a corresponding multiplicity of gods.

How then can he reveal himself save in an incarnation? We have exhausted our resources. The world grows weary of seeking him. The fulness of time is the hour of despair. He will now reveal himself, as declared in all prophecy, as announced in the evangel,—"The seed of the woman shall bruise the serpent's head." The great Father desires to communicate with his children. Our medium of communication is language. The Word of the Father will now be articulated for his children's use. The Word shall be made flesh that it may dwell among us.

IV. One thing remains to be said before the Magians

pass the threshold of Joseph's house; *they must have faith.* For spiritual things are spiritually discerned. The verities of the invisible world are beyond our finger tips. Faith is "the sixth sense." It is as really a sense as sight or hearing; consequently it is as unreasonable for a man to expect to grasp a spiritual truth without the exercise of faith, as it would be to insist on hearing a thing which can only be seen. One sense can not usurp the functions of another Hence all efforts to demonstrate spiritual facts by the so-called scientific method are futile.

A recent periodical contains an argument on "Physical Science and the Doctrine of Immortality", in which the writer undertakes to demonstrate by the scientific method that there is life beyond death. His concluding words are these: "We thus, in view of the advances of physical science, appear to have an infinite capacity of conceiving of impressions which may come from regions far transcending the narrow limits of this earth; and, in view of this capacity, can we believe that this little life is rounded with a sleep from which there is no awakening?" The learned disquisition closes with a mark of interrogation! But how could it be otherwise since faith, and faith alone, is "the evidence of things not seen"?

The most veritable facts in human life and experience are not infrequently beyond the necessity, not to say beyond the possibility, of argument. You will thank no man for tearing apart the leaves and petals of a rose to help your appreciation of it. It would be a useless task to dissect the vocal apparatus of a skylark; let me see it soaring through the ether and hear its matchless song! I watch the sun go down in golden glory; and a discourse on the refraction of light just then would be an impertinence. O man of science, be still and let me drink this beauty in! Or who shall argue as to a mother's love? Who shall estimate it by a mathematical computation of the number of kisses imprinted on an infant's cheek? So with this doctrine of the incarnation; you cannot reduce it to a dull scientific fact. Before you reach your *quod erat demonstrandum*, the life and glory have departed. Let this suffice. God is manifest in flesh. Let me bow and silently behold him. There is a magnetism in the presence of Christ, a light in his eyes, a warmth in his hands, a life out of his death, that forces me to cry like the centurion beneath his cross, "Verily, this is the Son of God!"

Not that the incarnation is contra-rational. It is above, but not against reason. It lies distinctly in the province of faith. The man who makes the assertion that no fact is to be received which cannot be apprehended by the senses, is in deep water; for we live and move and have our being in a realm of mystery. I will agree to explain to you the dual nature of Christ if you will explain to me the dual nature of man. I am flesh and spirit; no scientist in the world can elucidate the connection and co-operation of these two. I lift my hand. What does that mean? The power of mind over matter. My reason spoke to my will, my will commanded a sinew; and, behold, it was done! Thus spirit and flesh co-operate; my dual personality is a fact; no philosopher can explain it; none can deny it.

We are ready now to lift the latch and pass, with the Magians, into Joseph's house. Here is the mystery, God manifest in flesh. *Theanthropos!* This child wrapped in swaddling bands is the very God that sat upon the circle of the universe and called into being things that were not. This little hand, pink and dimpled, lying on its mother's breast, is the same that spun the new-created worlds into space, that rolls the rattling thunders through the skies. The mother soothes him with a lullaby, "Sleep, my baby, sleep." The lips that murmur in response are destined to speak the word whereat, in the process of the centuries, the thrones of all the Cæsars shall fall in irremediable ruin and give way to a kingdom of truth and righteousness on earth. He hath upon his vesture and his thigh a name written—a name to be made clearer and clearer in the progress of events—"King of Kings and Lord of Lords."

The wise men are at his feet, they have opened their treasures, and are laying them before him; myrrh and gold and frankincense. Then, falling on their knees, they worship him. "The kings of the earth do bring their glory and honor unto him." Thus all knees shall bow before him; for his kingdom is an everlasting kingdom, and his dominion is forever and ever.

The truth revealed to us thus at the advent season is fundamental to Christianity. It bears the same relation to our doctrinal system that a mainspring bears to the watch. Every pin and wheel and lever is important; but break the mainspring and the watch stops. Not only so, this doctrine is the touchstone of Christian sincerity; as it is written, "Hereby know we the Spirit of God: Every spirit that confesseth that Jesus Christ is come in flesh is of God; and every spirit that confesseth not that Jesus Christ is come in the flesh is not of God" (1 John 4, 2).

Here is the center of the gospel of reconciliation. If we reject the divine nativity, the cross of Calvary has no more significance than any other cross. The atonement derives its significance from the incarnation. The shadow of the cross is over the manger. Here is God's meeting-place with man. The story of the prodigal who went away into a far country and squandered his substance in riotous living, is the world's parable. He determined to return; but as he journeyed homeward, sleeping under hedges, begging a crust, the very dogs barked at him. He stood at length on a hilltop in sight of his home. He could go no further, but paused for very shame. He saw his father in the distance standing and shading his eyes; he saw him grasp his staff and hasten this way —coming as God came in the incarnation—coming to meet his wretched, poverty-stricken son. And now, behold the father has fallen upon his neck, and is kissing him. We are standing at the manger. God and man are reconciled here. Let us receive the mystery by faith, the truth with heart-felt gratitude. This is to come home. For only in the setting out of God to meet a wayward and helpless world is there a possibility of the world's return to God.

THE BREVITY OF LIFE

"We bring our years to an end as a tale that is told."—(*Revised Version*) Psalm 90, 9.

What is Life? I went to the dictionary and it replied, "Animal existence." I asked the scientists—those who call themselves "biologists" and should therefore certainly know—and Herbert Spencer, their illustrious spokesman, gave this translucent answer: "Life is a definite combination of heterogeneous changes, simultaneous and successive, in correspondence with external coexistences and sequences." Then I questioned the poets; Shakespeare likened it to a drama:

> "Out, out, brief candle!
> Life's but a walking shadow; a poor player
> That struts and frets his hour upon the stage
> And then is heard no more."

Sir Walter Raleigh, from his cell in London Tower, suggested the similitude of a journey:

> "Give me my scallop-shell of quiet,
> My staff of faith to lean upon,
> My scrip of joy—immortal diet!—
> My bottle of salvation,
> My gown of glory, hope's true gauge,
> And thus I take my pilgrimage."

But quaint George Herbert said it was a mere ramble through the fields on a summer's day:

> "I made a posie while the day ran by;
> Here will I smell my remnant out and tie
> My life within this band.
> But Time did beckon to the flowers; and they,
> By noon, most cunningly did steal away
> And wither in my hand."

I then took my query to the pagan dreamers; Pindar said, "Life is the shadow of a dream." Lucian likened it to a storm at sea, where men like bubbles rise, reflect the glory of the heavens for a brief moment, then vanish forever. Pliny's metaphor was of a larger sort: "It is a river," he said, "taking its rise at a fountain among the hills, gathering volume as it pursues its foaming, downward way, anon flowing calmly through the green valleys, and losing itself at last in the bosom of a boundless sea."

Then I opened the Book; and God said, "Thy days are swifter than a post; as the eagle that hasteth to the prey (Job 9, 25, 26). They are as a shadow (Job 8, 9); they pass away as the foam upon the water (Hosea 10, 7). As a flower of the field, so thou flourishest; for the wind passeth over thee and thou art gone (Ps. 103, 15, 16). Thou art like the grass which groweth up. In the morning it flourisheth and groweth up; in the evening it is cut down and withereth (Psalm 90, 5, 6); or as the grass upon the housetops which withereth before it groweth up (Psalm 129, 6). Thy years are as an handbreadth (Psalm 39, 5); thy coming and going are as the removal of a shepherd's tent (Isaiah 38, 12). Thy life is soon over, *as a tale that is told.*"

The story-teller is an interesting figure in the Oriental life of the olden time. He served not merely as a purveyor of news in the absence of books and newspapers, but also as the narrator of legends and traditions. He is still to be met with in the encampments of the Arabian Desert. At night the Bedouins gather in a circle, their swarthy faces glistening in the torchlight, their forms bent forward and eyes attent upon the story-teller, whose gestures, calm or violent, are adjusted to his theme. His voice is tranquil as he leads his hearers to the wars; monotonous along the weary march; rising to enthusiasm at the approach of the enemy; reaching a shrill frenzy amid the clash of arms; sinking again to monotone along the homeward trudge; closing with a song beneath a lady's window. The tale is told; the listeners have dispersed; the lights are out; the solemn silence of the desert is over all.

So is life. To-day, to-morrow and the day after, and then the end. Why not? Would you have it interminable, like a Chinese drama? Here is the ordinance: "The days of our years are threescore years and ten, and if by reason of strength they be fourscore years, yet is their strength labor and sorrow; for it is soon cut off, and we fly away." Our happiness depends in large measure on our cheerful acceptance of that decree. A recent writer defines life as "a continual struggle with death, with the certainty of being conquered at last." This is an unworthy view. There are considerations which make it clear to thoughtful people that our proper attitude is not one of stoical indifference or stolid surrender, but rather a calm and grateful acquiescence in the limitation of life.

First; the world was never intended to be the abode of immortal man. It is too little, and the tenant is too great. A man is made in God's likeness; his nature is overarched by infinity; his life is a bundle of incalculable potencies. The world is only twenty-five thousand miles in circumference, and the meanest man who walks upon its surface can belt it with a thought in the twinkling of an eye. It is inconceivable that God should have made such a creature and quickened him with a spark of his own being, to the end that he might walk on *terra firma* with leaden feet, eat, drink, laugh, die, and be shut up finally in a leasehold of six feet of earth.

No! Man is not for this world; and this world is not for him. The disparity is too great between the habitat and the inhabitant. When Darius offered Alexander all the country lying west of the Euphrates in exchange for his daughter's hand, his favorite, Parmenio, said: "If I were thou, I would accept it." To which Alexander replied: "So would I, were I Parmenio." If the narrow view which prevails in some quarters were correct—that man is the remote descendant of a mollusk, that he is merely a hundred and fifty pounds of bone and sinew with nothing but phosphorus in his brain-chamber, that he is "a stomach with its appurtenances,"—the world would, indeed, be quite large enough for him; but for immortal beings it is simply "an inn where travelers bait, then post away."

The second reason for acquiescence in the limitation of life is that *its machinery wears out*. In the Book of Ecclesiastes there is a striking picture of the decay of the physical powers. In old age, Koheleth says, "the keepers of the house do tremble and the strong men bow themselves [that is, the limbs are palsied and bowed with infirmity]; those that look out of the windows be darkened [poor old eyes!]; the doors shall be shut in the streets when the sound of the grinding is low [the shrunken lips are pursed]; he shall rise up at the voice of the bird [no need of chanticleer; the twitter of a sparrow awakes him from his light slumbers]; and all the daughters of music are brought low [or, as Shakespeare puts it, "His big, manly voice, turning again toward childish treble, pipes and whistles in his sound"]; he is afraid of that which is high [a long stairway is *via dolorosa* to him]; fears are in the way, the almond tree blossoms [his head is crowned with silver]; the grasshopper is a burden, desire fails." It is time to go!

The mental faculties also yield to advancing years. I remember well an aged figure that used to shuffle in slippers along the Yale campus. Time was when the voice of that man rang like a clarion and the multitude was swayed by his eloquence as by magic. Alas, he had become a "lean and slippered pantaloon," babbling and maundering as he tottered on his way. This is ever the dread of those who feel the burden of increasing years. They would not linger until memory fails and the wits go wool-gathering. Far better is it to go hence, pausing at the borderline of earth and heaven only to drink at the fountain of perpetual youth and then to live forever.

But ("sorrow's crown of sorrows!") the heart also wears out. At life's outset it puts forth tendrils, clasping a friend here and another there, which as years advance are sundered one by one. "I feel like one who treads alone some banquet hall deserted." In the art gallery at the Columbian Exposition was a picture by Josef Israel, representing an old man sitting with his face bowed between his wrinkled hands. On the bed beside him lay his wife—dead. The light of his eyes gone out! The title of the picture was "Alone." Who would care to linger under such circumstances? The home empty, the hearthstone cold, the heart desolate. Aye, surely, it is time to go.

The third reason for acquiescence in the divine decree as to the transitoriness of life, is that *a place is prepared for us in a better world.* So Jesus said: "In my Father's house are many mansions; if it were not so, I would have told you; I go to prepare a place for you." The world to which we go is adjusted to our nature; it will afford ample room for the exercise of our divine energies. It is the world where Immanuel, the Ideal Man, holds dominion. Our life there will be free from the limitations of time and space. "Now are we the sons of God, and it doth not yet appear what we shall be."

Our days here are school days. This world is just the place for preparation for a better one. Its pains and disappointments, its sorrows and adversities have in them the possibilities of character. The real life is beyond. In Heidelberg I saw once a group of students coming down the street in merry mood, one of whom was quite gray with age. I was told that he was of noble blood and independent fortune, and that he had been more than forty years in the curriculum of the University with no ambition, seemingly, to be graduated from it. So is the man who has no outlook beyond this present life.

Death is "Commencement." It is the gateway into the larger and more real world of affairs. It is promotion to higher tasks and nobler responsibilities. It was a sad day for the Class of Sixty-seven when, at the close of our college course at New Haven, we gathered on the Campus for our mutual farewell. Our friendship had been cemented by four years of loving comradeship, and the tears we shed that day were tears of genuine sorrow. Yet, had the opportunity been given to remain in the University, there was not one among us who would not have answered, "No! Our preparation is finished; the world beckons; our hearts are beating fast with hope and high purpose and aspiration; we must go!"

The solemn thought that we emphasize at the threshold of the New Year is this: *Let us make the utmost of our opportunities of preparation for the larger life.* Two things are necessary: one is *to get rid of sin;* and this can only be done by a simple acceptance of Christ who died to redeem us. Until we have attended to that matter, all "good resolutions" are futile. When Sir Thomas More was a prisoner in the Tower of London a friend suggested that his unkempt beard should be shorn. His answer was, "There is a controversy between the king and myself as to my head; and until that be settled, I will take no trouble with it." The soul's welfare is the prime consideration; pending its reconciliation with an offended God, all other matters are of minor consequence. An acceptance of Christ is the final determination of destiny; it should therefore be attended to this day.

Having thus gotten rid of sin, the total remainder of preparation is to *get used to service.* By our apprenticeship here in the kingdom of Christ we should be fitting ourselves for the larger duties and responsibilities that await us. He who squanders his study hours is naturally affrighted by the thought of the "examination" incident to graduation. Let us be scrupulous in the discharge of every duty, knowing well the eternal issues that flow from faithfulness here and now. "Do ye nexte thynge." Follow close in the footsteps of Jesus, of whom it is written, "He went about doing good." A pastor in this city tells of a humble parishioner, a hunchback —confined to her room, but ever zealous of good works—who placed in his hands these lines as expressing the purpose of her life:

"I must be doing something for the weary and the sad,
I must be giving forth the love that makes my heart so glad;
For God so fills my spirit with a joy that passeth show,
I fain would do his bidding in the only way I know.

"So to suffering and to sorrow I shall always give my heart,
And pray to God that every day I may some good impart,
Some little act of kindness, some simple word of cheer,
To make some drooping heart rejoice or stay some falling tear.

"And when I've crossed the river and passed its waters o'er,
And feel that some will miss me upon the other shore,
My grateful spirit ever shall bless the Lord divine,
Who crowns the humblest efforts of a human love like mine."

The year is before us. It is *terra incognita*, an unknown country of duties and dangers. One of the customary admonitions at the border line is, "This year we may die." It is far more pertinent to say, "This year we must live." For living is more solemn than dying. It means responsibility, day by day, hour by hour. Patience is heroism, faithfulness is success, steadfastness is ultimate triumph. These are the virtues that shine brightest in the divine inventory. On Riverside Drive, just under the shadow of the Grant Monument, is a solitary gravestone inscribed, "To an Amiable Child." It was over a century ago that this child, who, "the gates of heaven being left ajar, had wandered forth with dreamy eyes," lived sweetly, unselfishly, amiably for a little while and then returned to God. But who shall estimate the value of that little life? Or who shall say that in the final reckoning the modest gravestone may not overshadow the monument of the great commander? For it is not success but faithfulness that tells, after all.

And now I wish you *a happy New Year;* a year of God's peace in the consciousness of duty done; a year of simple faith in the divine goodness and of clear outlook toward the heavenly hills; a year of sweet communion with Jesus and close following in his steps; a year like that pleasant walk to Emmaus of which the disciples said, "Did not our hearts burn within us while he talked with us by the way?"

THE DELAYS OF PROVIDENCE

"The Lord is not slack concerning his promise, as some men count slackness; but is longsuffering to us-ward, not willing that any should perish, but that all should come to repentance."—2 Peter, 3, 9.

All men believe in Providence. The world is obviously under law; and reason suggests that behind the law is a Lawgiver. It is not too much to expect of this Lawgiver a just distribution of rewards and punishments among men. This finds expression in the Hindu doctrine of *Karma*, or the Law of Consequences. The Scriptural statement is, "Whatsoever a man soweth, that shall he also reap; he that soweth to the flesh, shall of the flesh reap corruption; and he that soweth to the Spirit, shall of the Spirit reap everlasting life."

But there appears to be something wrong in the administration of this law. We can discover no exact or immediate *quid pro quo*. The time between the seed-sowing and the harvest is sometimes beyond reason. God warns, entreats, admonishes, condemns and—suspends sentence. The execution hangs fire. The wicked persist in their wickedness and laugh at all omens of calamity. They live prosperously and "there are no bands in their death."

There were the antediluvians, whom God threatened to destroy because he "saw that the wickedness of man was great in the earth and that every imagination of the thoughts of his heart was only evil continually." Then what? The ark was one hundred and twenty years in building! Meanwhile the world went on with its carnival of crime. Those who saw the patriarch building his ship at a great distance from any navigable water and heard his prophecies of the coming deluge, looked at each other sagely and said, "Old Noah has gone into his dotage!"

And there were the Ninevites, of whom God said, "Their wickedness is come up before me." He sent Jonah to cry up and down through the city, "Yet forty days, yet forty days and Nineveh shall be overthrown!" And when the forty days were over, the people having put on sackcloth in token of repentance, the city was spared; as it is written, "God repented of the evil that he had said he would do unto them, and he did it not." Was it strange that Jonah, whose veracity was thus compromised, should sulk in the shadow of his gourd, saying, "O Lord, I knew that thou wouldst repent thee of the evil; wherefore, let me die, I entreat thee!"

And there were the Jews, who rejected the well-beloved Son of God. They crowned him with thorns, robed him in the cast-off purple of a petty magistrate, mocked and smote him, spat in his face and crucified him, saying: "His blood be on us and on our children!" Yet the heavens did not rain fire upon them, and their children are the chancelors of the world's exchequer to-day.

We need not go so far, however, to observe these delays of recompense. Our streets are full of sinners who persistently violate the divine law, mock at the admonitions of Holy Writ and tread on the precious blood of the covenant. We ourselves are monuments of the divine procrastination; as it is written,

"He hath not dealt with us after our sins, nor rewarded us according to our iniquities." If he had, indeed, we should not be worshipers in his sanctuary to-day, but prisoners of the outer darkness enduring the penalty of persistent sin.

How shall we account for these delays? Why is "the long shrift" given to those who are said to be "condemned already?" The law is clear: "The soul that sinneth it shall die." Why do not the lifted thunders fall? "God is slack" reply the thoughtless; "his warnings are intended merely to frighten us; he does not really regard our sins, or intend to punish them." But Peter gives a different answer. "God is not slack," he says, "as some men count slackness." And Peter should know. If ever a man had tempted Providence, it was he. He had been a rough fisherman, of an inflammable temper and not above profanity on occasion. Yet he was spared to join the company of Christ's disciples. And in that goodly fellowship he had thrice denied his Lord; yet Jesus gave no heed except to "turn and look upon him." That glance had in it all the potency of heaven's lightnings; but for Peter it was fraught with the utmost tenderness. He must have known how it was written, "If ye seek me, I will be found of you; but if ye forsake me, I will cast you off forever." Yet he forsook his Lord and was not cast off. And this is the man who says, "God is not slack concerning his promises, as some men count slackness."

But if this unpunctual administration of affairs be not "slackness," what is it?

First: It is not due to Ignorance on the part of God. He is fully cognizant of our sins. It is said that when the Romans saw the eyes of their great statue of Jupiter covered with spiders' webs, they gave themselves up to an abandon of vice, saying, "He doth not see, neither doth he regard us." But God's eyes are never dimmed. He neither slumbereth nor sleepeth. O the eyes of the Lord! "They run to and fro through all the earth to behold the evil and the good." "All things are naked and opened unto the eyes of him with whom we have to do." He needs no detectives to spy upon us. He needs no bloodhounds to trace his fugitives. If we take the wings of the morning and fly unto the uttermost parts of the sea, even there shall his hand hold us. He hears our faintest whisper in the solitudes. He knows the secret imaginations of our hearts. No, it is not because he is unaware of our sins that he fails to visit immediate retribution upon us.

Nor, secondly, is it because of Indifference on his part. It cannot be said of him, "He does not care." The School of Epicurus said, "The God we worship is a large god—too busy with the affairs of universal government to heed our peccadillos. He presides over the splendid feasts of Olympus. He wheels the worlds around their orbits. We are but little people; what cares he for us?" Our God, dear friends, is so great that he gives heed to infinitesimals. He cannot be indifferent to our ill-doing. He knows what sin has done; how it has ruined souls, desolated homes, overthrown governments, depopulated the world and peopled hell. He is a jealous God. His wrath is revealed from heaven against all ungodliness and unrighteousness of men (Rom. 1, 18). He is "angry with the wicked every day."

Nor, thirdly, is it because he is Impotent to punish sin.

His name is the Almighty. It is as easy for him to destroy a world as for me to crush an insect. Not long ago a well known infidel took occasion, in a spirit of bravado, to blaspheme publicly in this city, challenging God to strike him dead. Why did not God take him at his word and destroy him on the instant? Was it because he could not? No, indeed; but rather because a man spared is a more impressive proof of the divine greatness than a man slain. A like thing happened on a larger scale when Korah and his followers offered incense of blasphemy in the Jewish camp. And the Lord said to Moses, "Speak unto the congregation that they depart from the tents of these wicked men. Then Korah and his followers stood by themselves swinging their impious censers, and, behold, the earth opened her mouth "and they and all that appertained to them went down alive into the pit." Thus has the Lord on occasion demonstrated once and again his power to inflict an instant penalty on sin.

Why then are the unrighteous spared? The case stands thus: They have offended God; his warning has been spoken; instant retribution would be obviously just; God knows their guilt, is deeply grieved; is able to punish them; yet they live. Let us turn to Peter's observations respecting this matter:

I. He says the delays of Providence are to be accounted for by the fact that *God " is longsuffering to us-ward."* The name by which he revealed himself to Moses hiding in the cleft of the rock, was this: "I am the Lord. I will be gracious to whom I will be gracious, and will show mercy on whom I will show mercy." And the name by which he revealed himself from the cloud on Mount Sinai was this: "The Lord, the Lord God, merciful and gracious, longsuffering and abundant in goodness and truth; keeping mercy for thousands, forgiving iniquity and transgression and sin, and that will by no means clear the guilty." His word is Yea and Amen; but he can afford to wait: since, as Peter says, "one day is with him as a thousand years, and a thousand years as one day." He never "loses his temper" as men do. He experiences no caprice, no paroxysms of wrath. He is slow to anger because "the eternal years are his."

If we could stand beside his throne for a moment, and see with his eyes the sin and shame, the vice and uncleanness, the rebellion and blasphemy—if all the roofs were lifted and all men's hearts made naked and open before us as before him—we should cry, "Burn up the world, O Lord! Consume these rebels who have so defied thy mercy and offended against thy holy law!" But this is because our ways are not as his ways, nor our thoughts as his thoughts. He spares until the resources of his mercy are exhausted. He is the God of an infinite patience.

II. "*He is not willing that any should perish.*" He knows the meaning of that word "perish." He will not that any shall go forth into the region of eternal shame and remorse "where their worm dieth not and the fire is not quenched." "As I live, saith the Lord God, I have no pleasure in the death of the wicked; but that the wicked turn from his way and live." Could anything be more pathetic than his lament over Ephraim? "O Ephraim, how can I give thee up? How can I make thee as Admah and Zeboim?" It is like the wail of a mother at the death-bed of her child.

If further proof of God's unwillingness that any should perish be required, we shall find it in his exceeding great and precious promises: "Him that cometh unto me I will in no wise cast out";—"The Spirit and the Bride say, Come; and let him that heareth say, Come; and let him that is athirst come; and whosoever will, let him take the water of life freely";—"To-day if ye will hear his voice, harden not your hearts";—"Turn ye, turn ye; for why will ye die?"

III. *He desires "that all should come to repentance."* Here is the kernel of the whole matter. This is the objective point of the divine longsuffering. It is God's purpose that every man shall have opportunity to repent up to the full limit of his own immeasurable love; so that as many as possible may turn from their unrighteousness, accept the generous terms of grace and enter into life.

Once on a time a man made himself notorious as a highwayman along the "Bloody Way" from Jerusalem down to Jericho. God saw his deeds of violence, his murders and robberies, yet spared him. The civil authorities, however, were not so "slack"; they pursued the bandit, arrested him, placed him on trial and sentenced him to death. It was during his execution that the reason of the divine longsuffering was made manifest; for in the very article of death he repented, saying, "Lord, remember me!"

A wilful girl forsook her home once on a time and abandoned herself to a shameless life. She fell lower and lower until she became a common drab; so that society cast her out and pure women withdrew their garments as she passed. But God had not abandoned hope of her. She heard a voice one day in the street of Capernaum, saying, "Come unto me all ye that labor and are heavy laden, and I will give you rest." Her sins had palled upon her; she was "weary" of her vicious pleasure; she was "heavy laden" with fear of retribution. She sought the presence of the Merciful One, anointed his feet with spikenard and consecrated her life to him.

A lad, reared in the rabbinical schools of an Asian city, became possessed of an evil spirit of fanaticism. He went up to Jerusalem, joined the straitest sect of the Pharisees and ultimately became a member of the Sanhedrin. He was appointed an inquisitor to search out the followers of Jesus and hale them to judgment and death. His heart was wholly in his work. His guilt was none the less heinous because he thought he was doing his duty; yet the Lord spared him in prospect of the time when he should see, in a sudden burst of light from heaven, the divine beauty in the face of Christ, and penitently cry, "Lord, what wilt thou have me to do?"

What, now, are the practical conclusions? To begin with, "*It is a fearful thing to fall into the hands of the living God.*" The wrath of an irascible man is not so much to be dreaded as the calm indignation of one who, naturally patient, has been provoked too long. What then must be the anger of the patient God? "When he shall whet his sword, who shall stand before him?" His mills grind slow, but they grind woe. It is written that the incorrigibly wicked shall, in the judgment, call upon the hills to fall upon them and hide them from the wrath of the Lamb. What a paradox is there—"*the wrath of the Lamb!*"

And again, *There can be no room for complaint on the part of those who shall ultimately incur the penalty of sin.* God's love shall be vindicated in their doom. The warden of one of our penitentiaries relates that on the cell of a prisoner, who had been executed for murder, he found written everywhere along the walls, "God is love." It is not easy to surmise what prompted that inscription; but this I know, the regions of eternal night must be filled with irrepressible tributes to the goodness of God. The lost know the meaning of God's long delays. They know their doom is just, and confess that the scepter of the Lord is a right scepter.

Finally, *what shall be said of the inexcusable folly of those who persist in going down to death?* Why should any man be lost? God so loved the world that he gave his only-begotten Son to save it. The shadow of the cross is over us. The Spirit strives with all. The hands of Christ are stretched out still.

It is said that when Alexander besieged a city he kindled a beacon on a neighboring hilltop and announced that all who surrendered while it burned, should be spared. The beacon of God's mercy has been burning long for some of us. We have heard the invitations of the heavenly mercy, lo! these many years. Shall the tokens of the divine longsuffering to us-ward be vain as the roses that dropped upon Faust from heaven, turning to fiery coals as they fell? Is it not time to make an end of our folly? I beseech you, beloved, by the mercies of God, that ye be reconciled unto him. Now is the accepted time; and to-day is the day of salvation.

WHAT IS THAT TO THEE?

"Peter saith to Jesus, Lord, and what shall this man do? Jesus saith unto him, If I will that he tarry till I come, what is that to thee? follow thou me."—John 21 : 21, 22.

In the dusk of the morning a company of fishermen were cruising in their little boat along the margin of Lake Gennesaret, now and then letting down their nets. A solitary figure was seen walking along the shore. The men whispered to each other, "It is the Lord." And Peter could not wait; he girt his fisher's coat about him, leaped in and swam ashore. The others landed presently from the boat; and all gathered about their Lord.

It was a picturesque scene: The sun was rising over the trans-jordanic heights, tinging the snowy crown of Hermon with a red glory, while a golden mist rose slowly from the western sea. In the midst of the group stood Jesus, and nearby Peter, in dripping garments, his face now fallen on his breast. He had forgotten for the moment, that when he last saw Jesus he had thrice denied him: now the bitter recollection overwhelms him. Thrice the Master asks, "Simon, son of Jonas, lovest thou me?" Never was heedless lad more embarrassed by stern catechist than this bold fisherman: yet with downcast eyes he answers thrice, "Thou knowest that

I love thee." And with vast compassion his Lord reopens to him the three doors of the apostolic office, saying "Feed my sheep." Then an announcement of grave import falls from his lips: "When thou art old, thou shalt stretch forth thy hands and another shall gird thee and carry thee whither thou wouldest not." It was a prophecy of martyrdom. Did Peter blanche or tremble when the cold shadow fell over him? Nay; this was what he had longed for: to be baptized with his Lord's crimson baptism, to drink of his bitter cup. Then Jesus added, "Follow me!" He had said it twice before but never under such circumstances, nor with such grave significance. It was as if he said, "Come, Peter; the servant is not greater than his Lord. Enter into the fellowship of my shame and agony. On to the cross! On to the martyr's crown!"

At this point occurred the discordant note. Peter, turning about and seeing John, was moved to inquire, "Lord, and what shall this man do?" John had been his fellow fisherman, his comrade in the Mount of Transfiguration, his familiar friend in the retinue of Jesus. It was not strange, therefore, that in the unveiling of his own tragic death, he should inquire, "How about this man?" And Jesus said, *"If I will that he tarry till I come, what is that to thee? Follow thou me!"*

Was this to reprove his curiosity? I think not. There are, indeed, state secrets into which we must not pry: but curiosity was not a Petrine fault. Nor yet did Jesus intend to rebuke the jealousy of his disciple, as some suppose. For Peter was too large **a man** to look on John, "the beloved disciple," with green eyes. I can discern in the Master's words no rebuke at all, but rather the announcement of a great truth; to wit, *The solitariness of an earnest life.*

A man comes into the world by himself; alone he bears his burdens, endures his sorrows, meets his obligations; and alone he must stand in judgment before God. It behooves him, therefore, to know his personal responsibility. That was a great discovery of Descartes, when, walking by the bank of the Danube on a November night, he saw himself endowed with sovereign will and conscience as against all fashion and authority, and was moved to cry aloud, "*Ich bin ich!*" It is a momentous hour when that discovery dawns on any soul. It lifts us to the solitary dignity of Manhood created after the image of God.

I. *As to our personal Responsibility in the formulation of a Creed.* This is of supreme importance; for a man's life and character are founded on his faith. It has been observed that when our forefathers were casting about for a suitable day to be observed as a national anniversary, they did not select that whereon the Thirteen Colonies bound themselves together by formal enactment, but rather the day wherein the great principles of civil and religious liberty were announced in the historic Declaration. This was strictly philosophic, since government rests not on formal enactments nor on solemn covenants, but rather on eternal, rudimental principles. So a man's creed or code of religious tenets is the true foundation of his life and character. Thus it is written, "As a man thinketh in his heart, so is he."

How, then, shall we formulate our creed? By reference to tradition? Due weight must indeed be given to the results of historic controversies, to the calm deliverances of councils and the wise opinions of the fathers. But these must not be permitted to prevent the exercise of individual judgment, or blind the eyes to progressive revelation. There is a very solemn and inspiring truth in what John Robinson said to the Pilgrims embarking at Delft-haven, "Remember that new light shall ever spring forth from the word of God."

Are we, then, to derive our religious beliefs from current opinion? It is greatly to be feared that many are content to seek no further. The press is the purveyor of passing thought; and there are those who imagine that, in adopting its suggestions, they are keeping abreast of the age. But no ready-made or custom-made opinion can fit a self-made man. A passing thought is poor stuff to place in the foundation of an enduring life.

We are Christians. That means, among other things, that we have taken Christ to be our prophet, or instructor in spiritual things. He and his Book are ours; what more would we have? His word is ultimate to those who follow him. This matter of religious belief is between himself and us. It is of comparatively little consequence what the fathers said or what our contemporaries are saying. On one occasion Jesus asked of his disciples, "What do the people say of me?" And when they replied, "Some say one thing and some another," he added significantly, "But what say ye?" At that point Peter stood forth and witnessed his good confession: "Thou art the Christ, the Son of the living God!" It was for that very proposition that Athanasius in the third century faced the Arians, with the memorable words, "*Athanasius contra mundum.*" He was opposed by scholars, threatened by Constantine, displaced from his episcopal office, thrice exiled; yet he stood for his belief and was willing to stand *alone against the world.* This is the position for any self-respecting follower of Christ. It is himself against all authority and current opinion, if need be. His responsibility is to Christ alone, who said, "What is that to thee? Follow thou me."

II. *So, also, as to Rules of Conduct.* The path of duty is not a plain thoroughfare but a road with many divergent paths; so that we are ever at the cross-roads asking, "Which way?" I set out afoot in London once for Spurgeon's Tabernacle. As I supposed myself to be nearing the place, I ventured to ask a passer-by, "Which way to the Tabernacle?" He replied, "Follow the crowd." A little further on I met with the same advice, "Follow the crowd." In due time I reached my destination. But in questions of casuistry it is not safe to follow the crowd. "Thou shalt not follow a multitude to do evil."

One of the questions by which we are, unfortunately, apt to determine our personal duty is, "What will the world say?" Duty is distinctly a personal affair; conscience must determine it. When Franklin was at the court of France he found that all his fellow-ambassadors powdered their hair. He ventured, however, to preserve his own simple habit; of which Brancroft says, "It acted like a spell." A man's influence is always enhanced if he follows the bent of his own conscience in defiance of criticism.

It is no sin to be singular. The three Babylonish youths were alone in great Babylon in refusing to doff their bonnets before the great image; the outcry did not harm them.

Another question by which we frequently solve our ethical problems is, "What is the fashion?" The increasing sin of Sabbath desecration may be largely traced to this source. We are prone to justify ourselves by saying, "They all do it." Here again the Master's word is imperative: "What is that to thee? Follow thou me."

Let it be observed that some things are always right, under all circumstances and for everybody; for example, love toward God and love toward man. And some things are always wrong for everybody and under all circumstances; such as impiety, meanness and selfishness. Let it be observed further that some things may be wrong for others and right for you; and contrariwise, some things are right for others and wrong for you. Circumstances alter cases. As Macaulay has said, "Right and wrong actions are not always to be distinguished by marks so plain as those which distinguish a hexagon from a square." For want of considering this fact we indulge in much unjust fault-finding. "Judge not that ye be not judged," said the Master; "for with what judgment ye judge, ye shall be judged; and with what measure ye mete, it shall be measured unto you again." We must carry our own burdens of duty; each for himself must meet before his own conscience all questions of responsibility. Paul says, "Who art thou that judgest another man's servant? To his own master he standeth or falleth." In the sphere of duty as everywhere it behooves a man to attend strictly to his own business. And there is a tremendous truth in the old proverb, "Those who live in glass houses should not throw stones."

Our Lord put it on this wise: "How wilt thou say to thy brother, Let me pull out the mote out of thine eye; and, behold, a beam is in thine own eye? Thou hypocrite, first cast out the beam out of thine own eye; and then shalt thou see clearly to cast out the mote out of thy brother's eye." This is the law against censoriousness. It does not mean that we are to be tolerant of wrong or falsehood; it does mean that we have no jurisdiction over the consciences of our fellowmen. He is a tiresome man who has no definite views of right and wrong: but Paul Pry is a great nuisance. The proper course for a man to pursue is to let his own light shine so that others shall see his good works and glorify God. Do right, my friend, and worry less about the conduct of others. Do right and let the crowd sweep by. The world's fashion is of less moment than to keep one's conscience pure. Hear the Master saying: "What is that to thee? Follow thou me."

At a critical period of our Civil War the President was severely criticized for his conduct of affairs. A member of his cabinet suggested the propriety of making a formal explanation. His answer was, "If we begin that, we might as well close the shop. I am doing the best I can, the best I know how; and I intend to keep on doing so. If the end justifies me, all my traducers will be silenced; if not, a legion of angels from heaven, all testifying to the purity of my motives and the wisdom of my course, would make no difference. I must keep on following my conscience and leave the issue with God."

III. *As to service in the Kingdom of Christ.* A place is here appointed to every earnest man. There are diversities of gifts, but the same Spirit: and there are diversities of administration, but the same Lord. To one is given, by the Spirit, the word of wisdom, to another the word of knowledge by the same Spirit; but all these worketh that one and the selfsame Spirit, dividing to every man severally as he will." This being so, it should be obvious that every man is responsible to God alone for the faithful discharge of duty.

Yet we are ever disposed to criticize those who do not adjust themselves to our methods. No doubt there were some who found fault with "blundering Peter," who yet scarcely lifted their hands to advance the cause. As I was coming to my study yesterday on the Broadway line, the car was somehow displaced from the track. The passengers stood around, eager but unable to help. There was, however, one fussy gentleman with cane and gloves, who showed an eloquent acquaintance with the entire business of traction. He felt wholly competent to criticize and advise the gripman and all concerned in the affair; but I perceived that when all was over this fussy gentleman had not soiled his gloves. Good people, let us cease finding fault. The world would go far better if all would keep sweet and abide in their appointed places. Give others credit for doing their best. Or if they fail, what then? The Master's word is still, "What is that to thee? Follow thou me."

And while prone to criticize others, we are blind to our own shortcoming and malfeasance. We make no scruple of standing idle in the market place. If reminded of the proverb, "Nine-tenths of the work of the Christian church is done by one-tenth of its members," we comfort ourselves with the thought that we are in a respectable majority. The Master goes by with the sweat of the harvest on his brow, and after him the laborers with sickle in hand. Alas that we should be so little disturbed by his call, "What is it to thee that others are indolent? Follow thou me!"

At the beginning of the present century the General Assembly of Scotland was much exercised as to the duty of foreign evangelization. The controversy waxed warm. The proposition was opposed on various grounds. At length Dr. Erskine, ex-officio member of the Assembly, seated close by the pulpit in recognition of his advanced years and honorable service, rose and said, with a deep, tremulous voice, "Moderator, rax me yon Bible, wull ye?" He took the volume, opened it, and read aloud these words: "Go ye into all the world and preach the gospel unto every creature"; and adding, "Thus saith the Lord," he sat down. It was enough. Christ is our prophet; his word in matters of faith and conduct is ultimate to those who follow him. No argument can stand against his precept. No authority, no array of multitudinous influence can have a feather's weight against "Thus saith the Lord."

A word now to non-Christians. The injunction of the Master was addressed primarily to his disciples; but it is not without significance for those who do not profess to follow him. The plea most frequently advanced for this default is the inconsistencies of Christians. It is said, "They do not live up to their profession." *This is true.* We are not what we ought to be, and nobody knows it better than ourselves. In fact, however, we are not in the church because we profess to be good people, but only because we are trying to be good. We know our infirmity and feel the need of association for mutual help. The best we can say for ourselves is, "We are not what we ought to be; we are not what we mean to be; but by the grace of God we are what we are."

But *the criticism is not true as intended by those who make it.* The inference they draw is that there is no benefit in the fellowship of service or in the open confession of Christ. The falsity of that conclusion may be easily demonstrated. Let all the church members of New York be drawn up in line; let all others be arrayed in an opposite line; then walk between them, my friend, and pass judgment. We are humbly willing to abide the issue.

Furthermore *if the criticism were true*, this would nevertheless not affect your personal responsibility. The question is a purely personal one. If Christ be the Son of God, it is your duty to believe in him. If he said of the Eucharist, "Do this in remembrance of me," it is your duty to partake of it. If he said, "Let your light shine before men," it is your duty to confess him. And if all the so-called Christians on earth were arrant hypocrites, your duty in these premises would remain the same. "What is that to thee? Follow thou me."

No excuse for holding aloof from the Christian profession can be considered valid which will not stand in the Judgment. A fine showing a man would make on that occasion who, when God asks, "What hast thou to say for thyself, in that thou didst not follow the Christ?" should answer: "Yonder is Noah who lay drunken in his tent; yonder is Peter who thrice denied thee; yonder is David who sinned in the matter of Bathsheba." No, friend, you would not dare. The sophism is too plain. No man refuses good money because there are counterfeits abroad. How shall you absolve yourself from sinning against your own conscience by the fact that professing Christians are not what they should be?

And, finally, as to the application of this particular sermon: *It is not for the man in the next pew.* It is our infirmity, that we know too well our neighbor's need. How natural it was for David to grow indignant with the landlord who robbed his poor tenant of the one ewe-lamb that had eaten of his bread, drunk of his cup and lain in his bosom. "As the Lord liveth," he cried, "the man that hath done this thing shall surely die." But how hard it was to take the application to himself, when the prophet added, "Thou art the man!" Take the truth to yourself, my friend; let God's word find you out. Cease asking, How about this or that man? As to your concern with truth and duty, there is but one man, yourself. Alone you live; alone you must die; alone you must answer for the conduct of this life before the Judgment-bar of God.

RHODA, THE GATEKEEPER

"And as Peter knocked at the door of the gate, a damsel came to hearken, named Rhoda (*Greek* for Rose or Rosa). And when she knew Peter's voice she opened not the gate for gladness, but ran in and told how Peter stood before the gate. And they said unto her, Thou art mad. But she constantly affirmed that it was even so."—Acts 12, 13-15.

The place is familiar but the circumstances are strange. This is the upper room in Salome's house, where Jesus was accustomed to meet his disciples. It is fourteen years, however, since he was crucified and many things have happened in the interim. His followers in Jerusalem were permitted for a time to worship unmolested: but now the sword has been unsheathed. James, the faithful pastor of the Jerusalem church, has been beheaded. Peter has been thrown into prison and is reserved for death. It is a fear-stricken company that assembles in the upper room. They are come together to pray Peter out of prison. Can they do this? It remains to be seen. They unite their supplications with suppressed earnestness, for there is danger in the air. The doors are locked; and Rhoda the handmaid is stationed at the outer wicket.

Meanwhile Peter is in prison, guarded by four quaternions of soldiers and bound with a double chain. He is as secure as resolute foes can make him. But no walls are thick enough, no chains are strong enough, no guards are watchful enough to hold a man prisoner when God resolves to free him. The excitement of the day has wearied Peter and he rests, lulled to sleep by a good conscience, despite the fact that this may be his last day on earth.

In the upper room not far distant his comrade, John, is leading the sorrowful disciples in prayer: "O Lord, leave not thy servant in the power of the enemy, but deliver him for thy great mercy's sake!"

On a sudden a great light shines in the dungeon; the hand of an angel is laid upon Peter and a voice says, "Arise up quickly." (In the upper room John is pleading, "O thou who hast promised never to leave nor forsake thine own, be present with thy beloved servant, we entreat thee, and bring him forth out of darkness and the shadow of death!") As Peter struggles to his feet, his chains fall off; the angel says, "Gird thyself and bind on thy sandals ; cast thy garment about thee and follow me." He obeys as one in a dream; the great doors open before them noiselessly as if their bolts were drawn by unseen hands; the last one opens and closes behind them, and they are standing under the starlit sky. (In the upper room the petition rises: "O God, thy ways are not as our ways, nor thy thoughts as our thoughts; we are at our wits' end, but the thing which is impossible with men is possible with thee.")

Then the angel vanishes. Peter rubs his eyes, wonders, comes to himself. Whither now shall he go? There is but one place; to the upper room where he knows the disciples are praying for him. (The voice of John is pleading: "O Lord, we believe thy promises; thou art the hearer and answerer of prayer; we beseech thee restore our beloved Peter to us.")

A knock at the door! How it startles them. Is it an officer come to summon another of their number to prison and death? Who next? Their faces are blanched; the voice of prayer is hushed. Another knock, and a distinct voice without. The portress comes running in, breathless with excitement, crying, "It is Peter; he stands before the gate!" This is too good to believe. "The damsel is mad," they say. They have been praying for Peter's deliverance, and hoping against hope; the answer to their prayers has come in person, is knocking at the gate. O ye of little faith, unbolt the door and let your answer in!

Let us leave Peter at the gate and the disciples within—eager, questioning, still hesitating to believe,—while we fasten our eyes on Rhoda, the gatekeeper, who stands there as an embodiment of faith. She was well named "the Rose;" for among those disciples, older and cleverer than she, there is not one that renders a sweeter service: it is indeed the very attar of devotion, acceptable as frankincense before the gracious God.

I. *Observe the Simplicity of her Faith.* It was a great truth that Jesus uttered on one occasion, when, placing a child in the midst of his disciples, he said, "Except ye become as this little one, ye shall in no wise enter into the kingdom of heaven."

The question is as to the Philosophy of Prayer. The parties to the controversy are those outside the upper room, who believe not, those within who have been driven to their knees, and Rhoda the gatekeeper.

The discussion runs on this wise: "Our *first* objection to prayer," say those without, "is the immobility of God. His plans and purposes are from all eternity. It is inconceivable that he should be turned aside by the breath of his creatures. The imprisonment of Peter is but part of an Eternal plan; it is therefore a vain impertinence to pray for him."—To which those within reply, "God is indeed immutable; but immutability is one thing and immobility another. He is not like the Sphinx, that abides in imperturbable serenity while the storms of centuries sweep by. He has a heart that can be touched with a feeling of our infirmities; his name is 'Our Father'; and as a father pitieth his children, so he pitieth them that fear him."—But while the argument goes on in this manner, the little gatekeeper has merely this to say: "You have been praying for Peter; and, lo, he is at the door; shall I run and let him in?"

"Our *second* objection to prayer," say those without, "is *the inviolability of nature's laws*. There is a fixed order of the universe, and it cannot be supposed that the voice of an humble petitioner should interfere with it."—"But this inviolability," argue those within, "must be understood with reference to higher law. If I lift my hand, I violate the Law of Gravitation; if I put down my foot, I violate the Law of Momentum; if I shield my head from the pelting rain, I violate the Law of the Elements: but this is because I am myself the depository and agent of a higher law. If this is possible to me, it is surely possible to God who is above all."—And still the weightiest contribution to the argument comes from Rhoda, who can only say, "You have prayed, and your answer is waiting; shall I admit it?"

"But *thirdly*," say those without, "while denying the objective benefit of prayer, we are quite willing to admit its reflex influence. If you go into the mountain like Moses to commune with the Infinite and Eternal One, it is reasonably certain that you will come down with your faces shining."—"Aye, but there is something more," say those within; "else what is the meaning of assurances like this: 'Ask and it shall be given unto you; seek and ye shall find; knock and it shall be opened unto you'? Such promises are indeed given under certain conditions, as that the petitioner must have faith, must urge his suit with humble importunity, must assume an attitude of filial acquiescence."—But Rhoda, still waiting, can only say, "I do not understand your argument; only this I know; you have been praying for Peter long and earnestly, and Peter is knocking at the door. Shall I admit him?"

O sweet simplicity of faith! The Rose takes what God gives and asks no questions. It receives the air, the sunshine and the benignant elements of the soil, assimilates them and transmutes them into beauty and fragrance. Would that all our hearts were likewise open to truth!

> "If our faith were but more simple,
> We should take him at his word,
> And our lives would be all sunshine
> In the beauty of the Lord."

II. *Here is an illustration of the Reliability of Faith.* I hear one saying, "Simple folk like Rhoda may receive dogmas and promises without question; but for thinking men and women an ounce of reason is worth a pound of faith." This suggestion, however, rests on a misunderstanding. What is faith? Is it to take things on hearsay? Is it to believe without evidence? By no means; "faith is the substance of things hoped for, the evidence of things not seen." Faith is substance. Faith is evidence. It yields the strongest certitude because it rests on the surest foundations. Faith is stronger than reason. Its argument is more irrefutable than any in the Baconian philosophy. The inductive method reasons from facts to a conclusion: and what can be more satisfactory? "Facts cannot lie," they say. It is true that one fact cannot lie; but when you bind two facts or more into a bundle of premises, the *nexus* is your own and the conclusion may be false. There is no sophism in facts, but there are tremendous possibilities of sophistry in reasoning from facts. Let it not be supposed that the faith of Rhoda was credulity; far from it.

(1) To begin with, she had the evidence *of her senses*. She had heard the voice of Peter without the gate. All great spiritual truths are substantiated in like manner. Coleridge heard God in the Vale of Chamouni as really as one hears the roll of thunder. I have seen regeneration and so have you. Jerry McAuley was regeneration made visible and walking about among men. We have felt immortality; felt it as really as if spirits from the unseen world had clasped our hands. What else are these "intimations" of which philosophers have written and poets sung? We are drawn as with invisible cords. The unseen world is all around us.

(2) Rhoda had, furthermore, *the testimony of the divine word*. As an inmate of the home of Salome, she must have been acquainted with the Scriptures and familiar with the promises. There is a sense in

which a promise, with authority behind it, is more satisfactory than a visible and tangible fact. Here is a bar of yellow metal said to be worth ten thousand dollars, and here beside it is a government bond for the same amount. Which will you choose? The shining bar? Nay; take heed how you trust your eyes; for many a countryman has been deceived by a "gold brick." You will of a certainty choose the government bond; since there is unquestioned value in a promise to pay issued by a nation with a vast exchequer. Thus faith is more reliable than sight. The little gatekeeper might, indeed, have been deceived in Peter's voice, but she was quite confident of the veracity of God.

(3) She had, still further, *the response of her inner consciousness.* This is called the ultimate test of truth. A man is not loyal to himself, if he rejects the voice of divinity within him. It is a grave mistake to say, "I will believe only that which can be verified by the physical senses." Here was the fault in Tyndall's prayer-test. A photographer who has just taken your portrait may, yielding to your insistence, expose the sensitive plate to the light; but in doing so he will confim your doubt instead of dispelling it, since the picture, affronted by the test, vanishes in an instant. God and the great invisible truths which center in him can not be subjected to mathematical demonstration. If that were possible, faith would be not only unnecessary; there would be no place for it.

We have one form of evidence which Rhoda had not; to wit, the testimony of a great cloud of witnesses. We must decide here between negative and positive testimony. On the night of the 13th of November, 1898, there was a meteoric shower. You were probably asleep and did not observe it. Will you believe that there was such a shower, or not? There are hundreds of astronomers who say that they watched it from their observatories. There are tens of thousands of others who sat up all night to observe it. On the other hand, there are multitudes who are prepared to testify that they saw nothing of it. What then, will you conclude?

There are millions of people on earth who certify that they have had personal communion with God, that they have experienced the mystery of regeneration under the power of his Spirit, that the blood of Jesus Christ has cleansed them from the shame and bondage of sin, and that they have received answers to prayer again and again. It is respectfully submitted that the credulous man is not he who accepts this mass of evidence, but he who prefers the negative testimony of those who were asleep and did not see the falling stars. It is incredible that rational men should not give immense weight to the word of hosts of well accredited witnesses who testify with reference to the great truths of the Christian religion: "That which we have heard, that which we have seen with our eyes, that which we have looked upon and our hands have handled of the Word of life, declare we unto you."

III. We perceive here, still further, *the Comfort of Faith.* It was a sorrowful company that surrounded Rhoda in the upper room. They were overwhelmed with fears and misgivings; the traces of tears were on their cheeks. The little maid alone was happy among them. Dear, absent-minded Rhoda! So transported was she by the sound of Peter's voice that she neglected to open the door and let him in.

There are four stages of progress from spiritual pain to peace. I see a man walking along a country road, alone, shivering in the cold, muttering to himself in bitterness of soul, "Who will show us any good?" This is Unbelief.—I see him again pausing before a gate, looking toward the lighted windows of a home in the distance, listening to faint sounds of music, wondering, fearing, scarce venturing to hope. This is Doubt.—I see him now coming down the garden path and looking in at the windows; he notes the fire on the hearth and the well provided table, the dancing and merrymaking in which he has neither part nor lot. This is Knowledge.—I see him once more in his place at the table; there is a ring on his finger, there are shoes on his feet, he is eating of the Father's bread and drinking of his wine. This is Faith. The joy of life is not in perceiving things, but in appropriating them. The comfort of our religion is not in gazing at objective truth, but in making it ours. The secret of heaven is in the possessive pronoun; it is to say of Christ, "He is my Saviour"; of his cross, "This is my salvation"; of his people, "These are my friends"; and of his glory, "I shall have part in it."

We have thus pursued the argument of faith plus reason as against reason alone. Truth yields not to the demand of philosophers, but of little children. We must stoop to conquer. Let Faith and Reason go side by side to Calvary. Ask, "What is the meaning of this cross?" Reason replies, "The cross is two transverse beams of wood on which malefactors are slain." But Faith says, "The cross is the wisdom and the power of God."—Ask, "What is this superscription?" Reason answers, "It is written, 'Jesus of Nazareth, King of the Jews,' and is in three languages, Greek, Latin and Hebrew." But Faith says, "This is the King of the Universal Israel; my Lord and my God."—Ask, "What is this blood?" Reason replies, "Blood is a thin colorless liquid, known as *plasma*, filled with infinitesimal disks or corpuscles, involving somehow the mystery of life." But Faith says, "This blood is the love of God, the mercy of God, the power and pity of God; there is life in apprehending it, there is heaven in a glimpse of it, there are oceans of bliss in a drop of it!"

Let us away, therefore, with cold Reason that refuses to accept what lies beyond the finger tips, and welcome Faith. Stand out of our light, ye mere analysts and naturalists, who darken counsel by words without knowledge. One hour of Rhoda's simple faith in the great verities is worth a thousand cycles of proud groping among the shadows of doubt and unbelief. There is many an old woman in the chimney corner, with her Bible on her knee, who sees further along the great vistas of truth than all the Magians who lean on their own understanding. There is many a blind beggar who lifts his sightless sockets toward heaven and penetrates more deeply into the invisible than those who boast of their acquaintance with the schools. What is man whose breath is in his nostrils that he should reply to God's manifesto? An earthworm raising its head before the royal chariot! A mote in a sunbeam, with an infinitesimal glint of light borrowed from the sun, prating of itself as a rival luminary.

We have kept Peter waiting at the door too long. He enters, and his friends can doubt no more. He clasps their hands and kneeling down makes recognition of God's goodness. They had, indeed, been seeing through a glass darkly but now face to face. No more will they question, no more discuss the Philosophy of Prayer. That problem is forever solved for them.

One greater than Peter waits at the door asking to be admitted that he may reveal to us, in clear and indubitable form, all the sublimities and profundities of the spiritual life. He knoweth the Father, and none other can, except those to whom he shall reveal him. He knoweth heaven and immortality, and the glory that eye hath not seen nor ear heard. He knocks and calls; but, alas, we prefer to linger in the company of our doubts and misgivings. He knocks and calls: we know his voice. Why not withdraw the bolts, admit him and behold Truth, face to face and eye to eye? Here is his word: "Behold, I stand at the door and knock; if any man will open unto me, I will come in and sup with him and he with me."

THE MARKS OF THE LORD JESUS

"From henceforth let no man trouble me; for I bear in my body the marks of the Lord Jesus."—Gal. 6, 17.

An old soldier was at bay. His opponents were pressing him hard. At this time Paul was worn and weary. It was not easy to be patient under false accusation, particularly when his accusers were from the house of avowed friendship. The same had occurred a year before when certain ones in the Corinthian church had impugned his teaching and called his apostleship in question. It was on that occasion that Paul stooped, as he says, to "play the fool" in self-defense. His plea is one of the classics of eloquence:

"Would to God ye could bear with me a little in my folly; and indeed bear with me. I say again, Let no man think me a fool; if otherwise, yet as a fool receive me, that I may boast myself a little. That which I speak, I speak it not after the Lord, but as it were foolishly, in this confidence of boasting. Seeing that many glory after the flesh, I will glory also. For ye suffer fools gladly, seeing ye yourselves are wise. For ye suffer, if a man bring you into bondage, if a man devour you, if a man take of you, if a man exalt himself, if a man smite you on the face. I speak as concerning reproach, as though we had been weak. Howbeit, whereinsoever any is bold (I speak foolishly), I

am bold also. Are they Hebrews? so am I. Are they Israelites? so am I. Are they the seed of Abraham? so am I. Are they ministers of Christ? (I speak as a fool) I am more; in labors more abundant, in stripes above measure, in prisons more frequent, in deaths oft. Of the Jews five times received I forty stripes save one. Thrice was I beaten with rods, once was I stoned, thrice I suffered shipwreck, a night and a day I have been in the deep; in journeyings often, in perils of robbers, in perils by mine own countrymen, in perils by the heathen, in perils in the city, in perils in the wilderness, in perils in the sea, in perils among false brethren; in weariness and painfulness, in watchings often, in hunger and thirst, in fastings often, in cold and nakedness. Beside those things that are without, that which cometh upon me daily, the care of all the churches" (2 Cor. xi. 1, 16–28).

And now he was under fire again, and the poignancy of the attack was heightened by its coming from his dear missionary churches of Galatia. The Judaizers there, not content with antagonizing his teaching as to divine grace, had challenged his credentials But who were these recent recruits, and what were their noble achievements, that they should turn upon him? It was now twenty-six years since he had been converted on the way down to Damascus, and they had been years of hard fighting. He had earned his knighthood; where was their service chevron? He knew the smell of prison mold: had felt the tang of the leaden-pointed scourge. He had been tanned by the suns of Asian deserts; had been swept about in the mountain-torrents of Macedonia; had drifted, helpless and forlorn, upon the open seas. He was familiar with hunger and cold, with poverty and persecution. It was hard under these circumstances to be assailed by professing Christians. The *Epistle to the Galatians* is his masterly reply. He presents here a calm argument for the Doctrine of Grace, which his opponents had sought to controvert; the great doctrine which Luther characterized as "The article of a standing or a falling church." As he approaches the imputations made upon his apostolic authority, the fire of just indignation waxes hot, until, in his closing sentences, he outvies the fervid eloquence of Desmosthenes in his oration on "The Crown." What righteous scorn is here! What just contempt! "Hands off!" he cries. *Noli me tangere!* Shall carpet-knights assail a tried and proven soldier of the cross? "From henceforth let no man trouble me; I bear in my body the marks of the Lord Jesus!"

Our inquiry has reference to these "marks of the Lord Jesus." What were they? The word is *stigmata*; there are suggestions of practical value in it.

I. *The apostle speaks as a Slave.* The word *doulos*, "slave," used frequently in Paul's writings, is borrowed from the teachings of Christ. It means absolute ownership, such as was shown by the puncturing of the master's name, with hot needles, in the forehead. Paul thinks of himself as no longer his own, having surrendered all faculties and powers of body and soul to the domination of Christ. "If ye have aught against me," he says, "go to Jesus, whose I am and whom I serve. I bear his marks in my forehead. To him alone am I responsible. To my own Master I stand or fall."

It is apparent that here is the Christian's coign of vantage as against all criticism whatsoever. But it is a high position to take, and quite impossible except as we have submitted ourselves to Jesus Christ in an absolute surrender. Thus is it written: "Ye are not your own; ye are bought with a price. Forasmuch as ye know that ye were not redeemed with corruptible things, as silver and gold; but with the precious blood of Christ, as of a lamb without blemish and without spot." Have we been subjugated thus? And do we gladly and triumphantly avouch our Lord's control? Do we bear his marks of ownership? If so, it matters little what man may say against us.

II. *But Paul speaks, also, as a Devotee.* The god-mark was familiar in those days. It 'is still to be seen among the Hindoos, the cabalistic sign of Siva or Vishnu on the forehead. It tells at what altar a worshiper pays his devotions, to whose temple he brings his daily offering of rice. It is an open confession, as if he said, "This is my god." But you need not go to India to find the god-mark. All men wear it in their lives and characters. Observe it as you pass along the street. Here is one whose restless eyes betray his consecration to Mammon. Here is another whose countenance is seared with the red brand of Bacchus; and others wear the mark of the Beast in their sensual features (Rev. 13, 16).

If a man believes in the true God, it is his plain duty to declare it; but confession does not wait upon an open manifesto. No more is it a matter of fringes and phylacteries. Get once into the divine presence and you must, like Moses, go your way with a shining face. Jacob met God by the brook Jabbok and there his thigh was touched, the sinews shrank and the man thenceforth went limping on his way. In like manner Saul of Tarsus, as he journeyed to Damascus met God face to face, was blinded by a sudden flash of his glory, and ever afterward bore the trace of that interview in his blinking eyes. There is a real sense in which God leaves his mark on every man who comes into close, vital touch with him. Our walk and conversation is a plain avowal of spiritual allegiance. "Thy speech," said the high priest's servants to Peter, "bewrayeth thee."

III. *And Paul speaks as a Soldier.* His loyalty was vindicated by honorable scars. The members of the dueling corps of the University at Heidelberg are proud to display in their slashed features the sign-manual of the sword. But the service of Christ is no mere flourish of foils: it is a real campaign on the high places of the field. "We wrestle not against flesh and blood, but against principalities, against powers, against the rulers of the darkness of this world, against spiritual wickedness in high places." Our foes are said to be "the world and the flesh and the devil." The man who goes forth against these with a courageous heart is quite sure to be marked for life.

Let a man array himself *against the world*, and it will straightway smite him in the face. Have you ever defied its fashion or gone athwart its custom? Then you were stigmatized as "singular" or "eccentric": or if in dead earnest, you were characterized as a bigot or a fanatic.

He who makes a brave struggle *against the flesh*, that is, his own lower or baser nature, must bear the tokens of that struggle with him. But they are honorable scars: for "he that ruleth his own spirit is greater than he that taketh a city." It is no small matter to get the better of your envy, your avarice, your evil habit, your hot temper. This is "hard pounding", as Wellington said of Waterloo; and no man gets off unscathed. If you have seen Tissot's pictures of the Magdalene, you will remember how in one she stands in her doorway, decked with jewels and radiant with smiles. In the other, both smiles and jewels are gone; her face wears a serious look: and the sparkling brightness of her eyes has given way to a calm light which betrays the peace that passeth understanding. She has fought a great fight and won back her womanhood. She has entered into the fulness of the sweet promise: "To him that overcometh will I give to eat of the hidden manna; and I will give him a white stone, wherein is a new name written, which no man knoweth saving he that receiveth it."

And what shall be said of him who *confronts the devil* face to face? To deny the personality of this prince of the power of the air is to betray a frivolous mind. He is a man of shallow experience who cannot say, "I have measured swords with him." The early masters were fond of representing Christ in the Wilderness as dwelling among wolves and hyenas and lions; but there was one shadowy presence with him during those awful days, more real than ravenous beasts. He was led of Satan hither and thither and tested at every point, ever replying "Get thee behind me!" And when those days of temptation were over, his physical strength was so reduced that angels must needs come and minister unto him. Thus it is with every man who meets the adversary; he has the sympathy of One who can be touched with the feeling of our infirmities, having been tempted at all points like as we are, who holds out the promise of a splendid triumph and a glorious reward: but when that conflict is over its marks are evermore upon him.

IV. *Still further, the apostle speaks as a Sufferer for Jesus' sake.* There are fiery trials in Christian experience which sear the features. Pain drives its ploughshare in furrows across the brow. These also are marks of the Lord Jesus, "if so be that we suffer with him."

Much of our affliction is merely passive. There are many who lie on beds of languishing, racked and twisted with anguish, sustained by the presence of One who taketh note of their patience and "putteth their tears into his bottle" (Psalm lvi.8). All service is not active service. He is a faithful follower of Christ, who, able to do nothing but lie and cough, does that contentedly for Jesus' sake.

But the thought of the apostle goes deeper. He speaks elsewhere of his desire "to fill up that which is behind of the afflictions of Christ"; as if he felt himself to be in some wise a participator in the redemptive pain of his Master. It is true that we may not pass into the deep darkness of Gethsemane to drink of our Lord's purple cup of vicarious death; for He treadeth the wine-press alone; but we may abide in the outer shadow of the olive-trees, wakeful and prayerful, sympathizing with him. The passion of Christ is a passion for souls; and this must be the passion of his people as well. If thus we suffer with him, we shall also reign with him. It was in view of this phase of suffering that he said, "If any man will come after me, let him take up his cross and follow me." Our cross gets its significance from the analogy of his cross. It is a work to be voluntarily taken up by every one who follows Jesus, for the sake of delivering souls from the bondage and shame of sin. He who has apprehended this truth can say, like Paul, "I am crucified with Christ"; and again, "I protest that I die daily." He need not cut the nail-prints in his hands as St. Francis did; the world will put the *stigmata* upon him. But, blessed is the Christian who, like Simon of Cyrene, can feel the cross of his Lord resting upon him.

V. *Once more, the apostle speaks as one who Labors in his Master's field.* The hands of the toiler are marked with callous ridges. A farmer is proverbially the proudest of men. Why not? He knows himself to be a producer, not merely a consumer of the earth's substance. He plants a handful of corn and reaps a sheaf; he helps to feed the hunger of the world. To similar work the Christian is called, in the Master's words, "Say not it is yet four months and then cometh the harvest; lift up your eyes and see! The fields are already white unto the harvest." It is for us, who follow and serve him, to thrust in the sickle and reap.

The late James Tyson of Australia, a multi-millionaire, on being asked what he proposed to do with his money, replied: "I have never troubled myself about that. As for the money, I care nothing for it; my pleasure has been in the game of making it. I set out in my early manhood to fight the desert. I have put water where there was no water; and beef where there was no beef. I have put fences where there were no fences; and roads where there were no roads. Nothing can undo what I have done. I have fought the desert, and I have won!" It is, indeed, a great satisfaction for a man to feel that he has made an industria. success. But let us exalt that thought to a higher level, and rejoice in that we are called to be "laborers together with God." Our supreme joy should be, not in our escape from sin's penalty, nor in the hope of reward, but in glorious service for its own sake. Happy is he who can finally show the marks of faithfulness, the callous ridges made by sickle and flail, the evidences of unremitting and cheerful toil in fellowship with his Lord.

I see the coming of a great multitude to heaven's gate. They are the Overcomers, such as have grown weary in the service of Christ. They cannot keep step in the ranks as militiamen do, for they are veterans, worn and crippled. They have been through forced marches and fierce conflicts; they bear the marks of the Lord Jesus. Their uniforms are torn and tattered, and covered with dust. They carry a red-cross banner, sun-stained and winter-worn and riddled with tempests of lead. But as they approach, with labored step, faint and limping, the angels and archangels lean over the parapets to give them welcome. Make way for the Veterans! And now the gates roll back and One comes forth to meet them; One who hath upon his vesture and upon his thigh a name written, King of Kings and Lord of Lords: One who was seen upon the heights of Bozrah with garments dyed red, whose name is The Mighty to Save. On his brow are the scars of a thorny crown; in his lifted hands are the nail-prints. The great Veteran comes forth to meet and welcome his own. "Come, ye blessed of my Father! Ye have suffered with me," he says, "and ye shall also reign with me. Ye have been faithful unto death, receive ye the crown of life. Enter into the joy of your Lord!" Was there ever a triumphal entry like that? Were ever more exultant hearts than theirs? Were ever prouder men? Would you, my friend, be among them? Why not?

SILENCE IN HEAVEN

"And when he had opened the seventh seal, there was silence in heaven about the space of half an hour."—Rev. 8, 1.

A door was opened into heaven and the dreamer stood in the presence of the Great Assize. On the throne, beneath an overarching rainbow, sat One whose glory was "like a jasper and a sardine stone," to whom a great multitude of angels and archangels did obeisance, crying, "Holy! Holy! Holy!" In his right hand was a sealed book, the Record of the Divine Administration of Human Affairs. A voice was heard, "Who is worthy to open the book, and to loose the seals thereof?" And the dreamer says, "I wept much, because none was found worthy to open the book." But one of the elders said, "Weep not; behold, the Lion of the tribe of Judah hath prevailed to open the book and to loose its seven seals." Then this Hero of Redemption took the book, amid ascriptions of praise, "Thou art worthy! for thou hast redeemed us by thy blood out of every kindred and tongue and people and nation, and hast made us kings and priests unto our God!"

At the breaking of the *first* seal the White Horse of peace was revealed; and Shelomith sat upon him, wearing a diadem and armed with a bow.—The *second* seal was opened and the dreamer saw the Red Horse of war, his rider armed with a dripping sword. There was the confused noise of battle, and garments rolled in blood; the clang of weapons; the fierce cry of victory, mingled with lamentation.—At the opening of the *third* seal appeared the Black Horse of famine. He that sat upon him had a pair of balances; and a voice proclaimed, "A measure of wheat for a penny, and three measures of barley for a penny; and see thou hurt not the oil nor the wine!"—The *fourth* seal was opened, and, behold, the Pale Horse of pestilence. The earth is strewn with corpses and the stench of corruption is in the air.—At the opening of the *fifth* seal a great Altar appears, and under its shadow the souls of the martyrs. And they cry with a loud voice, "How long, O Lord, holy and true, dost thou not judge and avenge our blood?"— The breaking of the *sixth* seal reveals a terrific scene of confusion. The earth reels and totters, the sun is black as sackcloth of hair and the moon is as blood; the stars of heaven are falling as when a fig-tree casteth her untimely figs; the heavens are rolled together as a scroll; kings and potentates are crying to the mountains and rocks, "Fall on us and hide us!"

At this point comes a parenthetic vision. An angel is seen wearing the signet of Jehovah, with which, going abroad through the earth, he marks the foreheads of the righteous. Then, as in a dissolving view, the scene is shifted and a multitude of saints triumphant are seen arrayed in white robes and with palms in their hands; and one of the elders announces, "These are they which came up out of great tribulation and have washed their robes, and made them white in the blood of the Lamb. Therefore are they before the throne of God, and serve him day and night in his temple: and he that sitteth on the throne shall dwell among them. They shall hunger no more, neither thirst any more: neither shall the sun light on them, nor any heat. For the Lamb which is in the midst of the throne shall feed them, and shall lead them unto living fountains of waters: and God shall wipe away all tears from their eyes."

Then the *seventh* seal was opened; and "there was silence in heaven about the space of half an hour"; that is, the dreamer waited for such a period expectant, but no vision came and no word was spoken. Silence! The harpers on the sea of glass stood leaning on their harps; the elders, and the angels and archangels ceased from their ascriptions of praise. Silence! Silence in the High Court of Heaven. Silence as on a battle-field when the conflict is over and the dusk of evening falls.

Why this silence? Because there was nothing to say. The opening of the seventh seal revealed the mystery of the Divine Administration of Human Affairs; and the denouement was so satisfactory that all questioning and disapproval were put to shame. What was revealed we cannot say; but it convinced the assembled multitude of the absolute wisdom and goodness of God.

The world is noisy with controversy. The air is full of whys and wherefores. Our lesson is an algebraic problem, in which we are ever perplexed by an unknown factor; but at the opening of the seventh seal the x will be reduced to known terms, and our bewilderment will cease.

I. The Problem in its larger form is called *History;* that is, God's hand in universal affairs. Not every man can write history. David Hume was disqualified by reason of his failure to perceive the development of a divine purpose in the world. He was a compiler of facts; fortuitous events, bound together like a bundle of fagots. He saw the shadows of the Apocalypse, peace and war, famine and pestilence, galloping fast like riderless horses on a desolate field of battle. But as to any "philosophy of history" he was not competent to frame it.

For the clear solution of the problem we must await the final apocalypse; but the centuries thus far have revealed some indisputable facts. One is, that a definite plan pervades the present order. Nothing happens; all things are preconcerted; all work together in a progressive scheme.—Another fact is that all events center in and radiate from the cross. What we call civilization is merely its effulgence. The limits of civilization and Christendom are co-extensive. The voice of Jehovah is to be heard above all the confusion of passing events, saying, "I will declare the decree: *'Thou art my Son; this day have I begotten thee. Ask of me and I will give thee the heathen for thine inheritance and the uttermost parts of the earth for thy possession.'*"—And still another fact is that there are no real reverses in Christian progress. Everthing is going right; century by century, year by year, day by day. Events are clearly, irresistibly moving on toward the restitution of all things.

I have sometimes stood on the seashore when it seemed impossible to determine whether the tide was going out or coming in. But let me wait awhile and the tide will speak for itself. It advances, leaves its impress in a lace-like outline on the beach for a moment, and then recedes. And so again and again, making no apparent headway: yet I must surely retreat as the tide rolls in. There are those who deny the cumulative influence of the Gospel, saying, "There is no real progress. The thing that hath been shall be; and there is nothing new under the sun." Yet there has not been a year within our memory when they have not been obliged to shift their position to avoid the overwhelming logic of events.

The law of progress is as sure as gravitation. If there be a momentary arrest, it is only for the regathering of force. A man who had always dwelt in darkness would be greatly bewildered if brought forth to see the day break. What would this mean to him? A tremulous shimmer in the east; a flaming arrow shot upward; another and another; then ghosts and specters flying noiselessly as if from an unseen bowman; now arrows flying thick and fast; now crimson fingers stretched aloft, as of some radiant angel; the glories brightening, fading, brightening again; now a shining forehead followed by a resplendent face; the unseen Bowman is at hand, and "jocund Day stands tiptoe on the misty mountain tops." Such a conflict of light and darkness would be wholly bewildering to one unfamiliar with it; to one who did not know the end from the beginning as we do. The eyes of faith, as well as the logic of experience, are needed to assure us that the progress of truth and righteousness is as this shining light which shineth brighter and brighter to the perfect day.

Yet there are doubts to be solved and questions to

be answered, and we must needs await the opening of the seventh seal. "He calleth to me out of Seir, 'Watchman, what of the night?' The watchman said, 'The morning cometh and also the night!'" But when the curtain is lifted at last, we shall be awestruck by the convincing tokens of God's wisdom in the procession of events. It will appear then that the ups and downs of history were alike in the interest of progress, and we shall see the divine glory shining through all.

In the meantime we are always in danger of darkening counsel by words without knowledge. Carlyle speaks of "that chaotic hubbub in which men's souls run to waste." I preached in a country church last summer where I could see through the open door a group of young people in the porch; their suppressed voices and laughter were an interruption to the calm current of thought. Far better would it be for our faith could we withdraw from the noisy diversion of argument. There are larger truths to be learned in the closet than in the forum. "The world is too much with us."

II. Let us turn now to the more personal phase of the problem; that is, *Providence.* For Providence is merely history with an emphasis on the personal factor; it is God's hand in my affairs and yours. And here we observe a like confusion. The riderless horses run up and down in our changeful lives. We recognize the general principle of compensation; but the law is in question because of numberless exceptions. The fabric seems all threads and thrums. The righteous man is abased while the wicked flourishes like a green bay-tree. Justice is out of joint.

Was Koheleth right when he said, "The wise dieth as the fool, and there is no profit. All is vanity and vexation of spirit"? Or is there something yet to be revealed before the problem of Providence shall be solved?

Ask Worldly-wiseman and he will overwhelm you with his volubility. He holds the clew of the maze. Job sits in the ashes of his prosperity with potsherd in hand, and his neighbors come to comfort him. Many are their wise suggestions; and Job murmurs: "If your soul were in my soul's stead, I also could heap up words against you and shake my head at you." Once and again they urge their consolations in vain and the afflicted man cries: "Miserable comforters are ye all!"

We open the Scriptures; and here are words of genuine help and comfort: "He sitteth as a refiner of silver"; "All things work together for good to them that love God"; "There remaineth a rest." Yet these are but glimmering lights. The whys and wherefores still remain. We abide in patience because we can do nothing else. The unknown factor holds the most important place in the problem; and we await the time when God shall express its value in known terms. We remember how he said: "What I do thou knowest not now, but thou shalt know hereafter"; and again, "In that day ye shall know."

Here is the true philosophy of life. We were restive in childhood under restraints that seem quite reasonable now. Why was I kept at my lessons in school when the birds were singing and the fields were green? Why must I be kept at my boyish tale of bricks when the show was passing along the streets, with the gilded band-wagon in front and the lads of the village following after? Why was I allowed to read only Peter Parley when the others were reading Sylvanus Cobb? Why was I shut in the closet for a peccadillo, for such a little thing? Ah, now I see. "When I was a child I thought as a child." I said many things in those days that would not bear the test of later wisdom. We are but children after all. God's thoughts are not as our thoughts; one day he will share his thoughts with us. The developments of the future will satisfy and silence us.

The man who wrote "God moves in a mysterious way," had set out for Blackfriar's Bridge, in melancholy mood, to drown himself. He wandered to and fro, puzzled in the labyrinth of streets, until the merciful Lord brought him to himself. He returned to his apartment, fell upon his knees in gratitude, and then arose and wrote:

"God moves in a mysterious way
 His wonders to perform;
He plants His footsteps in the sea,
 And rides upon the storm.

"Deep in unfathomable mines
 Of never-failing skill,
He treasures up His bright designs,
 And works His sovereign will.

"Ye fearful saints, fresh courage take;
 The clouds ye so much dread
Are big with mercy, and shall break
 In blessings on your head.

"Judge not the Lord by feeble sense,
 But trust Him for His grace;
Behind a frowning providence
 He hides a smiling face.

"His purposes will ripen fast,
  Unfolding every hour;
The bud may have a bitter taste,
  But sweet will be the flower.

"Blind unbelief is sure to err,
  And scan His work in vain:
*God is His own Interpreter,
  And He will it plain.*"

What then? *Let us talk less and believe more.* Isaac, meditating in the fields at eventide, gets nearer to the truth than men in noisy arenas of debate. The most provoking man in Pilgrim's Progress is Mr. Talkative. God has many truths for listeners, but few for the garrulous. He sows in fields apart, where chattering crows are ever watching for the scattered seed. The doctrine of the Incarnation has been discussed in historic councils with scanty results. But once it pleased God to reveal it to a woman in such wise as never before or since; and it is written of her, "Mary kept these things in her heart and pondered them." God has messages of duty, also, for you and me; but they can scarcely be received or apprehended amid the strife of tongues. A prophet knelt on the summit of Carmel, with his head between his knees. A mighty wind swept over; but the Lord was not in the wind. The earth shook and trembled beneath him; but the Lord was not in the earthquake. The forests glowed and crackled in a mighty conflagration around him; but the Lord was not in the fire. And after that a still small voice said, "What doest thou here, Elijah?" Faith is fostered thus in quiet hours. God reveals himself to those who come apart with him.

If you, my friend, have discovered aught of the

Lord's secret, let it be as a sweet confidence between you and him. There are some things to speak aloud and others to cherish in the breast. It is written, "The secret of the Lord is with them that fear him: and he will show them his covenant." What the Lord whispers to his chosen, in the inner place of his pavilion is but the faintest prophecy of that which shall ultimately be revealed in explanation of his wise dealings with us. It is recorded that as Alexander the Great was reading a letter, he detected his favorite Hephæstion looking over his shoulder; whereupon he uttered no reproof but significantly placed his finger on his lips. God's sweetest revelation to our souls is incommunicable. Men caught up into the third heaven see things "which it is not lawful to utter." The great truth is convincing beyond all words. Wherefore, let us be swift to hear, slow to speak. Speech is silver; but silence is golden. The essence of practical theology is here: "Be still and know that I am God."

"WHERE THE PATHS MEET, SHE STANDETH"

"In the top of high places by the way, where the paths meet, she standeth."—Proverbs 8, 2 (R. V.).

In the Book of Proverbs—which is a dramatic presentation of the duties and responsibilities of human life—you have observed a figure passing in and out among the madding crowd, of kindly face and friendly speech. She is described as having in her right hand length of days and in her left hand riches of honor; "her ways are ways of pleasantness and all her paths are paths of peace." Her name is Wisdom, and her purpose is to counsel and admonish those who are unmindful of their own good. Now in the gateway, where merchants do congregate; now with the crowd surging along the streets; anon, at the crossing of the ways, she stretches forth her hands, warning, exhorting, promising, pleading: "My voice is unto the sons of men. O, ye simple, understand wisdom; and ye fools, be of an understanding heart!"

We have come to the sanctuary, each by his own road and going his ain gait. Are we quite sure we have been going right? Let us hear the call of Wisdom to a calm consideration of life's responsibilities and issues. Here, "where the paths meet, she standeth." All readers of Dickens are familiar with Seven Dials, in London: it is a center where streets converge, like the hands on a dial or the spokes of a wheel. One midnight I stood there, bewildered: knowing well by what thoroughfare I had come, but questioning, "Which way now?" Let us pause here as at Seven Dials and consider. We are desirous of reaching the highest possibility of character and usefulness; but are our faces set thitherward? "There is a way which seemeth right unto a man, but the end thereof are the ways of death." Here is the possibility of an irreparable mistake. Let us, therefore, look around us, and at the meeting of the Seven Paths of Life enquire, Which way?

1. I see yonder a broad thoroughfare,—*The Street of the Breadwinners.* All who journey there are bearing burdens. They are honest people; but O how weary and troubled! What are they doing? Toiling to make both ends meet; struggling to keep the wolf from the door. And where are they going? To shops, factories, offices: and after that? Alas! they seem heedless of the outlook. They are worn and weary plodders, with no light in their eyes, no spring in their step. These are the people who make the work-a-day world go round. The heavens are open above them; but their faces are downcast and they do not see. They rise with the sun and, after making their tale of bricks, go joylessly to bed. Weary; O, so weary and heavy laden! Is a man then no better than a horse or an ox? Is life worth living at this rate?

But I see, going in and out among them, a Fellow-craftsman with a shining face and enheartening words.

The sweat of labor is on his brow: under his arm is a wooden plow which he has mended at his shop. His hands are as the hands of a breadwinner; but his voice is the voice of Wisdom: "O sons and daughters of toil, know ye not that the kingdom of God is among you? Life is not circumscribed by the narrow walls of our workshops. Lift up your eyes and see; the heavens are open; ye live forever! It is yours to dream dreams and see visions of the eternal life. Be laborers together with me in the service of truth and righteousness. Come unto me, all ye that labor and are heavy laden, and I will give you rest."

And alas, the many heed him not. How sordid their lives, and how hopeless! Their backs are breaking under burdens; and their hearts are breaking as well. All their energies are put into their lower tasks. They live like beasts of burden, and they die as galley slaves go scourged to their dungeons. No heaven above! No life beyond! Is life worth living in that way?

II. But here is another thoroughfare; *The Golden Way*. It is paved with gold; a golden mist is in the air. Those who journey here are not content with a mere livelihood; they long for fortune, affluence, opulence. They have set out to win the yellow prize. They know no god but Mammon; before him they bow and do obeisance.

Some are young and hopeful. The fever of the quest is in their veins, *auri sacra fames*. They are just "getting their hand in." If any such are present to-night, let them consider the wisdom of getting their hand in. Do you know how monkeys are captured in Algiers? A gourd is hollowed out, baited with rice and placed in a convenient tree. The silly creature reaches in, grasps the rice, struggles to be free, and is captured because it refuses to let go. The secret of getting rich without sorrow is in knowing when to open the hand and let go.

And others in this Golden Way are in the midst of the hurly-burly. They have learned the Midas-touch, so that all their investments turn to profit. The glittering coin before their eyes shuts out the sun and stars of heaven. The love of earthly good has blinded them to the eternal sublimities. Are they happy? Aye; *unless they stop to think*.

Others of the Mammonites have grown old and retired. They have little to do but repose in easy chairs and cut off coupons. They ride along the Golden Way in open carriages, enjoying the fruit of their labors. They are clothed in purple and fine linen, and fare sumptuously every day; but life's candle is burning to the socket. They set out years ago to conquer wealth, and they have won. They have thought of gold by day and dreamed of gold by night. They have sighed for gold, have lived for gold, have filled their bags and vaults and pockets with gold—and, alas! there is not one little pocket in a shroud.

For, shading our eyes and gazing afar to the end of the Golden Way, we see a highwayman, grim and merciless, who meets and lays a heavy hand upon them, crying: "Strip! Disgorge! Your money and your life!" And, lo! they vanish, cold, naked, penniless. They had made their wills; now they have left all.

III. Let us turn our eyes, now, to the *Path of Glory*,

leading up yon steep mountainside. Not many journey there, but they are choice souls. If their names were called, you would have no difficulty in recognizing them; for they are writ large on the world's muster-roll. There are scholars, with their arms full of parchments; scientists and philosophers; military heroes crowned with wreaths and decorated with badges of distinction; kings and potentates whose scepters have shaken the earth. A noble procession of ambitious souls!

But observe, as they journey, how they all arrive at the same place. It is an imposing cemetery in the far distance, where monoliths, carved with honorable epitaphs, are gleaming in the sun. On this very day a funeral cortege is passing thither, with tolling of bells and the sobbing of a bereaved nation. Who goes now to his last resting-place?* The President of the French Republic. As the hearse, with its sable plumes, passes under the great archway, I read there this inscription: "The Paths of Glory lead but to the Grave." And we remember the words of the Preacher: "Better is the sight of the eyes than the wandering of desire; this is also vanity and vexation of spirit."

IV. I see another road; broad and inviting and beaten with many footsteps; its name is *Vanitas Vanitatum*. Here go the pleasure-seekers; some reeling and staggering, many marked with the red brand of sensuality. The voice of Folly, leering and ogling from her door-way, is heard, "Turn in hither! Stolen waters are sweet." These votaries of the flesh are sowing wild oats and must reap the harvest of

---

* President Faure died on the Friday preceding this discourse.

eternal shame; they are sowing the wind and must reap the whirlwind. "While we live, let us live," they cry; "for what is better than that a man should enjoy the ways of his heart and the sight of his eyes?" The air is filled with laughter; crisp and hollow laughter, "like the crackling of thorns" (Eccl. 7, 6). I remember a dreary day on the prairie when, the night closing in with a falling temperature, a group of huntsmen gathered slender twigs and wisps of grass and kindled them for warmth. It was a ceaseless task, for their fuel was no sooner lighted than, crackling for a moment, it was gone. It made music while it lasted; but it died so soon! So, says Solomon, is the laughter of fools. They have, in very truth, their labor for their pains.

And at the end of the merry pilgrimage, what then? The Judgment. See the flashing in the heavens; hear the roll of thunder. The mummers have had "a good time"; has it never occurred to them that it might be wise to provide for a good eternity? They have reached the end of the road, still keeping up the pantomime of folly. Let them off with their dominoes now! God is not mocked; whatsoever a man soweth, that shall he also reap. And we hear the voice of the Preacher, "Rejoice, O young man, in thy youth; and delight thyself in the ways of thy heart and in the sight of thine eyes; but know thou that for all these things God will call thee into judgment." O the unspeakable shame of one who, chasing a butterfly, leaps into hell!

V. And yonder runs the *Road of the Merit-makers*. They are a serious folk who journey this way. They are sensible of sin and would earn their way into heaven. They are like prisoners who, fettered with ball and chain, work out their sentence on the turnpike. It is a thankless task: so much to be done and so little to show for it. Mistaken souls, who have not learned the largesse of heaven or the glorious liberty of the children of God!

I see many priests and pontiffs here, with bells and pomegranates on their robes, and broad fringes and phylacteries. They are fasting, paying tithes, intoning long prayers, forgetful that God looketh on the heart.

Here, also, go troops of flagellants, barefoot, clothed in sackcloth, lashing their bodies for the sins of their souls. They are sad-faced and sad-hearted; making merit, all. So have I seen the silent monks of La Trappe toiling in the fields, offering no greeting to each other or the passer-by but "Remember death!"

And here are legalists, earning their way to heaven by good works; unmindful that "by the deeds of the law no flesh shall be justified." What does all this come to? Not long ago in the Treasury Department at Washington a one-hundred dollar note was received which had been executed with a pen. It was calculated that three months of constant labor had been expended on this counterfeit. When finished, it was worthless, and its maker was arrested in endeavoring to pass it. Such will be the outcome of all spurious forms of merit-making. The product is nil. Merit, indeed, cannot be made by mortal man. There is no merit, no legal tender at the Judgment, save the righteousness which is by faith in Jesus Christ, who having expiated our sins on Calvary, imputes his righteousness to those who love him.

VI. And behold *Via Novissima!* There go the newsmongers; who, like the Athenians, do nothing but hear or tell some new thing. They are engaged, apparently, in opening up new avenues through trackless forests and over untraveled wilds; and their song is ever "Ring out the old! Ring in the new!"

All these are agreed that tradition goes for naught. It is enough for them to say of any doctrine that the fathers believed it. They call the scientists to aid them in proclaiming a new god,—Law, Energy, or All-pervading Soul; it little matters what, so long as there is a clear departure from the teaching of him who said, "When ye pray, say Our Father." And a new Bible, too; a new Bible by all means, since the world of progress has outlived the old fashioned Book which our fathers and mothers loved and touched with reverent hands. And a new Christ; yes; the edict has gone forth from one our Theological Seminaries that the time is ripe for "a restatement of the doctrine of Christ." And yet, with all this concerted effort to supersede the religion of the past, has it not occurred to these novelty-mongers that they are going backward and not forward? for, indeed, "there is nothing new under the sun." The "new departures" in belief which are proclaimed from time to time, are but revamped heresies. Christian Science, Theosophy, the Higher Criticism are old as the centuries. They are shop-worn goods laid out on bargain counters, and, alas! there are always foolish folk to purchase them. Not long ago, seeing some "Barlow knives" in a cutler's sample case, I said, "These are the sort that was popular when I was a boy; is there any market for them now?" He replied: "O yes; there's a great sale for Barlow knives on the Indian Reservations." So the heresies that pass out of fashion in one age are sure to come into vogue further on. It is an old world that we are living in, and things have been pretty well canvassed, and the things which have been canvassed have been fairly well tried; and tried truths are the truths for you and me.

We note, also, a current demand for new morals. The old views of the sanctity of marriage are passing away in some quarters: and there are signs of weariness with the old forms of Sabbath observance. "The smart set" in society are giving Sunday musicales and conversations. But they are mistaken in claiming novelty for these things. A thousand years before the Christian Era the Lord said to Amos, "What seest thou?"—He answered, "A basket of summer fruit."—"And what hearest thou?"—"The voice of those who cry, 'When will the new moon be gone and the Sabbath, that we may pursue our ways?'" On this very afternoon a secular performance is given at the Waldorf-Astoria by leaders of the social left-wing. They are threshing out old straw. They have fallen in with the vulgar crowd who for centuries have sought to circumvent the divine code of morals.

And such flatter themselves that they are "liberal" and "progressive." In reality they are but looking over their shoulders to a worn-out past. In blazing new roads through the forests, they merely make their way into a bog. They are reactionaries: the world is too righteous now, too sensible and respectable, to tolerate their methods. They have yet to learn the aphorism that "What is true is old; and what is not old is not true." The only new thing in the province of religion is that of which John Robinson spoke: "The new light ever breaking forth from the Word of God."

VII. But there is one other way; *Via Crucis.* It was once a narrow path, and few there were who found it; but a great multitude whom no man can number journey there. The cross throws its bright shadow all along the way. Men and women, weary of sin and longing for pardon and peace, lift their eyes to Christ crucified, saying, "Lord, I believe!" Then on they go, singing, "All hail the power of Jesus' name." Yet singing is but an incident of their journey. They have a great project on hand, nothing less than the conquest of the world by the deliverance of souls from sin. In their hands are sickles wherewith they toil in God's yellow fields. They believe in the Golden Age, in the coming of the King, in the uplifting of the race. God is saving the world by them. Oh, blessed copartnership of heavenly grace! God and they are saving the world; for are they not "laborers together with him"? His blessing is upon them; his Spirit is with them; his Pillar of Cloud goes before them.

> "This is the way I long have sought,
> And mourned because I found it not;
> Till late I heard my Saviour say,
> 'Come hither, soul, I am the way.'"

You may hear the lamentable sound of stumbling in their ranks; for they are sinners all, but, blessed be God, sinners saved by grace. On they go, wrestling with their baser selves and rejoicing in multiplied triumphs. Their ambition is to live devout and useful lives. Their gaze is toward the eastern skies; for they "love the appearing" of their Lord. They ask no reward of service but to hear him say, "Well done," and be forever with him.

"This is the old Way; "The way the holy prophets went; the way that leads from banishment." It is the plain Way; as Isaiah said, "An highway shall be there, and a way; and the wayfaring man, though a fool, shall not err therein." It is the straight Way; beginning at the cross and ending at heaven's gate. See them yonder, at the far end of *Via Crucis*—now *Via Lucis*—passing into the great glory, singing, "Bless the Lord, O my soul!"

We have tarried at Seven *Dials* long enough. We have observed the Seven Ways of Life. We cannot remain here; we must needs choose our path and move on. You will rise presently and go forth to meet the duties and responsibilities of another day. Which road will you take? "Come thou with us and we will do thee good." To journey by the Royal Way of the Cross means the pardon of sin by the washing of redeeming blood; the building up of character by the imitation of Christ; participation in service with those who are lending themselves to the betterment of the world; and heaven to crown it all. "We are traveling on to heaven above; Will you go? Will you go?" Are you not weary of the other paths? The Holy Spirit speaks: "This is the way; walk ye in it." Shall we go forth together, then? If so the cloudy pillar will lead on until, with all the ransomed, we shall come to Zion with songs and everlasting joy upon our head. May the dear Lord grant it.

"WAS CHRIST A CHRISTIAN?"

"For which cause he is not ashamed to call them brethren."—Heb. 2, 11.

A sermon was preached by a distinguished Rabbi in the Synagogue Emmanuel last Sabbath in answer to the question, "Was Christ a Christian?" The discourse, while controversial, was in a spirit of admirable courtesy. It is a pleasure to observe that a Rabbi can speak thus freely among us with none to make him afraid. Our prayer for the people whom he represents is that their eyes may be opened to see the fulfilment of the Hope of Israel: and may the Lord save us from Anti-Semitic prejudices.

The Rabbi said: "All real Christianity died with its founder"; and he proceeded to affirm that if Christ were now to return, he would not recognize current Christianity or acknowledge any of the existing denominations. This was his answer to the question, "Is Christ a Christian?" Let us venture to go back of his conclusion and also of his premises to enquire whether the question itself is a fair one.

I. *What is a Christian?* The poet Young wrote, "A Christian is the highest style of man." In Hare's "Guesses at Truth" a Christian is said to be "God Almighty's gentleman." The reference is obviously to the ideal follower of Christ.

A Christian is, to begin with, *a man*, subject to all the limitations of humanity, circumscribed by the common horizons of life.

He is *a near-sighted man*. His eyes are holden, so that however sincere his desire to apprehend truth, he sees "as in a glass darkly." The great verities are mere shadows fleeing before him. He perceives "men as trees walking."

He is, moreover, *a sinful man*. What? In spite of his new birth out of darkness into light? Aye. Regeneration is a tremendous fact indeed, but it does not extirpate sin. It effects a radical change in the ruling purpose; it finds a man devoted to self-gratification, and it turns him right about with his face toward righteousness and eternal life. It arrays him in spiritual armor and bids him fight his way to manhood, with an assurance of divine help and blessing. He has a hard struggle on hand; not against flesh and blood, but against principalities and powers. His passions and appetites often get the better of him; down he goes; and what then? Does he surrender? Ah, no! He has access to infinite resources of strength and encouragement; for "if any man sin, we have an advocate with the Father, even Jesus Christ the righteous." To his feet again, and at it more bravely than ever! Meanwhile, sin is an ever-present though diminishing factor in his life. This is true of all Christians; for "if we say that we have no sin, we deceive ourselves and the truth is not in us."

He is, still further, *a churchman;* that is, an associate of other penitent sinners. In his life of spiritual conflict and toil he feels the need of sympathy and longs for the uplift of mutual prayer. Another may feel strong enough to stand alone; but a penitent sinner knows his weakness. "Two are better than one; for if they fall, the one will lift up his fellow: but woe to him that is alone when he falleth; for he hath not another to lift him up." Wherefore, he naturally and perforce turns his face toward the fellowship of saints.—But the question arises "Which of the numerous branches of the Church shall I join? Greek, Catholic or Protestant? Baptist, Methodist or Presbyterian?" He suits himself. He is like one whose patriotism moves him to enlist in the army. Shall it be infantry, cavalry or artillery? What matters it so long as all are under one flag? So the follower of Christ, casting about him, says, "I must get into the atmosphere of associated prayer; must find my place somewhere in the great co-operative labor-guild. Which Denomination shall it be?" He is likely, as a sensible man, to decide that the best is the broadest, always providing the red-cross banner floats over it; while the worst is the one which thinks itself the best and cries, "The temple of the Lord are we."

And being in the church, the Christian finds himself at home. For are not all his companions, like himself, sinners saved by grace? Are they not all strugglers, desiring to grow to the full stature of manhood in Christ, all coming short and making the same lament, "'The good I would, I do not; and the evil I would not, that I do.' 'Sorrie I am, my Lord, sorrie I am'"?

What shall we say then? "Was Christ a Christian?" Could he fellowship with such feeble and imperfect folk? But we are not yet ready to answer until we have made a preliminary inquiry as to Christ himself.

II. *Who was Christ?* A singular personage every way.

He was a Man; yet his manhood was qualified by a stupendous fact; to wit, that he was also God. He stands solitary and alone as *theanthropos*. He had been "with the Father before the world was." He assumed flesh for a definite purpose; for the accomplishment of that purpose he must become a veritable man while remaining "very God of very God." And, having finished his redemptive work, he went back to "the glory which he had with the Father before the world was."

He was an omniscient Man. He knew no doubts, problems or questionings. He did not see truth in shadowy reflections, as we do, but swept the infinite horizons at a glance. All truth was ever present to his mind; indeed, truth had its primal source in him; it emanated from him as sunlight from the radiant orb; insomuch that he could say, "I am the Truth."

He was a holy Man. In this he was altogether unique. He felt no unworthiness; knew no accusations of Conscience; never prayed for the pardon of personal sin. His challenge was, "Which of you convicteth me of sin?" To this his Roman judge replied, "I find no fault in him at all!" the man who delivered him to death, "I have betrayed innocent blood!" and the soldier who had charge of his execution, "Verily, this was a righteous man!" So extraordinary was the holiness of Jesus that, while undisputed, it has ever puzzled the ingenuity of scholars. How could it be? Shall we say, "*Potest non peccare,*" or "*Non potest peccare*"? Origen suggested that this singular quality was due to the fact that Christ's humanity was interpenetrated by divine virtue as red-hot iron by fire. The explanation, however, little concerns us, so long as the fact itself is conceded on all sides. He was holy, harmless and undefiled. His seamless robe was a symbol of his flawless life and character.

The death of Jesus was as extraordinary as his life. Others have been crucified, but the world knows only one Cross. Heroes have died bravely, but never hero or martyr like this man. He had power to lay down his life, and power to take it up. He died because he had determined to die. He gave himself for the life of the world. He took the entire sin of the ruined race upon his great heart, which broke under the burden. It was considerations like these that moved the infidel Rousseau to exclaim, "Jesus died like a God!"

And his posthumous influence, also, is singular. For nineteen centuries all possible tests as of fire and acid have been applied to his life and character and work; and the testimony of history is, "I find no fault in him at all." Who of all the dignitaries of the centuries can compare with him? Call the roll, and let the procession of the mighties pass before us. Then call "Jesus of Nazareth!" and behold how the others shrivel like pigmies. He is the chiefest among ten thousand. "No mortal can with him compare among the sons of men." All the forces of civilization center in him. All the light of the nations is reflected from the shining of his face.

"*Was Christ a Christian,*" *then?* A thousand times,

No! So far above is he, so far removed from all. The impropriety of the question is as if one should ask, "Was Jehovah a Jew?" But if the enquiry be, "Has Christ a warm heart for his people?" A thousand times, Yes. How do we know? It is written, in connection with his farewell interview with the Twelve, "He, having loved his own, loved them to the end"! What forbearance, what consideration was there! He knew their sin and weakness. He foresaw that Thomas would doubt him, that Peter would deny him, that all would forsake him in the bitter hour; yet he *loved them to the end.*

If he were to come to New York to-day, he would enter into every fellowship of true believers; not as a Christian, indeed, but as the Lord of all Christians. Their denominational name would be as nothing to him, if only he were assured of their love and devotion.

He would come to some of our churches with a scourge of small cords, no doubt, to drive out much that justly offends him; as it is written, "Whom I love I rebuke and chasten." In some, where sumptuous mummery and dumb-show prevail, he would gravely say, "God is a Spirit; and they that worship him must worship in spirit and in truth." In others, seeing too much of worldly conformity, he would say, "Be ye holy as I am holy! Come out from the world, and be ye separate, a peculiar people, zealous of good works." In others, where his people have mutilated their Bibles and sought counsel at voiceless oracles, he would say, "Did ye ever hear me call in question the inerrancy of Holy Writ? Shall the servant be wiser than his Lord? Search these Scriptures, for in them ye think ye have eternal life and these are they which testify of me."

But he would not be blind to penitence or oblivious of earnest endeavor. He would utter words of sympathy and encouragement: "Fear not, little flock, it is your Father's good pleasure to give you the kingdom." He would take note of the purpose and aspiration. He would remind us of the parables of the leaven and the mustard seed. And without doubt he would stimulate our latent energies by calling to remembrance his great commision: "All power is given unto me in heaven and on earth; go ye, therefore, and evangelize; and, lo, I am with you alway, even unto the end."

If he were to come to our churches to-day, he would doubtless address himself to many of us who minister in sacred things. "Preach me," he would say; "Preach my atoning blood! Preach my quickening and invigorating Breath! Preach the exceeding great and precious promises of my Grace! Why will ye turn aside to questions that are without edification? Have ye forgotten how I said, 'I, if I be lifted up, will draw all men unto me'?"

He would pass along these aisles and look into the faces of many who have been following him afar off. It would be as when he turned and looked on faithless Peter; and we, like Peter, would go out and weep bitterly. He would speak to us gravely of our responsibilities, saying, "Ye are the salt of the earth; but if the salt have lost its savor, wherewith shall it be salted?" and, "Ye are the light of the world; let your light so shine before men that they may see your good works and glorify God."

He would stand, perhaps, where I am standing now, for the vindication of his people. It is a pleasure to remember how, when his disciples frowned on the penitent woman who anointed his feet, he looked around upon them, saying, "Let her alone; she hath wrought a good work upon me!" He would, in like manner, defend the feeble and penitent, not only from the unfriendly criticisms of their brethren, but also from the aspersions of the world. For, "to whom shall I liken this generation? It is like unto children sitting in the markets, and calling unto their fellows, and saying, We have piped unto you, and ye have not danced; we have mourned unto you, and ye have not lamented."

Best of all, he would stand here, as among his disciples in the upper room, and make this prayer: *"Father, I pray for them: not for the world, but for them which thou hast given me; for they are thine. And all mine are thine, and thine are mine; and I am glorified in them. And now I am no more in the world, but these are in the world, and I come to thee. Holy Father, keep through thine own name those whom thou hast given me, that they may be one, as we are. And now I come to thee; and these things I speak in the world, that they might have my joy fulfilled in themselves. I have given them thy word; and the world hath hated them, because they are not of the world, even as I am not of the world. Neither pray I for these alone, but for them also which shall believe on me through their word; that they all may be one; as thou, Father, art in me, and I in thee, that they also may be one in us: that the world may believe that thou hast sent me."*

If these things are so, what then? *First;* let us be humbly ashamed of ourselves, since we have come so far short of the possibilities of the Christian life. The world is quite right in asserting that we do not live up to our professions. Yet let us not be discouraged, but gratefully confess, "I am not what I ought to be; I am not what I hope to be; I am not what I mean to be; but by the grace of God I am not what I once was." The gold is in the crucible: the time is coming when its brightness will reflect the Master's face.

Second; let us not turn our backs upon any of our fellow-Christians, since he himself is not "ashamed to call them brethren." He is very jealous for them, insomuch that it is written, "He that toucheth them, toucheth the apple of his eye." Knowing our common infirmities, let us be tenderly affectionate one toward another. If any have gone backward, let us prayerfully seek to restore them. And let us love the Church Universal; for though constituted of imperfect men and women, it is nevertheless the consort of Christ. One of these days he will lead her "without spot or blemish" to the Marriage Feast. Meanwhile let us take heed how we cast reflection upon her fair repute.

And, *finally;* let us never be ashamed of Christ. "Nay, when I blush, be this my shame, that I no more revere his name." He is "the first-born among many brethren" here; and he will acknowledge the humblest of his true followers in the presence of the universe assembled at the Great Day.

It is recorded of Joseph that when his father and brethren came from Beer-sheba, he as Viceroy received them with most distinguished honors. He was not ashamed of the old farmer with his rustic sons who came in homespun with wagons to the royal city. Nay, he went out to meet them, he brought them to Court, he introduced them to the king, saying, "These are my brethren." So will our Elder Brother receive us when we go over to the Better Country. Here is his promise: "Whosoever shall confess me before men, him will I confess also before my Father which is in heaven."

THE SOVEREIGNTY OF GOD

"O Lord, thou art exalted as head above all."—I. Chron. 29, 11.

The work of King David was done. The kingdom was about to be handed over to Solomon. A solemn assembly had been called at which David commended his son to the consideration of the people and dwelt with pathetic emphasis on the unfulfilled dream of his life, the building of "the house magnifical." The address opened with an invocation of singular beauty: "*Blessed be thou,* Lord *God of Israel our father, for ever and ever. Thine, O* Lord, *is the greatness, and the power, and the glory, and the victory, and the majesty: for all that is in the heaven and in the earth is thine. Thine is the kingdom, O* Lord, *and thou art exalted as head above all.*"

The sin of our times is irreverence. We take great liberties with God. In prosperity we forget him, in adversity we murmur against him. In our controversies we bandy his august Name to and fro as in a game of shuttlecock. We pare the edges of his holy Law. We stand at the doorway of his oracles, crying, "Yea, hath God spoken?" Irreverence is a most heinous sin. It was called *nefas* by the Romans, and was regarded as a capital offense. Not murder itself had so short a shrift. The wind blows in a different quarter now. Is it not time to call a halt and to ask in all seriousness whether God has any rights which earthworms and ephemera are bound to respect? It is important to know God's place in the universe and our place with reference to him.

I. He is, at the outset, *the First Cause of All.* One phase of the current sin of irreverence is Materialism. Not a few so-called scientists are sedulously engaged in trying to eliminate God from the problem of nature. Because they cannot find him with telescopes and microscopes, they conclude that his being is a myth; as if, indeed, God were to be discovered floating about like a star or hiding somewhere like a microbe. In fact, he is not far from every one of us. He stands at the scientist's elbow with power enough in a breath of his nostrils to sweep an army of cavilers into nonentity; but he cannot be seen with fleshly eyes nor touched with finger tips. The sixth sense must be brought into requisition; as it is written, "By faith we understand that the worlds were framed by the word of God, so that things which are seen were not made of things which do appear." When Napoleon, to whom Laplace had submitted his system of philosophy, inquired, "Where does God come in?" the answer was, "We have no longer any need of God." But there are two points at which a godless scientist is at his wits' end.

The first is Creation. You say, "I do not believe in creation; I am an evolutionist." You are probably aware that evolution is as yet a mere hypothesis and that, except by novices, nothing more is claimed for it. Nor is it a working hypothesis as yet. At frequent intervals it utterly breaks down. It is like a railway along the summits of the Andes, which may look well enough on paper but has too many chasms for practical use. You have taken a hypothesis as your first premise and set out to substantiate it. You smile at bridgeless gulfs and chasms; "missing links" are of slight consequence. You are in search of origins. Matter is a fact; the question is, Whence came it? Follow it back to chaos, past chaos to the nebula, and beyond the nebula to the primordial germ: what then? The difficulty still remains. It is as hard to account for an atom as for a universe. You are facing an impenetrable wall of darkness; but for the theist a door opens just there and, amidst a burst of glory, he finds himself in the presence of the Infinite. Here is God's workshop; and behold, he is spreading out the heavens, hanging dawns and sunsets like tapestries, framing worlds and spinning them into their orbits. He stretcheth out the north over the empty place and hangeth the earth upon nothing; he maketh Arcturus, Orion, and Pleiades, and the chambers of the south; he measureth the waters in the hollow of his hand; he comprehendeth the dust in a measure and weigheth the mountains in scales. Here, then, is the solution of the problem. "In the beginning. God."

The second insurmountable difficulty of the godless scientist is to account for the maintenance of the present order. Law and energy are inadequate. Law without a lawgiver, order without an administrator, effects without causes, an engine without an engineer; these are not merely illogical, they are unthinkable. Furthermore, they yield no satisfaction to a seeking soul. A few days ago I watched a broken spar making a vain struggle to reach the shore through the boiling surf, beaten and buffeted to and fro, helpless, hopeless, a mere victim of the elements. So is a godless man in the grip of insensate laws: he is helpless amid the hiss and roar of machinery. There is unspeakable relief in the thought of Providence: "In him we live and move and have our being." A warm hand touches ours; and we are led forth to Olivet to hear him say: "Behold the fowls of the air; they sow not, neither do they reap, nor gather into barns; yet your heavenly Father feedeth them. Are ye not much better than they? And consider the lilies of the field, how they grow; they toil not, neither do they spin: yet I say unto you, that even Solomon in all his glory was not arrayed like one of these." In this philosophy we rest. God is over us and under us and round about us.

> The Lord our God is full of might,
>   The winds obey His will;
> He speaks,—and in his heavenly height
>   The rolling sun stands still.
>
> Rebel, ye waves, and o'er the land
>   With threatening aspect roar;
> The Lord uplifts his awful hand,
>   And chains you to the shore.
>
> Howl, winds of night; your force combine;
>   Without his high behest,
> Ye shall not, in the mountain pine,
>   Disturb the sparrow's nest.
>
> His voice sublime is heard afar,
>   In distant peals it dies;
> He yokes the whirlwind to his car,
>   And sweeps the howling skies.
>
> Ye nations, bend—in reverence bend;
>   Ye monarchs, wait his nod,
> And bid the choral song ascend
>   To celebrate your God.

II. God is also *the Power Behind the Throne.* Here we touch another phase of irreverence, to wit, Anarchy. Defiance of human forms of government is closely allied with Atheism, since the "powers that be are ordained of God." It is true that God does not approve of tyranny and oppression; but "order is heaven's first law." Wherefore we are forbidden to speak evil of dignities.

The political fabric which God constructed for his chosen people was ideal. It was known as the Theocracy, or "Government of God." Its constitution was the Moral Law. Its earthly Executive was the High Priest, on whose breastplate was inscribed, "Holiness to the Lord." Its center was the Ark of the Covenant, over which was the mysterious Shekinah, the pillar of cloud in which God manifested his presence and from which he made known his holy will.

As time passed, however, the people clamored for a monarchy. They wanted a visible king who should wear a glittering crown and wield a scepter and ride in a chariot before them. Wherefore God gave them Saul the son of Kish to rule over them. But in fact, neither Saul nor any of his successors was king of Israel. They were but viceroys, appointed to rule under God. There is no *jus divinum* but this. God is the king-maker; his is ever the power behind the throne. "By me," he says, "kings rule." This is recognized in all Christian monarchies. Victoria is "Queen of Great Britain and Empress of India by the grace of God."

But what shall we say of a Republic? Our fathers assembled in Independence Hall to formulate a government "of the people, by the people and for the people." Nevertheless a republic does not derive its authority from the consent of the people except as the maxim holds true, *Vox populi, vox Dei*. While the members of the Continental Congress were engaged in discussing the fundamental principles of civil and ecclesiastical freedom with such minor considerations as taxes and revenues, a suggestion of supreme importance was made by Benjamin Franklin; to wit, "As no government can endure and prosper without the blessing of heaven, I move that prayer be now offered to Almighty God." This was a just recognition of the ultimate authority; For "except the Lord build the house, they labor in vain who build it; except the Lord keep the city, the watchman waketh but in vain."

In the present juncture in our National affairs it is wise to remember what Thomas Carlyle said, "No government can stand on the mechanical utilities." We are just now searching for new outlets of commerce, making excursions of enterprise into Asiatic waters, dreaming dreams of national expansion. Who can estimate the issues? We are crossing the line of seclusion into fellowship with the world-powers. As a Christian nation we can have no interest in "national expansion" except so far as it may mean the expansion of the kingdom of Christ. Any other view is sordid and provincial. A great career is before us, but that is not the point. This is what counts: We are to have a splendid opportunity of serving God. The responsibility of the hour cannot righteously be avoided. "The White Man's Burden" is laid upon us. The poet's adjuration sounds like an echo of the Great Commission of our Lord:

> " Take up the White Man's burden—
>   Send forth the best ye breed—
> Go, bind your sons to exile
>   To serve your captives' need ;
> To wait, in heavy harness,
>   On fluttered folk and wild—
> Your new-caught sullen peoples,
>   Half devil and half child.
>
> Take up the White Man's burden—
>   Ye dare not stoop to less—
> Nor call too loud on Freedom
>   To cloke your weariness.
> By all ye will or whisper,
>   By all ye leave or do,
> The silent sullen peoples
>   Shall weigh your God and you."

It was four centuries ago that Spain began her foreign invasions with the power of the inquisition behind her. Two centuries later England set forth to the conquest of the seas. Her methods were mediæval; her broadest purpose was commercial enterprise. We are not so hampered and handicapped in our new departure. This Republic has the benefit of a hundred glorious years of civil and ecclesiastical freedom. We are a Christian nation, by profession and universal consent; as such we assume the white man's burden. If we bear it wisely and prayerfully, who knows how magnificently we may contribute to the triumphs of civilization and prepare the way for the coming of Christ. To this end let us ever remember that God worketh in us to will and to do of his own good pleasure. It is true that his name is not in our Constitution; but that is a matter of little moment if his authority be felt and manifest in the hearts and lives of rulers and people. Therefore our constant prayer should be: "Protect us by thy might, great God, our King!"

III. God is furthermore *the Alpha of Truth*. There are only two systems of theology: Arminianism and Calvinism; and these differ not as to the landscape of truth but merely as to the viewpoint. An Arminian makes man the center; that is, the sovereignty of the human will. A Calvinist begins at the sovereignty of God. I am a Calvinist by logical necessity; it seems impossible to me that the solar system should revolve around the moon. It cannot be said that God's love is the center, nor his justice; for these are mere attributes. God himself is the effulgent focus from which all great verities radiate. His sovereignty is not an attribute but the condition of his ineffable being. Love and justice are unavailing except as He who loves and judges, sits supreme upon his throne.

In a system thus buttressed by Omnipotence, we have a sufficient basis of Salvation. If our hope of a blessed hereafter rested on ourselves alone, we might well fear and tremble. What is more uncomfortable than for a little child to run after its mother, clinging to her skirts and crying to be cared for? But a child in its mother's arms—ah, there are safety and happiness. The man who hopes to be saved by clinging to God, may well speak of the danger of "falling from grace." But if the Almighty shall somehow lay hold upon him, then danger ceases. "No man," said Jesus, "shall pluck you out of my hand.—The gates of hell shall not prevail against you." Wherefore "work out your own salvation with fear and trembling, for it is God that worketh in you."

In this we have, also, a reliable staff of life. In the philosophy of self-culture there are three cabalistic words: Sin, Duty, Character; and each of these must be defined with reference to God. What is sin? *Lese majesty;* that is, Enmity against God. Thus David cried in his penitence, "Against thee, thee only have I sinned and done this evil in thy sight!" —What is duty? It is debt. To whom? To God. All questions of conscience are reduced to this ultimate form, Will it please God?—And what is character? Godliness; that is, God-likeness. On the negative side it is avoidance of sin, on the positive the right discharge of duty; and both of these are in the nature of a return to God.

Here, also, is the working postulate of the kingdom. The divine sovereignty furnishes a satisfactory franchise for Missions at home and abroad. "All power is given unto me," said Jesus, "wherefore go ye into all the world and preach the gospel to every creature." What is this gospel but the proclamation of the grace of one who is not only willing but infinitely able to save? "How beautiful upon the mountains are the feet of him that bringeth good tidings, that publisheth peace; that bringeth good tidings of good, that publisheth salvation; that saith unto Zion, *Thy God reigneth!*"

If these things are true, it behooves us to make much of God in our thinking and living. Let us walk softly before him. Let us take heed and beware of malapertness in the discussion of great verities; for "fools rush in where angels fear to tread." The man who imagines himself competent to pluck the heart out of divine mysteries will do well to read the thirty-eighth chapter of the Book of Job. It should never be forgotten that "the Lord our God is a jealous God."

In all our dealings with the high and holy One who inhabiteth eternity—and dealings we must have with him since we were created in his likeness—let us bow reverently as did Moses at the burning bush. This is the admonition: "Draw not nigh hither; put off thy shoes from off thy feet, for the place whereon thou standest is holy ground." Our burning bush is at Calvary, where Deity burned (yet was not consumed) for us. Here God reveals himself; his boundless love, his infinite justice, his sovereign grace. Come nigh, O sinner, and touch his wounded feet; but no nearer! The revelation of Godhood here rolls upon us like a floodtide. Bow low, speak softly; this is the Holy of Holies. "My Lord and my God!"

Now unto the King Eternal, Immortal, Invisible, the only wise God and our Saviour, be honor and glory forever and ever. Amen.

MINT, ANISE AND CUMMIN

"Woe unto you scribes and Pharisees, hypocrites! for ye pay tithe of mint, anise and cummin, and have omitted the weightier matters of the law."
—Matthew 23, 23.

In the Life of Dr. Johnson there is an interesting colloquy between Boswell and his great master, as follows:

Boswell. "Pray, sir, did you ever play on any musical instrument?"

Johnson. "No, sir; had I learned to fiddle, I should have done nothing else. I once bought me a flageolet, but I never made out a tune."

Boswell. "A flageolet, sir? So small an instrument. I should have liked to hear you play on the violoncello; that should have been your instrument."

Johnson. "Sir, I might as well have played on the violoncello as another; but I should have done nothing else. No, sir; a man would never undertake great things could he be content with small. I once tried knotting—Dempster's sister undertook to teach me—but I could not learn it."

There is the homely setting forth of a great truth; to wit, An undue attention to small matters disqualifies us for a just consideration of more important things. It was just here that the Scribes and Pharisees erred. They lived in a time of spiritual declension: and, as religious leaders, they should have distinguished themselves by holy zeal. But they were not equal to their opportunity. The time called for men of broad views, high purposes, noble aspirations; but these were "fiddlers," as Johnson would have said. They were gownsmen, doctrinaires; attentive to minutest details and particulars. They were like the Preraphælites, who cannot paint a poppy field but only a field of poppies. They were like that countryman who "could not see London for its houses." They were little men, living in a little world, thinking along narrow grooves, strenuously attentive to infinitesimals. A glance at these men suggests the importance of *Taking Large Views of Things.*

The initial mistake made by the Scribes and Pharisees was in their *Conception of God.* Surely as Doctors of Divinity they should have known him. They were Professors of Theology, which is defined to be the "Science of God;" but their views were most superficial. God was to them the supreme Ruler of a little strip of territory on the eastern border of the Mediterranean Sea; his province was scarcely greater than that of a Roman procurator. He had set the Jews apart as his chosen people and, unmindful of the rest of humankind, was minutely observant and exacting in his attitude toward them. The tithe of garden herbs was a proper oblation for such an One.

It is of the utmost importance that we should obtain an adequate view of God. We are measured, indeed, by our conception of him. The man who is entrusted with a single talent would never have wasted his opportunity as he did, but for his grievous error as to his master's character. He said, "Lord, I knew thee that thou art a hard man, reaping where thou hast not sown, and gathering where thou hast not strewed: and I was afraid, and went and hid thy talent in the earth."

Our God is a great God. His greatness is unsearchable. He is great in his being; for this is his name: I AM THAT I AM.—He is great in his attributes. How easy to say "Omnipotence," "Omniscience," "Omnipresence"; but who shall comprehend these heights and depths? It is to measure the ocean in a gourd.—He is great, moreover, in his demands upon us who were made in his likeness. His word is, "My son, give me thy heart"; and, behold, we offer him mint, anise and cummin!

The Scribes and Pharisees had also but a narrow view of *the great truths which radiate from God*. To them were entrusted the Oracles; and it was their special function as Biblical Experts, to know and explain great doctrines and precepts. But their scholarship was addressed to the jot and tittle. They made much of the letter which killeth and overlooked the spirit which giveth life. They were hair-splitters, wire-drawers, monstrous triflers. They did not enter into the great chambers of truth but had much to say of superficial considerations. So beggars stand hungry at the windows of the bake-shop. So, in our boyhood, we walked around the tents of the menagerie, hearing the roar and trumpeting of mighty beasts, the music of orchestras, and applause and laughter of the audience; in which we, alas, had neither part nor lot. These exegetes should have remembered the saying that is written: "The entrance of thy word giveth light."

The successors of these men are among us. We too have Biblical experts whose attention is given to mint, anise and cummin to the neglect of the weightier matters of the law. For forty years we have been listening to the arguments of the Higher Critics. The great truths that fill the temple with their glory have been held in abeyance while theologians have gravely discussed the question of flaws in the marble. And with what result? "The mountain has brought forth a mouse." Cardinal Wiseman said of the accumulated product of this controversy: "In all this mass, although every attainable source has been exhausted; although the fathers of every age have been gleaned for their readings; although the versions of every nation, Arabic, Syriac, Coptic, Armenian and Ethiopian, have been ransacked for their renderings; although manuscripts of every age, from the sixteenth century upwards to the third, and of every country, have been again and again visited by industrious swarms to rifle them of their treasures; although, having exhausted the stores of the West, critics have traveled like naturalists into distant lands to discover new specimens, have visited, like Scholz or Sebastian, the recesses of Mount Athos or the unexplored libraries of the Egyptian and Syrian deserts, yet has nothing been discovered, no, not one single various reading, which can throw doubt upon any passage before considered certain or decisive in favor of any important doctrine." A more recent opinion of the results of this controversy has been expressed by Dr. Green of Princeton, who affirms that of the propositions of the Higher Critics ninety per cent. have been disproven, five per cent. more are in the process of demolition, while the remainder may be regarded as a more or less valuable addition to the sum total of our knowledge. If this be so, there is some reason to inquire whether the game has been worth the candle.

Is it not time for laymen to lend a hand? Why should it be so generally assumed that specialists are the best judges of comprehensive doctrines, when the very opposite is true? Is it not apparent that minute scrutiny and explanation of infinitesimals may so contract the vision as to interfere with a just apprehension of larger things? Men who fiddle well, as Doctor Johnson intimated, are not likely to be accomplished in such matters as jurisprudence or international diplomacy. The Bible is a great book; it deals with great verities, such as sin, salvation, judgment and the endless life. These cannot be subjected to the processes of the microscope. The larger scholarship alone can grasp them.

At one time Greece was given over to the Sophists, whose entire outfit was an elaborate collection of juggling catches. They applied their methods to all great questions, and would with perfect equanimity maintain the truth of either side. The youth of Athens flocked to their schools, and were captivated by their plausible words. Then came Socrates, the reformer, who addressed himself in particular to these learned triflers. He maintained the importance of truth. He protested that there was a large and generous way of determining "between the worse and better reason." Great thinker that he was, sweeping the horizon with his far-reaching eyes, he could not endure quibbles and subtleties. And it was the hair-splitting sophists who put the cup of hemlock to his lips.

The larger way of looking at truth is not for specialists, but for the average man. The expert has his place, indeed, but not just here. He goes into the Yosemite with a geologist's hammer and, busied about "specimens," he cannot be expected to behold clearly the magnificence of nature. I stood once on the upper deck of a steamer, approaching the chalk cliffs of France, which were reddened by the glory of a magnificent sunset, and was lost in reverent wonder and admiration; a friend at my elbow, much given to scientific research, broke the silence with the observation that these cliffs had been formed by minute rhizopods. Rhizopods, forsooth! So does the small scholarship of our time break in upon the vision of stupendous truths. So did the Scribes and Pharisees tempt Christ with questions as to "the sevenfold widow" and the greatest commandment, while he was discoursing on the illimitable glories of the endless life. Not thus let us approach the Oracles. The things that make for life and character and usefulness are here. "Search the Scriptures," said our Master, "for in them ye think ye have eternal life and these are they which testify of me."

Another mistake was made by the Scribes and Pharisees in their *Treatment of Ethics*. As lawyers, that is, expositors of the Mosaic Code, it was their particular business to know and teach rules of conduct. In this they were masters of casuistry. They were scrupulous in particulars to the last degree. They subdivided the precepts of the Law; weighed and measured and compared them. The greatest, said some, was the Law of the Phylactery; the least was the Law of the Bird's Nest. They sifted and threshed, scrutinized and analyzed, quibbled and made fine distinctions. They dwelt much on the importance of ablutions. The arms "must be washed a pigmy's length," they said; that is, from knuckles to elbow, with the water dropping from the finger tips. Meanwhile, God was saying to them, "Your hands are full of blood; wash you, make you clean; cease to do evil, learn to do well."

As to the Sabbath, they had many *toldoth* or minute requirements. There were rules as to treading on the grass, as to kindling a fire, as to the number of steps that might lawfully be taken on the Holy Day. How like the sound of a clarion is the larger word of the Master, "The Sabbath was made for man!" Here is the criterion by which to settle all questions of Sabbath rest; this is a day for the soul, a day to bring us into closer sympathy with the divine purpose concerning us. Here is no place for trifling and wire-drawing. "The seventh day is the Sabbath of the Lord thy God!"

All similar questions of conduct were treated by these doctrinaires in the same way. It was a mere tithing of garden herbs. The Law is the expression of the divine mind. A true obedience is that which brings us into closer fellowship with God. We wrong ourselves by quibbling here. We offend God by our petty modes of casuistry. The Scribes and Pharisees were quite willing to bargain with Judas for thirty pieces of silver, but they drew the line at putting the thirty pieces into the temple treasury. Thus they were ever straining out the gnat and swallowing the camel. Not long ago a young man came to me with a sum of money, requesting that I would use it for the relief of the poor. A little later he came again with a like request: "I am a Christian man" he said; "and would like to be doing something for charity." I said, "Do you mind my asking how you made this money?" He replied, "Not at all: I play the races." "You play the races!" I exclaimed, "and profess to be a Christian man! How can you follow Christ without praying over your business?" He answered, "But I do pray about my business; I never attend a race, without previously getting down on my knees and taking counsel as to which horse will win." He proceeded to justify himself in this manner: "There is a certain amount of money up on these races and somebody must win it. The chances are that it will pass into the hands of wicked men. Why should I not get possession of that money, since I have told the Lord that I would give him a tithe of it?" Here is an extreme illustration of casuistry, such as enters, in less or greater measure, into our common considerations of right and wrong. The way to avoid it is to take the larger view. Virtue, character, usefulness; these are immense considerations. Let these be the measure of our life. "Ye are the salt of the earth; but if the salt have lost its savor, wherewith shall it be salted? it is thenceforth good for nothing but to be cast out and trodden under foot of men.—Ye are the light of the world; let your light so shine before men that they may see your good works and glorify your Father which is in heaven." Here is the criterion: nothing is right that belittles character; nothing is wrong that glorifies God.

The Scribes and Pharisees were astray also in *their Views of Worship*. They were high churchmen. They were punctilious to the last degree as to rites and ceremonies. ' They made much of bowings and genuflections, as if these could satisfy God. It was against such trivial observances that our Lord's words were directed: "Woe unto you, Scribes and Pharisees, mask-wearers! ye are like whited sepulchres, fair without but within full of dead men's bones and all uncleanness." At this point we touch upon one of the most portentous evils of our time, to wit, Ritualism. What is that? Lip service; the outward form of devotion with no corresponding regard for piety. It is drawing near to God with our lips while our hearts are far from him.

Down the road from his battle with Amalek came king Saul, who had been commanded to kill all that he captured, and, behold, he is driving before him the best of the sheep and oxen and fatlings. The prophet met him, saying, "What meaneth this bleating of sheep in mine ears, and this lowing of oxen?" And Saul said, "I have spared them to sacrifice unto the LORD thy God." Saul was a ritualist. The prophet rebuked him, saying, "To obey is better than sacrifice; and to hearken, than the fat of rams. Because thou hast disobeyed the word of the LORD he hath rejected thee."

A bandit of the Alps pursues his bloody calling the year round with no scruple; but on Good Friday he appears in the village, lays a tithe of his plunder before the bambino, makes confession, receives absolution; and straightway hies him back to his pursuits among the fastnesses of the hills. The bandit is a ritualist. But how, think you, does such offering of mint, anise and cummin appear to a just God?

In the temple of ancient Egypt was kept the sacred crocodile; attended by princes, fed with the rarest delicacies, adorned with chains of gold. When the stupid thing died, the whole city put on trappings of woe, and drained its revenues for sumptuous obsequies. That was ritualism: pagan, to be sure, but quite as reasonable as much that we are familiar with in these last days.

In the Anglican Establishment a body of "high churchmen" insist on swinging their censers and uplifting the mass. There is an outcry: "You are violating the national constitution; you are breaking your ordination vows; you are threatening the disruption of the Church; you are hurrying us on toward disestablishment!" But what of that? On with the mummery! What are laws and oaths and vows? But the incense that rises from such service surely giveth a stinking savor in the nostrils of God.

What is the mind of the Master? He met the woman at the well of Sychar, and spoke to her of the great questions of the endless life. At length he touched upon her personal sin; and, as the custom is, thinking to divert the conversation into less painful channels, she said, "Let us discuss a question of theology. Our fathers worshiped God in Gerizim, but ye on Mount Zion; now which is right?" Mark his answer: "Woman, believe me, the hour cometh when ye shall neither in this mountain nor yet at Jerusalem worship the Father; for God is a Spirit; and they that worship him, must worship him in spirit and in truth."

But the crowning error of the Scribes and Pharisees was in their *Thought of Salvation.* They were looking for a Messiah. His coming was "the Hope of Israel." All the prophets from Moses onward had spoken of him. But he was expected to come wearing a golden crown and with a jeweled scepter. Lo, here he stands before them: a man in homespun! He is as a root out of a dry ground; he hath no form nor comeliness; and there is no beauty that they should desire him. And they ask, "Is not this the son of Joseph the carpenter?" Had Jesus been willing to pose before them as a good man and nothing more, there would have been no outcry against him. But he insisted on his Messiahship; he claimed to be equal with God.

Nicodemus greeted him thus: "Rabbi, we know thou art a teacher come from God." This, however, did not satisfy Jesus; his reply was instantaneous: "Verily, verily, I say unto thee, except a man be born again he cannot see the kingdom of God."

A young ruler, on one occasion, threw himself before Jesus, saying, "Good Rabbi, What must I do to inherit eternal life?" Good Rabbi! More garden herbs. He would have none of it. "Why callest thou me good? there is none good but one, that is God." In other words, his claim was Godhood or nothing. Mint, anise and cummin would not content him.

The world on all sides is willing to admit that Jesus was a good man; but to say that and no more is to affront his majesty. It is to proclaim him an impostor, in that it rejects his larger claims. No man can go half way with Jesus. "If any will come after me, let him deny himself, take up his cross and follow me!"

Our constant temptation is to minimize the demands of Christ. Let it be remembered that he will accept no terms but unconditional surrender. He is nothing to us unless he be our Lord, our Life, our Sacrifice, our Saviour and our All. He will not undertake our salvation except as God's equal. This qualified acceptance of Jesus was in the mind of the apostle when he cried, "O foolish Galatians, who hath bewitched you, that ye should not obey the truth, before whose eyes Jesus Christ hath been evidently set forth, crucified among you?"

We conclude, then, with a prayer that God would enlarge our scope of vision, that he would enable us to treat great verities in a large way. The word *amplius*, with which Michael Angelo was wont to reprove his art pupils when their work was of too contracted sort, is the word for us. *Amplius!* Larger, broader, deeper, higher! What foolish men are we to fret our souls about the light of glowworms when the sun shines over us! Lift up your eyes and see. Immortality, Duty, Character, Heaven, Glory; these are splendid truths. They emanate from God. And the boast of manhood is, as Keppler says, that we can "think God's thoughts after him." He is a great God; his greatness is unsearchable. We are made in his likeness and after his image. He speaks, "My son, give me thy heart!" Let us look toward his throne with high purpose and noble aspiration. No mint, anise and cummin for our God. The best is none too good for him. For, "except your righteousness shall exceed the righteousness of the Scribes and Pharisees, ye shall in no wise enter the kingdom of God."

THE FIRST EASTER SERMON

"And they said one to another, Did not our heart burn within us, while he talked with us by the way, and while he opened to us the Scriptures?"—Luke 24, 32.

The road from Jerusalem to Emmaus was through a region of wild and rugged beauty; but these travelers had no eyes for it. "The noontide sun is dark and music discord, when the heart is low." A great sorrow had befallen them: their dearest Friend had been put to a shameful death. "O for the touch of a vanished hand and the sound of a voice that is still!" They were on their way to Galilee: discouraged and perhaps, as Matthew Henry says, "meditating a retreat." They had followed Jesus in full confidence of his Messiahship only to see him tamely surrender to his foes. They could not understand how, claiming omnipotence, he should have bowed himself to the mockery and scourging in the Judgment Hall; or how he should have submitted to the agonies of the cross when, with divine resources at his command, he might have called upon legions of angels to deliver him. Indeed, they were sorely disappointed in him; they had looked to him as David's Son for the restoration of the glory of Israel, and he had gone as a lamb to the slaughter and as a sheep before her shearers is dumb, so he opened not his mouth. Such were the sorrowful thoughts that pressed upon their hearts. So absorbed were they that they did not hear the footstep of a lone traveler who approached from behind and presently overtook them. It was Jesus himself; but their eyes were holden that they knew him not.

"What manner of communications are these," he asked, "that ye have one with another?"

They stood still, looking sad; and Cleopas answered, "Dost thou alone sojourn in Jerusalem and not know the things which have come to pass in these days?"

He said unto them, "What things?"

They replied, "The things concerning Jesus of Nazareth, who was a prophet mighty in deed and word." Then they related the manner of his cruel death; betraying their sore disappointment in the words, "We hoped that it was he that should redeem Israel." They made mention, also, of strange rumors that had come to their ears; how certain women had seen a vision of angels who declared that Jesus was alive; and how others had gone to the sepulchre and found it empty; but "seeing is believing," they said, "and as yet no one hath seen him."

At this the Stranger said, "O fools, and slow of heart to believe all that the prophets have spoken! Ought not Christ to have suffered these things, and to enter into his glory?" And beginning at Moses and the prophets he expounded unto them the Scriptures concerning himself. This was *the first Easter sermon*, and it is worthy of our attention for many reasons.

I. *It was addressed to the Universal Church.* For

what is the church? To-day in St. Peter's at Rome the Resurrection is being celebrated with much pomp and circumstance. The Pope enters, arrayed in magnificent canonicals, followed by an imposing retinue of Cardinals. Vested choirs sing antiphonal hosannas and hallelujahs. The imposing edifice is filled with clouds of incense. Is this the Church? Perhaps so. But there was a time when, beneath that same Imperial City, a little company of fugitives from sword and fagot met in the Catacombs to worship Christ. On the stone shelves hewn out on either side, lay the mangled bodies of their martyred dead. The company with muffled voices made their prayers and sang praises, while the night dews dropped about them and the roll of chariot wheels was heard above. A feeble folk they were, like the conies, and compassed about with fears and sorrows: but they loved Christ, worshiped in sincerity and were prepared, if need be, to seal their covenant with their blood. Was this the Church? I think so. "Where two or three are gathered together in my name, there am I in the midst of them": this is the Master's definition. It was seen in miniature in this little company on the way to Emmaus. The Romanists say, "Where the church is, there is Christ:" but precisely the reverse is true; where Christ is, there is the church. Had you been going along the road that day and passed this little group of wayfarers in homespun, you would scarcely have turned a second look upon them. Yet there was a vivid suggestion of the great energy which through the centuries has been working for civilization as leaven in the three measures of meal. This is the living organism through which God's

Spirit is working for the deliverance of our race: the mighty Archimedean leverage by which he is lifting our sin-stricken world into the eternal light and glory. And the discourse which Jesus preached to those dusty travelers, though recorded in merest outline, must be of absorbing interest to the Church of all ages.

II. *Observe that Christ here spake of "the things concerning himself."* In any other preacher this would be preposterous. By all considerations of just modesty we are required to hide ourselves behind the truth. It was needful, however, that Christ should speak of himself in this manner, since he himself is the living centre of his Gospel. Christianity stands alone as distinctly the religion of a Person. Christianity is Christ. He is more than its central fact; he is first, last, midst and all in all. It is for this reason that all attempts to found a living system on Christian doctrine or on Christian ethics apart from Christ himself, have been lamentable failures. Neo-Platonism, Arianism, Unitarianism, the Hindu Somajes, "Ethical Culture," and Altruistic Socialism are illustrations in point. It is impossible to omit Christ and save his teaching; for He himself is the life which animates his doctrine.

In this we perceive the necessity of his resurrection. Had the record ended with the cross, the system of doctrine and ethics which he had established, must have shared his fate. Thus when Oliver Cromwell died one stormy night in September, 1658, there was consternation among the friends of civil and religious freedom. His body had been scarcely laid away in Westminster, when Charles Stuart and his cavaliers came marching back to London to assert the *jus divinum;* and the Commonwealth—because it was so closely identified with the Great Commoner—was dissipated like an ice palace in the sun. But suppose that, as the royal cortége passed along the streets the Lord Protector himself had reappeared at Temple Bar, crying, "God with us!" and rallying his Roundheads about him. How would these cavaliers have fled like leaves before an autumn blast! This is precisely what Jesus did when he returned from the sepulchre and, meeting his disciples, marked out for them the campaign of the future propaganda, saying, "All power is given unto me in heaven and on earth; go ye, therefore, and evangelize; and, lo, I am with you alway, even unto the end of the world!"

It is obvious, from these considerations, that our preaching must ever exalt Christ as Center and Head of all. Our constant temptation is to turn aside to trivial themes. The Jews require a sign and the Greeks seek after wisdom; but we must needs preach Christ and him crucified; to the Jews a stumbling-block and to the Greeks foolishness, but to them which are saved the very wisdom and power of God. It behooves us who are appointed to declare the unsearchable riches of the gospel, to accept the homiletic rules which our Master has laid down. And would that our people might never ask for truth that lies outside that vast circle of light which radiates from Christ! Our secret of success is in the true word that he uttered, "I, if I be lifted up, will draw all men unto me."

III. *Let it be noted furthermore that the Scriptures furnished the sum and substance of this Easter sermon.* "And beginning at Moses and all the prophets, he expounded to them in all the Scriptures the things concerning himself." It is not to be presumed that he carried with him the bulky scroll of Revelation; but, better than that, he had it stored in memory and at his fingers' ends. He had learned the Scriptures in the Rabbinical schools and memorized them at his mother's knee. He loved them, he believed in them, he understood them, he made them the man of his counsel, he set them forth as an infallible rule of faith and practice. So far as the record indicates he never uttered a word that could prejudice the minds of his hearers against their absolute truth and inerrancy. On this occasion he began at the beginning and proceeded along the luminous path of prophecy concerning himself as the Saviour of the world. This was what his doubting and bewildered hearers needed; for, as Trench says, "man's word, woman's word and angel's word they had heard and heeded"; but they had yet to hear and heed the inerrant word of God.

It is probable that Jesus began his exposition with the protevangel, " The seed of the woman shall bruise the serpent's head "; which, uttered at the gate of Paradise, set forth in dim outline the mighty proposition that God would manifest himself in flesh for the world's deliverance from sin.

He called attention to many predictions of his singular birth; such as, "A virgin shall conceive, and bear a son, and shall call name Immanuel" (Isa. 7, 14); and, " For unto us a child is born, unto us a son is given: and the government shall be upon his shoulder: and his name shall be called Wonderful,

Counselor, The Mighty God, The Everlasting Father, The Prince of Peace" (Isa. 9, 6).

He noted the prophecies touching his life, character and ministry among men; such as, "He shall grow up before him as a tender plant, and as a root out of a dry ground: he hath no form nor comeliness; and when we shall see him, there is no beauty that we should desire him" (Isa. 53, 2). Also the words of Moses, "The Lord thy God will raise up unto thee a Prophet from the midst of thee, of thy brethren, like unto me; unto him ye shall hearken" (Deut. 18, 15). And the words of David; "The Lord hath sworn, and will not repent, Thou art a Priest forever after the order of Melchizedek" (Psalm 110, 4). And the prophecies concerning his Kingship, as in Daniel's vision of the great image and the stone that, crushing the image, became a great mountain and filled the whole earth (Dan. 2, 31–35).

He dwelt, no doubt, with special emphasis on the predictions of his vicarious death; such as, "He was wounded for our transgressions, he was bruised for our iniquities: the chastisement of our peace was upon him; and with his stripes we are healed. All we like sheep have gone astray; we have turned every one to his own way; and the Lord hath laid on him the iniquity of us all" (Isa. 53, 5–6); also, "After threescore and two weeks shall Messiah be cut off, but not for himself" (Daniel 9, 26). He showed how the elaborate rites and symbols of the Old Economy were all eloquent of his death and the saving power of his blood. Perhaps he led his two companions to the doorway of the Tabernacle, saying, "What is the meaning of this lamb offered in sacrifice and the blood flowing over the sides of the brazen altar? What is the meaning of this blood sprinkled on the golden candlestick? this blood on the table of shew bread? this blood on the brazen ewer? this blood on the golden altar of incense? this blood on the curtain of fine twined linen? this blood sprinkled on the mercy seat?" Aye, what was the meaning of that blood if it did not point always to the Lamb of God slain from the foundation of the world; if it did not point forward to One whose death was to expiate the world's sin?

He must also have emphasized the predictions of his resurrection from the dead. This was the typical significance of Aaron's budded rod preserved in the Ark of the Covenant. This was also the prophetic interpretation of that strange episode in Jonah's life of which the Lord himself had said, "As Jonah was three days and three nights in the whale's belly, so shall the Son of Man be three days and three nights in the heart of the earth." Likewise emphasis was put upon the divine promise, "Thou wilt not leave my soul in hell· neither wilt thou suffer thine holy one to see corruption" (Psalm 16, 10).

But the time would fail us to indicate the multitudinous references to himself pointed out by this great Teacher in Holy Writ.* Let it suffice to say,

---

* The distance from Jerusalem to Emmaus was about seven miles; a journey of perhaps two hours. This was time enough for a considerable setting forth of the particulars of Messianic prophecy. Among the passages of Scripture to which Jesus may have referred on this occasion, are these: the place of his birth, Micah 5, 2; the visit of dignitaries, Psa. 72, 10; his poverty, Isa. 53, 2; his purity of character, Isa. 53, 9; his zeal, Psa. 69, 9; his ministry, Isa. 61, 1-2 and 9, 1-2; his teaching by parable, Psa. 78, 2; his miracles, Isa. 35, 5-6; his rejection, Psa. 69, 4-8 and 118, 22; his public entrance into Jerusalem, Zech. 9, 9; his betrayal, Psa. 41, 9 and 55, 12-14; the thirty pieces of silver, Zech. 11, 12-13; his sufferings, Psa. 22, 14-15; the indignities heaped

in passing, that we as Christian ministers and teachers fall short of our great advantage if we also do not set forth Christ in the Scriptures. Let the quaint prayer of Nicholas Breton be ours:

> "I would I were an excellent divine
> Who had the Bible at my finger's ends;
> That men might hear out of this mouth of mine
> How God doth make his enemies his friends."

IV. *Let us not lose sight of Christ's purpose in this discourse.* He was proving a "needs be"; as he said at the outset: "O fools and slow of heart to believe all that the prophets have spoken! *Ought not Christ to have suffered these things and to enter into his glory?*" This was his *quod erat demonstrandum.*

A fourfold obligation rested on Christ with reference to his birth, life, death and resurrection: *First;* it was made imperative by an Eternal Decree, since from the beginning God had resolved thus to save the world from sin. *Second;* the Scriptures which were written in pursuance of that decree must needs be fulfilled. *Third;* the burden of inevitable Duty was laid upon the heart and conscience of Jesus as the ideal Man. And *Fourth;* Love itself commanded and he must obey;—as it is written, "God so loved the world."

The plan thus marked out was the only one, so far as we can conceive, by which the desired result could have been accomplished. So Jesus said, "Except a corn of wheat fall into the ground and die, it abideth

---

upon him, Micah 5, 1; Isa. 50, 6; Psa. 69, 21; Psa. 22, 7-8; his being nailed to the cross, Psa. 22, 16; the parting of his garments, Psa. 22, 18; his intercession for his enemies, Isa. 53, 12; his being pierced, Zech. 12, 10; his burial with the rich, Isa. 53, 9; his ascension, Psa. 68, 18; his exaltation, Psa. 110, 1; his universal dominion, Psa. 72, 8; the perpetuity of his kingdom, Isa. 9, 7.

alone; but if it die, it bringeth forth much fruit." And again, "As Moses lifted up the serpent in the wilderness even so must the Son of Man be lifted up, that whosoever believeth in him should not perish, but have everlasting life." *Must* is the word. Here lies the world's only hope, and God stood pledged to its realization. In vain do the kings of the earth set themselves, and the rulers take counsel together against it; He has declared the decree, "*Thou art my Son, this day have I begotten thee! Ask of me and I will give thee the heathen for thine inheritance, and the uttermost parts of the earth for thy possession.*"—(*Psalm* 2).

V. *We have the testimony of the two wayfarers as to the effect of this discourse upon them.* They had set out on their journey from Jerusalem with hearts as heavy as if they were going through a graveyard: but as this Stranger conversed with them, hope revived and they seemed to be walking through the King's garden, amid the music of murmuring waters and singing birds. The journey ended ere they knew it; and here they were at Emmaus, standing before the door. At their urgent entreaty their Comrade consented to tarry with them. "And it came to pass as he sat at meat with them, he took bread, and blessed it, and brake, and gave to them. And their eyes were opened, and they knew him."—They knew him perhaps by the nail-prints in his lifted hands, or by the shining of his face, or by the kindliness of his familiar voice. They gazed in silent amazement upon him; and, lo, he vanished out of their sight!

Then they said one to another, "Did not our heart burn within us while he talked with us by the way, and while he opened to us the Scriptures?" Ah, beloved friends, this is what we want; the heart that burns in view of solemn truth. We are so dull, so apathetic in the presence of great verities. We are like the multitude who at Calvary "stood beholding." Would we enter into a full appreciation of truth? Shall it take possession of us, filling our souls, as with the speechless joy of glad discovery? Then let us walk with Jesus and keep silent while he opens unto us the Scriptures; let us be willing, without cavil or questioning, to behold him in his exposition of his Word. Let us accept from his lips the *"needs be"* which runs like a crimson path through the blessed Book, leading from the councils of eternity, past the manger at Bethlehem and the workshop and the cross and the rifled sepulchre, to the open heavens whither he has vanished to prepare a place for those who love him.

Have you, my friend, been walking alone thus far? If so, give welcome to the heavenly stranger who would join you. Have you been absorbed in the cares and sorrows of life? Hear his footstep as he draws near. He would fain open to you the Scriptures and reason with you of the things concerning himself. So shall life be made worth living; no longer a confusion of threads and thrums, but the orderly casting of a shuttle to and fro, the weaving of a white garment in which, by divine grace, you shall yet appear at the marriage of the King's Son. So shall history seem no more a mere discord of fortuitous events, but a calm and irresistible movement toward an ultimate triumph, an oratorio through which runs, like a dominant note, the voice of the Knight-errant of Bozrah, "I am he that speaketh in righteousness, traveling in the greatness of my strength, mighty to save!" So shall the future open up before you, as a journey through the night indeed, but a night filled with music and bright with multitudinous stars of promise. In the pathway of those stars, we shall still behold a graveyard. God's Acre in the distance is all astir; and beyond it is the city that hath foundations whose builder and maker is God. Its gates are open and within sitteth the King upon his throne, high and lifted up, bearing the scars of his passion and proclaiming, "I am he that liveth and was dead, and behold, I am alive forever more, and have the keys of death and hell!" And round about him is a great multitude which no man can number, ceaselessly singing, "Blessing and honor and glory and power be unto him that liveth forever and ever! Amen."

THE GREAT LAW OF CHRIST

"Bear ye one another's burdens, and so fulfil the law of Christ. For if a man think himself to be something, when he is nothing, he deceiveth himself. But let every man prove his own work, and then shall he have rejoicing in himself alone, and not in another. For every man shall bear his own burden."
—Galatians 6, 2-5.

A controversy had been going on among the Christians of the Galatian Churches as to the necessity of obedience to the Ceremonial Law. Not a few were of the opinion that all candidates for admission to the Church should be made to pass through the little wicket-gate of Mosaism; that is, to observe its prescriptions as to fasting, circumcision and the like. The apostle says, "If you want a law, let me suggest one that will adequately employ your energies, a large and comprehensive law worthy of broad-minded men; namely, the Great Law of Christ."

Many Galatians who professed to be Christians, were bringing reproach upon the Gospel by walking unworthily. Some who had come out of the bondage of Judaism, were more devoted to the external forms of religion than to the weightier matters of righteousness; others who had been converted from Paganism, were yielding themselves to the vices of their former life. What should be done? The ready answer would be, "Let them be excommunicated." And, indeed, Paul would be the last man to deny the

THE GREAT LAW OF CHRIST.

importance of wise discipline. But "alas for the rarity of Christian charity under the sun." The kinder methods should first be exhausted. "If a man be overtaken in a fault," says Paul, "ye which are spiritual restore such an one in the spirit of meekness." Just here he suggests, for the solution of the difficulty, the Law of Christ. It is called by Apostle James, "The Royal Law"; he says, "If ye fulfill the royal law, Thou shalt love thy neighbor as thyself, ye shall do well," (James 2, 8).

This Law of Christ as related to the Law of Moses, was illustrated in the case of the adulterous woman whom the enemies of Jesus brought to him as he was teaching in Solomon's Porch. "Moses in the Law," they said, "commanded us that such should be stoned; but what sayest thou?" In his reply there was no minimizing of the offense but the saving wisdom of mercy: "Let him that is without sin cast the first stone at her." See them stealing away, self-convicted, beginning at the eldest! Then to the woman he said, "Go, and sin no more."

The Law, thus exemplified by Christ himself, is set forth by his apostle in three propositions, as follows:

The first is this: "*Every man shall bear his own burden.*" Here is an announcement of the vital duty of personal independence. "Every man for himself" is a much abused precept; but there is a great truth in it. We are like soldiers on the march. It devolves on every one to shoulder his own musket and bear his own knapsack. There must be no shirking, no murmuring or complaining. "Every man for himself" is a rule to be recognized in all the important affairs of life.

As to pain, poverty, bereavement and the like: there is much to be said for the teaching of the Stoics, "What can't be cured must be endured." A mother would gladly bear the suffering of her ailing child, but this she cannot do. "Each for himself" is the order of nature. An Indian at the stake, smiling scornfully amid the flames which his foes have kindled about him, is a true philosopher. What is there to do, indeed, but to make the best of it? Much of the misery of life comes from our assuming a wrong attitude toward such inevitable facts. Wealth that has vanished would better be forgotten. If a physical malady be incurable, the wisest course is to submit and prepare for the sequel. Here are burdens for us to bear without complaint. My friend, brace up to your burden like a man. God alone can help you. The sole consolation is that your Heavenly Father knows, stands by and promises, "My grace shall be sufficient for thee."

And there are moral responsibilities, also, which are intransferable. Duty is a personal matter. A man lives in a world of responsibility which is wholly his own. *Ich bin Ich.* It is impossible to serve God by proxy. The great sin of Christian people is shirking. It is a common saying that nine-tenths of the work of the Christian church is done by one-tenth of its members. If this be true, then nine-tenths of Christ's people are shirking their responsibility. If you are a Christian, my friend, get under your burden and bear it. Don't cringe, don't complain, don't shirk. No man can do your duty for you any more than he can eat, drink or sleep for you. "You have a work that no other can do."

It is related that when the Duke of Wellington was ordered to the Cape of Good Hope, a young officer in his regiment applied for leave of absence. The Duke made this laconic reply, "Sail or sell." Let us be grateful that God is so wonderfully patient with us. If the policy of the Iron Duke were to be enforced among the churches, what disturbance there would be! Our Lord expects every man to do his duty; and his requirement is greatly emphasized by the fact that he promises all necessary help, saying, "As thy day, so shall thy strength be."

As to temptation also: A man must fight his own battle with the world, the flesh and the devil. "There is no discharge in this war." Here is the test of manhood. This is my own fight; and my strength is in the Saxon motto, "Will, God and I can!" Saul's armor will be of no avail. I must go out for myself against the giant of Gath. But nothing is required of me beyond the possibilities of courage. No temptation is permitted beyond what I am able to bear. Let me go forth in the strength of Jehovah alone and I shall come back, like David from the valley of Elah, dragging the gory head of the adversary by its shaggy locks. This is the gospel of manliness. Lift thy burden and bear it. Be strong. Quit thyself like a man.

The second proposition of the Great Law is this: "Bear ye one another's burdens." For, after all, we cannot escape the important fact of mutual dependence and interdependence. Did I say we are an army on the march? Aye, comrades all. And if one at my side staggers under the heat and burden of the day, what then? In the name of comradeship give him a lift!

Put your canteen to his lips, shoulder his musket, strap his knapsack to your back. For the strong should bear the burdens of the weak.

The church is likened to a body; as it is written, "The body is not one member but many. So that the eye cannot say unto the hand, I have no need of thee: nor again the head to the feet, I have no need of you. But God hath tempered the body together, that there should be no schism in it; but that the members should have the same care one for another. And whether one member suffer, all the members suffer with it, or one member be honored, all the members rejoice with it."

The Great Law here referred to is exemplified in sympathy. We are exhorted to "rejoice with them that do rejoice and weep with them that weep." Who shall estimate the power of a warm hand-clasp in the hour of adversity? "And a word in due season, how good it is; it is like apples of gold in a silver basket." The world is full of sufferers, prisoners of poverty, victims of misfortune; and a kind word costs so little. It was for lack of sympathy that poor Robert Burns, weak by nature, spoiled by adulation, driven hither and thither by mighty passions, was forced out of Christian fellowship and moved to resentful philippics against it.

> "O ye wha are so guid yersels,
> Sae pious and sae holy,
> Ye've naught to do but mark and tell
> Your neebor's fauts and folly."

Who knows but a kindly word, a due regard for his peculiar nature and circumstances, an earnest entreaty, might have changed the tenor of his life?

But sympathy is not enough; there must be practical beneficence. To a starving beggar an ounce of bread is worth a ton of commiseration. An old woman who had known Oliver Goldsmith when he was a student of medicine, called on him long afterward in behalf of her husband, who, as she said, was suffering from loss of appetite and melancholy. He went with her to the bedside, made his diagnosis and presently sent her a box containing ten—borrowed—guineas, marked, "Pills: To be taken as necessity requires. And be of good courage." It is burden-bearing like this that makes the whole world kin. It is this that binds the Church together in the true fellowship of Christ.

> We share our mutual woes,
> Our mutual burdens bear,
> And often for each other flows
> The sympathizing tear.

The third proposition, without which the two former would be antagonistic, is this: A part of every man's burden is to share the burden of the next man. It is impossible to separate individual from social duty. One who undertakes to bear his own burden, with no regard for the burdens of others, will be sure to fail. A selfish Christian is a contradiction of terms. The true Christian is a member of the body of Christ, so closely associated with his fellows that all their interests are his. It is like the intercommunication kept up in our physical organism by the nervous system, so that if one tread upon my foot, the pain goes flying along the electric wires of sympathy clear to the finger tips.

Here is where the Anchorites made their fatal error.

The man who retires to solitude for self-culture flies from his burden. Our Lord frequented the great centers of life. He joined himself to the multitudes who were going up to the annual feasts. He visited the porches of Bethesda. He came up close to the beating heart of humanity. He heard the cry for help on every side and sought to relieve it. No greater mistake can be made than to imagine that we are imitating Christ when we retire from the world to read mystical literature and devote ourselves to "the deepening of the spiritual life."

The Great Law of Christ is so-called for three reasons: *First*, because he gave it.—*Second*, because he exemplified it in his own life among men. He bore his own burden; for, indeed, there was a burden which he alone could bear; in which no friendship could relieve him. At the gateway of Gethsemane he said to his disciples, "Tarry ye here while I go and pray yonder." And there, under the deep shadow of the olive-trees, he drank his bitter cup; as it is written, "I have trodden the winepress alone and of the people there was none with me." He made no complaint, no murmuring. His prayer was, "If it be possible, let this cup pass from me;" but when it became manifest that the bitterness of death was the necessary condition of the world's redemption, he calmly acquiesced, saying, "O my Father, not my will but thine be done." And thereupon he set his face steadfastly toward the cross. Such was the courage of the Perfect Man.—But furthermore he exemplified the Great Law in bearing the burden of others. It is written "He bare our griefs and carried our sorrows. We did esteem him stricken, smitten of God and afflicted; but he was wounded for our transgressions and bruised for our iniquities. The chastisement of our peace was upon him." His heart went out toward all sufferers. His ears were open to every cry for relief. He fed the hungry, opened the eyes of the blind, wiped away the leper's spots, ministered to sorrow, wept by the open grave; and at last he climbed up Calvary staggering under the burden of the whole world's sin. Ah, that was the sublimest deed of sympathy, of self-sacrifice, of practical beneficence, that the world ever saw. His heart broke in compassion for the world's pain, and his hands were stretched out in divinest charity to all the children of men.—*And third*, the Great Law of Christ is so called because he laid it down as the fundamental principle of his Kingdom. The universal observance of this Law will bring in the Millennium. It corresponds to the physical Law of Gravitation, by which all the worlds of the solar system are kept in proper relation to each other and to the central sun. If those for whom Jesus died were under the domination of this Law, as the stars of heaven are under the control of gravity, there would not be one lost or wayward soul in the universe. This was in the mind of Jesus when he said, "I pray for these; that they all may be one; even as thou, Father, art in me and I in thee, that they also may be one in us: that the world may believe that thou didst send me."

In the Great Law, thus briefly stated, we find the sum and substance of the duties of the Christian life. Our success in right living is measured by our imitation of Christ as the Burden-bearer. Mere sentiment is little worth. Our religion is a matter of practical import; it is to do good as we have opportunity unto all men. St. Francis of Assisi is said to have retired from all human fellowship in his desire to attain to the higher life. He gave himself up in solitude to penance and maceration. He lashed his body for the sins of his soul. He fasted and wept. At length, as he knelt under his crucifix, the sign of divine approval is said to have been given him. He rose with the *stigmata* in the palms of his hands. The legend is false; the process is impossible. The nail-prints are not thus given in solitude. Nor is it by this method that we enter into the fellowship of Christ's suffering. We come into sympathy with him in the thick of the world's conflict. We die with him when our hearts break in sympathetic touch with the world's agonizing heart. This is "the cure of souls"; this is the law of charity; this is the fellowship of Christ. He entered into our estate; he passed under the lintel of human homes, toiled in the workshop, joined the company of wayfaring men, knelt by the bedsides of the sick and dying, gave comfort to the sorrowing in God's Acre. This was his burden because it was the burden of his fellow-men.

Our invitation to the Christian life is couched in such terms as suggest the Great Law: "Come unto me, all ye that labor and are heavy laden," that is, weary with bearing the burdens of life, "and I will give you rest." But this rest is no exemption from burden-bearing, for he immediately adds, "Take my yoke upon you and learn of me; for I am meek and lowly of heart, and ye shall find rest unto your souls." Our rest then is in our fellowship with Christ in the bearing of life's burden, our own and others'. "For my yoke is easy," easy because a yoke is ever for two. He stands beside me, helping me to bear it. Aye, blessed Lord, the yoke is half thine and half mine; and the burden too; wherefore thou sayest truly, "My yoke is easy and my burden is light."

THE LOGIC OF EVENTS

"The Pharisees also with the Sadducees came, and tempting desired him that he would show them a sign from heaven. He answered and said unto them, When it is evening, ye say, It will be fair weather: for the sky is red. And in the morning, It will be foul weather to-day: for the sky is red and lowering. O ye hypocrites, ye can discern the face of the sky; but can ye not discern the signs of the times?"—Matthew 16, 1-3.

It is the part of wisdom to interpret signs. He is a poor skipper who, trusting to his compass, makes no observation of the heavens. He is a poor ranchman who does not round up his cattle or fold his sheep when the thickening air tells of a coming storm. A week ago, in Virginia, I saw a bunch of wild violets in the hand of a little maid; and straightway the verdant forests and the blooming fields were all before me, and I heard Charles of Orleans singing:

> "The Time hath laid his mantle by
> Of wind and rain and icy chill;
> And stream and fountain, brook and rill,
> All in their new apparel vie;
> For Time hath laid his mantle by."

He is but a poor reader of the newspapers who cannot dream dreams and see visions between the lines. The duty of the hour is suggested by current events, as clearly as a farmer's tasks from the marginal references of *The Farmer's Almanac*, "Now plant corn" or "Now gather in your barley."

At the time of our context a great crisis in Jewish history had come, and the religious leaders did not know it. They were familiar with the wisdom of the schools, but could not "take an observation." So busy were they with minute inspection of the jot and tittle of ceremonial requirement that they were in grave danger of overlooking the advent of their long-expected Christ. The fulness of time was at hand; the scepter, falling from the trembling hand of Judah, had signaled the great event; the seventy weeks of years spoken of by Daniel the prophet were accomplished; there was a universal feeling of expectancy; a star had risen out of Jacob; the voice of Elias the forerunner had been lifted up in the wilderness. But these soothsayers had lost their cunning: they were weatherwise but stupid in spiritual things. Thus Jesus reproved them: "At evening ye say, It will be fair weather: for the sky is red. And in the morning, It will be foul weather: for the sky is red and lowering. O ye pretenders, can ye not discern the signs of the times?"

We are drawing near to the border line of the centuries; and there is a universal conviction that mighty events are before us. The last century was marked by the introduction of new forces in the province of spiritual as of material things. Steam and electricity, inventions and discoveries were paralleled by the development of great spiritual energies. With this propulsion, who shall prophesy the forthcomings of the next century? "Men of thought and men of action, clear the way."

One of the most significant Signs of the Times is the Opening of the Doors of the Nations. A familiar prayer in the Missionary Concerts of forty years ago was that God would prepare the way for the propagation of the gospel and incline the Pagan nations to receive it. That prayer is obsolete. The great gates have rolled back on their hinges and the messengers of salvation may go without let or hindrance to the uttermost parts of the earth.

One hundred and sixty years ago an epoch-making book was published, entitled, "An Inquiry into the Obligation of Christians to Use Means for the Conversion of the World." It created a great stir among the churches. The author was William Carey, "the consecrated cobbler" of Northamptonshire. He desired to go as a commissioned herald of the gospel to India, but so great was the opposition that he was obliged finally to sail in a Danish ship. On reaching his destination, he supported himself by working in an indigo factory, meanwhile studying the Bengali language. The first seven years of his work were without apparent result; then Krishna-Pal was converted. A single soul for his hire! But since that day the enterprise has so justified itself that opposition has practically ceased. The original proposition of William Carey was reproved in his Conference by a venerable minister who cried out, "Sit down, young man!" It would require great courage to repeat that injunction now; for not less than seven hundred thousand native Christians are in evidence in India. The land of the Vedas glows with the radiance of the Sun of Righteousness.

In 1853 the ports of Japan were opened by Commodore Perry to the commerce of the world. The Church with some hesitation sailed in and not without misgiving began her work of evangelization. To-day Japan is the Young America of the Orient. And at this moment the enterprising people of that country are discussing the propriety of substituting for their ancient establishment the religion of Christ. This is the Lord's doing and it is marvelous in our eyes.

It was only twenty-six years ago that David Livingstone died on his knees in mid Africa. The Dark Continent is now cobwebbed by thoroughfares of commercial enterprise. A railway has been projected from the Mediterranean to the the Cape of Good Hope. The slave trade has been practically extirpated. And the gospel is preached from Tanganyika to the Congo and from the Nile to the country of the Boers. Thus the prophecy is fulfilled: "Ethiopia shall soon stretch out her hands unto God."

The Empire of China, surrounded by its great wall, has until recently resisted all foreign innovations. No railway could be built for fear of disturbing the historic rest of Fung-shui, "the spirit of the past." But the Great Powers of Europe have seized on many ports of entry; the territory of the Celestial Empire is being apportioned among them. "Where the carcass is there the vultures are gathered together." What this portends remains to be seen; but one thing is clear, an highway is being cast up for the Evangel. The light of the morning is on the vultures' wings.

Thus, one by one, the gates have been thrown open. God's providence is manifest. "Not by might nor by power, but by my Spirit, saith the Lord." The fable of Aladdin before the cave, crying "Open Sesame!" has been realized; and by this circumstance a tremendous emphasis is put upon the great commission of the Master, "Go ye into all the world and preach the gospel."

Another of the important Signs of the Times is the Volunteering of Men and Women for the Propaganda. The old-time prayer for the opening of the gates was accompanied by another, to wit, that God would send laborers into his harvest. That prayer, also, has been answered abundantly. It was a difficult matter half a century ago to persuade a theological student to enlist for foreign work; and, with rare but notable exceptions, such as offered themselves were of smaller intellectual caliber than those who remained at home. To-day, however, our Missionary Boards are confronted by an embarrassment of riches. The choicest men and women who are graduated from our institutions of secular and theological learning are clamoring to enter the Foreign field.

The preaching of Peter the Hermit who went up and down portraying the sufferings of Christian prisoners in infidel hands was followed by the uprising of a multitude who, with the cry, "*Deus vult!*" set forth to the conquest of the Holy Sepulcher. Wonderful was the power of enthusiasm in that historic movement; it is difficult for historians to account for it.

In like manner at the beginning of our Civil War, when our national life and freedom were jeopardized, the call of President Lincoln for troops was answered by a militant host, who swung into line with the song, "We're coming, Father Abraham, a hundred thousand more!" But here is something far more wonderful. There is no appeal to the passions, but a calm address to brain and conscience. There is no sudden cry, "To arms!" nor kindling of red beacons on the hills; only the calling up of an old and half-forgotten edict, "Go ye into all the world and preach the gospel!"

Here is a most eloquent fact: there are two thousand of the very best and brightest of the educated young men and women of America, who stand pledged, ready and clamorous, to adventure their lives in the regions of darkness and the habitations of death for Jesus' sake. No longer need we pray, "O Lord, send laborers into thy harvest." The laborers are here, awaiting only their commissions from our Missionary Boards. They jostle one another in their eagerness to reach the yellow fields, to thrust in the sickle and reap.

Still another of the significant Signs is the Success which has attended all Efforts at Foreign Evangelization. However this may have been disputed hitherto, it is no longer an open question. None but the wilfully blind can ask, "Do Foreign Missions pay?"

The pioneer of Missions was Christ himself, the immediate result of whose labors was comparatively insignificant; not more than five hundred converts could be reckoned at the time of his death. His work was to prepare the way for the faithful disciples, of whom he said, "The works that I do shall ye do also, and greater works than these shall ye do, because I go unto my Father"; that is, larger ingatherings were to occur through their labors after he had breathed the power of his Spirit upon them.

When Paul set forth on his missionary tours, the miracle of Pentecost had occurred and there were thousands of believers. He traversed the plains of Asia Minor and the mountains of Macedonia, established churches in coigns of vantage everywhere and was greatly prospered in his work. Afterward for more than three centuries the church seemed to fully realize the imperativeness of the Great Commission, aiming at the conquest of the world. There was no dearth of revivals then; souls sprang up as willows by the water courses.

In the fifth century a Scotchman named Patricius, familiar to us as Saint Patrick, went over to Ireland and won the people of that barbaric country to an acknowledgment of Christ.—In the seventh century the monk Augustine, passing through tne slave market at Rome, saw a group of fair-haired Saxons on sale. On being told that they were Angli, he uttered the historic words, *"Non Angli sed Angeli, si essent Christiani"*; and forthwith set out to the evangelization of their native Britain. But for that missionary journey we ourselves, the descendants of those Angles, might be still going about clothed in skins and making our living with clubs. What an ingrate, then, must the Anglo-Saxon be who says, "I do not believe in Foreign Missions"!—In the eighth century the monk Boniface carried the Gospel to Germany, hewed down the Thunderer's Oak and brought the people under the power of the cross. Great successes these!

Then came the Dark Ages. For a thousand years the Church forgot her commission; for many centuries she spent her strength in vain controversies and vainer crusades. This culminated in an overwhelming visitation of darkness, leading on to that period of infidelity when Voltaire, Rousseau and Thomas Paine won the ear of Christendom; the faithful meanwhile lamenting, "Who will show us any good?"

And then the Church came to herself. The missionary epoch began with the nineteenth century. There are now seventy Missionary Societies. The annual contributions to Foreign Missions are not less than fifteen millions of dollars. There are three thousand five hundred missionaries on the field, aided in their work by seven thousand five hundred native assistants. There are four millions of communicants; and whereas there were two hundred millions of nominal Christians at the beginning of the present century, there are not less than five hundred millions to-day. We are justified in saying, therefore, that no earnest effort looking to the conversion of the heathen has ever been fruitless. God's promises are Yea and Amen. "He that goeth forth and weepeth, bearing precious seed, shall doubtless come again with rejoicing, bringing his sheaves with him."

And still another *Sign of the Times is the Church's Return to Reason.* This has been brought about by the inevitable logic of events. God's people have come to see that their business is the conquest of the world, the setting up of the kingdom of Christ.

For centuries the Church was busied with the formulation of creeds and symbols. Her energy was expended in controversies bearing on the clear and proper expression of more or less fundamental doctrines. No doubt this was necessary by way of preparation for other work lying further on; but the time for such business has gone by.—A new creed or catechism has recently been put forth as an expression of the faith of the Nonconformist Churches of England. However perfect this may be, there is little likelihood that it will awaken any considerable enthusiasm. We are too busy in these times, with the larger affairs of the Kingdom, to consider it gravely. —The President of Bowdoin College has just now called for a "Reconstruction of Christianity"; but his is a lone voice like that of the bittern. "We are doing a great work and cannot come down." We have creeds enough, some good, some otherwise. He is an over-critical thinker who cannot pick and choose to his own satisfaction from the abundant product of the past.

The Church was also employed for centuries in Polemics, in the internecine strife of words. The great guns of the denominations were set over against each other, each seeking to "prove its doctrine orthodox by apostolic blows and knocks." That time however has gone by, thank God. You know how Bazaine, in the Franco-Prussian War, surrendered his magnificent army of a hundred and eighty thousand men at Metz. When brought before the court-martial he sought to defend himself by pleading, "We knew not what to do. We could not determine the source of authority. We were not sure as to the complexion of the government at Paris. We sat in council discussing and debating in vain." The president of the court, moved by indignation, interrupted him again and again with the words, "But France, sir! What of France, sir?" Is there not a suggestion here for those of us who insist on retraversing old questions of creed and ethics? Shall the conquest of the world be kept waiting on our deliberations?

Shall we hold in abeyance the Master's injunction, "Seek ye first of all the Kingdom," while we retire to discuss the *pros* and *cons* of "free will, fixed fate, foreknowledge absolute"? Up with the red cross standard! On to the front! The gates of the world are open; the Man of Macedonia beckons us; the word of command rings loud and clear through the centuries, "Go ye, evangelize!" All other considerations sink into insignificance. We believe in Christ's Crown and Covenant. This is no time for parley. The battle is on; the call of the Captain of our salvation is, "Go forward!"

One other Sign of the Times demands consideration; namely, the Spiking of Hostile Guns. The voice of infidelity is suppressed. How marvelous the change since a century ago! The one great infidel who keeps himself ever before the public gaze in America gets his only hearing among the curiosity-mongers and has no more influence among thoughtful people than if he were a swallow in a chimney.—And the False Religions are moribund. It was said by Max Müller a quarter of a century ago that, aside from Christianity, there were but two living religions on earth, Mohammedanism and Buddhism. The former —representing the three great horrors, war, slavery and polygamy—is fighting for life in its ancient strongholds, making no conquests except among the hordes of darkest Africa: The latter, whose adherents have been variously estimated at from one to four hundred millions, is yielding everywhere to the advancing light of civilization and Christian thought.

The only obstacle to the progress of Christianity worth considering to-day is within the Church. It lies partly in the ignorance of Christian people. There are some who profess to be followers of Jesus, yet refuse to lend themselves to missionary enterprise because they are blind to current events. They would do well to give heed to John Wesley, who said, "I read the newspapers to see how God is governing the world."—Other Christians seem to be indifferent; and their indifference rests in unbelief. They are like the spies who came back from Canaan, saying, "The inhabitants thereof are Anakim and we were as grasshoppers in their sight." O that they might be persuaded to believe in God's leadership; for courage ever rests in faith. "Let us go up at once," said Caleb, "and possess the land, for we be well able to overcome them!" The word for the hour is the watchword of the Covenanters, "God with us!" The world is at our feet if we believe. All things are possible to the man or the church that believeth. "I can do all things through Christ which strengtheneth me."

And now as to the personal application. *First:* It devolves on every Christian to heed the injunction of the Master, "Go ye." It was addressed to every one. No Christian is excused. Go, my friend, in person or by proxy. Go or send your substitute. "I will descend into the mine," said Carey, "if you will hold the rope." Have you sent your substitute down into the mine, my friend? Then stand by the rope! Let the man who has jeopardized his life as your substitute, toiling amid privation and danger, with fire-damp all about him, know that you are loyally and vigilantly standing by. This is an individual matter. "What did you see?" asked Dr. Cook of a Waterloo gunner. "I saw nothing," he replied, "but dust and smoke."—"And what did you do?"—"I stood by my gun!"

Second: It behooves every follower of Christ to give, up to the full measure of his ability, for the carrying on of this work. The nations will never be evangelized until God's people realize that they are not their own but are bought with a price, even the precious blood of Jesus. It is estimated that the annual contribution of Christian people throughout the world for foreign Missions is about ten cents *per capita.* Is it not wonderful that with such a meager showing of consecration, the Church should have achieved any results at all? We sometimes wonder why Christ does not come to establish his throne. "Why tarry the wheels of his chariot?" cried the mother of Sisera, looking out at the window. It is plain to see why the wheels of the Lord's chariot tarry; they are fast in the mire of avarice and parsimony. Ten cents per annum, for each Christian, for the conversion of the world! Is there not truth in what Dr. Duff said, "We are playing at missions"? O for a baptism of the Holy Ghost to open the hearts of God's people! The old historian Diodorus tells of a fire in the Pyrenees which burned off the forests and penetrated the soil until a stream of pure silver gushed forth and ran down the mountain sides. This is a manifest fable. But there will be a more marvelous story to tell when the fire of God's Spirit shall touch the hearts of his people. What a burning there will be, and how the silver and the gold will flow together at the feet of God!

Finally, let us pray without ceasing for the coming of the kingdom of Christ. To your knees, O Israel!

"For him shall endless prayer be made." We pray for ourselves, we pray for our friends, we pray for our enemies; now let us pray for Christ, that his kingdom may stretch from the river unto the ends of the earth. "Help me to my knees!" said one of the fathers when informed that he had but an hour to live; "help me to my knees that I may pray for the conversion of the world." And there he knelt, his pulse growing feeble, his eyes growing dim; until his last word was spoken, "Thy Kingdom come!" Let us offer that prayer *once*, with all our hearts, in a spirit of absolute abandon of surrender,—"Thy Kingdom come!"—and we shall never be again the same men. The world will grow little; the things of the Kingdom will fill the horizons of life; nothing will seem important but the salvation of souls. Use us, O Lord, for thy great purposes! Stimulate us to holy endeavor, kindle our zeal, enlarge our faith, baptize us with thy Spirit! Use us to thy glory! Thy Kingdom come in our hearts! Thy Kingdom come among all the children of men! Amen.

PETER'S SALUTATORY

" Peter, an apostle of Jesus Christ, to the strangers scattered throughout Pontus, Galatia, Cappadocia, Asia, and Bithynia, elect according to the foreknowledge of God the Father, through sanctification of the Spirit, unto obedience and sprinkling of the blood of Jesus Christ: Grace unto you, and peace, be multiplied. Blessed be the God and Father of our Lord Jesus Christ, which according to his abundant mercy hath begotten us again unto a lively hope by the resurrection of Jesus Christ from the dead, to an inheritance incorruptible, and undefiled, and that fadeth not away, reserved in heaven for you, who are kept by the power of God through faith unto salvation ready to be revealed in the last time."—I. Peter 1, 1-5.

The world loves Peter. His faults, his virtues and his blunders were those of a large-hearted, open-handed man. We love him for his frankness; he "wore his heart upon his sleeve for daws to peck at." We love him for his enthusiasm; when his blood was up let the servant of Malchus take heed! We love him for his courage; once indeed he played the coward before the pointed finger of a maid; but once was enough; he shook and trembled no more until the day when he entered into full fellowship with his Master in glorious martyrdom.

It was a great day for Peter when the Lord found him mending his nets by the lakeside, and said, "Arise, and follow me." He left all—boats, comrades, the bickering in the fish-markets, the fierce joy of the bracing winds of Gennesaret — and thenceforth devoted himself to the service of Christ.

This meant much for a sunburned fisherman, who had little acquaintance with schools and less taste for the forum. He set out, like our bold Genoese, blindly feeling his way, but sure of something beyond, an Eldorado of duty and usefulness with gold at its heart and harvests on its bosom. As he passed on the heavens lifted and the horizons receded before him. There came dreams and visions; graces and manifold graces. His mind was broadened, his heart enlarged, and Simon the son of Jonas became "Peter, the Rock."

For thirty years after his conversion he did not venture to exercise the functions of a teacher. In the words before us we have his Salutatory, in which he shows himself an expert in clear and succinct statement of truth. He goes straight at the heart of the matter, as we should expect from one whose upbringing has been in the school of experience. This was better than to be a university-bred man. He had walked with Jesus, had seen him in the Mount of Transfiguration, had witnessed his crucifixion, had looked into the rifled grave in Joseph's garden. He had heard the mighty rushing wind at Pentecost, was familiar with persecution, had traversed many lands to preach the unsearchable riches of Christ. This was great training, the best indeed for a teachable man. An alchemist may theorize about gold, but he is a better financier who digs gold out of the bowels of the earth. Sir Isaac Newton said to Dr. Halley, "I am always glad to hear you speak of astronomy or mathematics; for those are subjects which you have studied and understand. But you should not talk of Christianity; for you have never tasted of it. I have, and I am certain you know nothing about it."

In these words, with which the apostle prefaces his General Epistles, we shall find that he practically sweeps the horizon of truth. He gives us, indeed, a System of Theology; none the less complete because so brief and simple. Let us see:

I. *Here is the Doctrine of Election.* The words are, "Peter, to the elect." He knew that he was approaching a great mystery, but that did not appal him. Observe, he does not undertake to explain it; he simply receives and commends it to believers as an indubitable and most comfortable fact. And incidentally he has several things to say about it.

First: It is "according to the foreknowledge of God." So far he is on secure ground. Yet just here the Calvinists and the Arminians part company. All parties agree as to the premises; but the question is, Was God's foreknowledge antecedent to his decree or *vice versâ?* Peter is neither a Calvinist nor an Arminian. Probably he would have said that the question of priority had no relevancy here. There can be no chronological sequence, no "before" or "after" with God. He is not subject to the limitations of time. Yesterday, to-day and to-morrow are alike with him. He whose goings forth are from eternity cannot be supposed to adjust his movements to the vibrations of a pendulum or to keep step with our procession of days.

Second: Election is "through sanctification of the Spirit"; rather "in sanctification of the Spirit" (R. V.). This indicates the method by which the decree is carried to its conclusion. The function of the Holy Ghost is to produce holiness: the process is sanctification; the result is Character or Godlikeness. This operation of the Spirit is not momentary, as in the new birth, but progressive. There are persons who speak of themselves as though they "were already perfect"; but their lives are always in evidence against them. We grow "from grace to grace" under the influence of the Spirit, coming nearer and nearer continually to the likeness of Christ. Thus Peter says in another place: "Add to your faith virtue; and to virtue, knowledge; and to knowledge, temperance; and to temperance, patience; and to patience, godliness; and to godliness, brotherly kindness; and to brotherly kindness, charity," (2 Pet. 1:5-7). In which manner, as Paul says, "we all with open face beholding as in a mirror the glory of the Lord, are changed into the same image, from glory to glory, even as by the Spirit of the Lord": (2 Cor. 3:18).

Third: Election is "unto obedience and sprinkling of the blood of Jesus Christ." The prevailing aversion to the Doctrine of Election is largely due to a misapprehension, to wit, that God by his decree set apart certain ones to the mere enjoyment of special honors and privileges. In fact the objective point of election is not privilege so much as duty and responsibility. We are not to imagine that God surveyed the coming race, as if passing them in solemn review, saying, "Thou to heaven" and, "Thou to hell." The call is to obedience and sprinkling of the blood; that is, to a life of purity and usefulness. James defines religion thus, "to visit the fatherless and widows in their affliction and to keep oneself unspotted from the world." And Peter follows a description of Christian living with an exhortation,— "Give the more diligence to make your calling and election sure."

II. *Here, also, is the Doctrine of Regeneration.* "Blessed be the God and Father of our Lord Jesus Christ, which according to his abundant mercy hath begotten us again"; that is, regenerated us. This also is a mystery, but not to be rejected on that account. Jesus said, "The wind bloweth where it listeth and thou hearest the sound thereof, but canst not tell whence it cometh, and whither it goeth; so is every one that is born of the Spirit." Regeneration is a mysterious but visible and tangible fact. It is to be seen every day in the walk and conversation of those who have been delivered from the bonds of iniquity into the glorious liberty of the children of God. It is vitally important that we should apprehend this fact, since regeneration is prerequisite to the eternal life; as Jesus said, "Verily, verily, I say unto you, Except a man be born again he cannot see the Kingdom of God."

Peter goes on to say of this doctrine, *First*, that we are regenerated "unto a lively hope"; better, a living hope. The hope referred to is not to be thought of as something which can be put away and produced on occasion, as a man shows his railway ticket when the conductor calls for it. The only hope that is worth having is like the angel that awoke Peter in the prison at Philippi, loosed his chains with a touch, bade him arise and gird himself, went before him through doors that opened successively at their approach as if the bolts were drawn by unseen hands, led him from ward to ward and did not leave him until he stood under the starry canopy of heaven.

Second: Our regeneration is "by the resurrection of Jesus Christ from the dead." Is it not then by the power of the cross? The death of Jesus is, indeed, the ground of our pardon, but the new birth is by the influence of that Spirit which the risen Christ breathes upon us. Thus it is written, "He was delivered for our offenses and raised again for our justification." A deed of conveyance is ineffective without the seller's signature. So if Christ had not risen our faith would be vain, we would be still in our sins (1 Cor. xv. 17). But because he liveth, we live also. In the sprouting grain the farmer sees visions of yellow harvests and loaded wains and full granaries: so is the resurrection of Christ the prophecy and assurance of our newness of life. Regeneration is wrought by the Breath of him who, in his triumph over death, brought life and immortality to light.

Third: We are begotten again " to an inheritance incorruptible and undefiled, and that fadeth not away." In regeneration we are received, by the Spirit of Adoption, into the rights and privileges of sonship : "If sons, then heirs, heirs of God and joint heirs with Jesus Christ." We partly enter upon our inheritance here and now. In some portions of Scotland it is the custom for the seller of a field to give to the purchaser a bit of turf which is "the earnest of the purchased possession." In like manner we have foretastes of heaven as we journey on through this present life. But, O! who shall describe what lies beyond? Who shall say what surprises await those who are "made meet for the inheritance of the saints in light?" In moments of spiritual exaltation we climb the slopes of Nebo and catch glimpses of the country that is afar off. In our Father's Will and Testament we read of "joy unspeakable and full of glory." Our hopes are thus quickened: as when Christian, in The Pilgrim's Progress, standing at the gateway of the Celestial City, was dazzled and bewildered by a momentary vision of angels, of which he said, "which when I saw, I wished myself among them."

III. *And here is also the Doctrine of Perseverance.* Peter speaks of this inheritance as "reserved in heaven for you who are kept." A great word that, "kept!" It means, once a Christian, always a Christian. There is no "falling from grace." A man may fall from self-confidence, from fallacious hopes, from ill-grounded opinions; but from God's grace, never.

This is evident from the *first* observation which Peter makes concerning this Doctrine; he says, we are "kept by the power of God." To expect to persevere in right living by our own unaided efforts is as vain as it would be to seek shelter in one's shadow. The secret of continuance is in the motto of a famous Crusader; a wine glass, with a broken foot, bearing this inscription, "Hold thou me up!" If God lays hold of a man, who shall pluck him out of the almighty hand? One reason why the *Te Deum* has been kept so long in the hymnology of the Church is because it advances to this climacteric statement and petition: "In thee, O Lord, do I put my trust; let me never be confounded!"

But *second;* we are "kept through faith." By faith

we co-operate with the power of God. Faith is the reaching up of my hand to clasp God's hand. This is the grip that makes our perseverance sure. A woman stood at the window of a burning house, stretching out her hands and calling piteously for help. A ladder was raised from the street but did not reach. A fireman pushed his way up the stairways and into the room, fastened a rope to the lintel, and grasped the trembling woman saying, "Hold fast!" As they were thus descending he felt a sudden relaxing of her grip and knew she had swooned; whereupon he tightened his hold and at length brought her to safety. It often happens thus in our relations with God. Our faith wavers, our strength fails; he merely holds us closer. Thus we are "kept," kept in our weakness, kept amid all the vicissitudes of our wayward life, kept by his great power; and "no man shall pluck us out of his hand." The gates of hell shall not prevail against us.

One thing more: we are "kept unto salvation ready to be revealed in the last time." This salvation begins here and now. For "there is no condemnation to them that are in Christ Jesus." And "he that believeth hath entered into life." But salvation is a cumulative fact; it increases more and more as life passes on. We are constantly entering on larger measures of hope and character, of usefulness and assurance. We know more of Christ: we drink deeper of spiritual peace. This is what Paul means when he says: "Work out your own salvation with fear and trembling, for it is God that worketh in you." Work it *out*, to its logical results, day by day, until the fruits of the Spirit shall be realized in you.

But this salvation can only be fully revealed "in the last time." The end is glory. "Now are we sons of God, and it hath not yet been manifested what we shall be." God's purposes do not stop short of the full, final, perfect consummation. As it is written: "Whom he foreknew, them he did predestinate to be conformed to the image of his Son, and whom he did predestinate, them he also called; and whom he called, them he also justified; and whom he justified, them he also glorified" (Rom. 8, 29).

Thus Peter in his Salutatory gives us a System of Theology in brief. It covers the whole ground: Election goes back into eternity; Regeneration marks the beginning of the Christian life; and Perseverance brings us to heaven's gate.

The words of Peter were immediately addressed to saints under persecution. He speaks of them as being "in heaviness through manifold trials." The doctrines which he so simply enunciates were intended to alleviate their sufferings by the strengthening of their faith. We, also, are oftentimes in heaviness; and our deepest comfort lies in the contemplation of the same mighty truths. "If God be for us, who can be against us?"

A martyr in Queen Mary's time, while on the way to execution, said, "One more stile and I shall be at heaven's gate." The pains and trials of the pilgrimage are made lighter by the thought that we are drawing nearer "the end of our faith, even the salvation of our souls." Meanwhile, not life nor death can separate us from the love of God. We know whom we have believed and are persuaded that he is able to keep that which we have committed unto him against that day.

Do our souls respond to these truths of the Kingdom? Or are they mere dreams and visions? Are they no more than problems worthy of serious thought; or have they so entered into our personal experience as to be interwoven with the tissues of life? Objective truth is of little moment. The important matter is that we should see truth with our eyes and handle it with our hands and give expression to it in walk and conversation. When Merle d'Aubigné was a theological student at Geneva, his teacher Robert Haldane said to him, "You tell me you accept this doctrine: There it is in the Scriptures; but have you received it into your inmost heart?" He was moved by that inquiry to self-examination. The iron entered into his soul, and, whereas he had previously been an enthusiastic student of theology, he became a living Epistle of Christ. We have contemplated the three great doctrines which cover the Christian life: Election, Regeneration and Perseverance, ending in "salvation ready to be revealed in the last time." Would that these truths might press themselves in upon mind, conscience and heart, so that we might be able to say, "I believe!" and thenceforth to hope unto the end for the grace that is to be brought unto us at the revelation of Jesus Christ!

THREE HUNDRED YEARS*

"And I said, This is my infirmity; but I will remember the years of the right hand of the Most High."—Psalm 77, 10.

"The hound when he hath lost his scent," says Dr. Gurnall, quaintly, "hunts backward and so recovers it, and pursues his game with louder cry than ever." David was in low spirits: he had been complaining of a "sore which ran in the night and ceased not;" he had been asking, "Will the Lord be favorable no more?" He perceives however that this is an unworthy view of divine providence, and plucks up courage by a review of past mercies, saying, "This is my infirmity; but I will remember the years of the right hand of the Most High."

The three hundredth anniversary of the birth of Oliver Cromwell is an occasion for serious thought and grateful remembrance. A cursory view of the intervening period will serve to show that God has been constantly in the world and that everything is going right. We shall dwell on the personal factor only so far as may be needful to emphasize the contrast between our present civilization and that of three centuries ago.

The birth of Cromwell was on April 25th, 1599, at Huntingdon, in the Fen Country. Those were de-

---
A sermon preached on the three hundredth anniversary of the birth of Oliver Cromwell.

generate times. In England the people were overburdened with taxes, likened to the frogs of Egypt that came up into the bedchambers and the kneading-troughs. In Ireland the Romanists were carrying matters with a high and bloody hand. In Scotland the faithful were upholding "Christ's Crown and Covenant" and sealing their devotion with their lives.

The Tudors were making way for the Stuarts, the meanest family that ever wielded a scepter. Down from the North Country came James I, on his way to Westminster. The royal cortége paused at Huntingdon: where, among the entertainments, was a wrestling match on the green. Oliver, a promising lad of four years, was pitted against Prince Charles of corresponding age, and threw him. It was ominous sport; for in coming time there would be many a bitter contest betwixt these two, ere the one would throw the other—on the headsman's block.

The star of Popery was in the ascendant. The air was vibrant with the recent clangor of the bells of St. Bartholomew's. Only eleven years had elapsed since the Great Armada, sailing forth to the suppression of Protestantism, had been scattered by God's breath in lamentable wreck. In Oliver's sixth year he must have heard of certain kegs of powder discovered under Westminster Hall, placed there with the purpose of blowing Parliament into the air. In his twelfth year the King James Version of the Holy Scriptures was given to the world. Up to that time the Bible was practically unknown to the common people, but thenceforth, as Wickliffe had prophesied, "a mere ploughman might know the whole counsel of God."

In 1616 Cromwell was matriculated at Cambridge. Here we note a strange coincidence: at the very time when his name was entered on the roster of the University, thus,—"*Oliverius Cromwell, admissus in commeatum sociorium*"—another inscription was being made on the stone floor of Stratford Church not far away, "Here lies William Shakespeare. Good friend, for Jesus' sake, forbear to move these bones." This marked the passing of the Golden Age of English Literature to make way for the Great Controversy of civil and ecclesiastical freedom.

On leaving Cambridge the youth went up to London to the Inns of Court. While there, bending over his law books, he could not have been unmindful of events occurring about him. No doubt he followed the crowd to Tower Hill to witness the execution of Sir Walter Raleigh; he may have seen him on the scaffold, drawing his finger along the edge of the headsman's ax with the remark, "This is a sharp medicine, but it cures all ills." He must have learned, also, at about the same time, of the sailing of a ship called the Mayflower from Delft Haven, in which an historic company of adventurous souls set forth in earnest quest of freedom to worship God.

The times were out of joint, indeed. And what room was there in the cloisters for a youth whose soul was vexed with the great problem of human rights? In sore trouble and bewilderment he returned to Huntingdon, to busy himself in "mowing, milking and marketing," meanwhile, as Milton says, "enlarging his soul in a quiet bosom for more exalted times."

His call to public service came in 1628, when the

people of the Fen Country sent him to Parliament to defend their rights. They had by persistent toil recovered four thousand acres of swamp land, of which the King now claimed a moiety. It fell upon Cromwell to resist this claim. In Parliament, where he was known as the "Lord of the Fens," he attended strictly to the business in hand. His only speech on any question of general importance was brief and to the point, as follows: "Mr. Speaker: I have heard that Doctor Alabaster hath preached flat Popery at Paul's Cross; and that the Bishop of Winchester hath promised him promotion. Is this the path of ecclesiastical preferment? If this be done in the green tree, what shall be expected in the dry?"

So little stir did he make in Parliament that he almost failed of re-election. One vote determined it —a slight margin when we consider that the body now to assemble was the Long Parliament, in which must be discussed with white-hot earnestness the question, *Jus divinum* versus Popular Rights. The climax of that controversy was reached when Cromwell moved that the power of the militia should rest no longer in the Crown but in the Parliament. Then came the tug of war. The King entered Westminster Hall with a band of soldiery and sought to arrest the prime movers. Never had the privileges of the place been so violated. As the King passed out into the street his chariot was followed by a multitude. Ominous voices were heard: "To your tents, O Israel!" His majesty, fearing the rising storm, betook himself to flight, to be seen no more in London until he stepped upon the scaffold whereon he was to die.

It is now 1642. We salute Captain Cromwell of

the 7th Troop. His followers, recruited from among the short-haired yeomen, are called "Roundheads." He is to share with Prince Rupert of the Cavaliers the honors of military leadership in the approaching conflict. You may see the portraits of these men in Warwick Castle. The death-mask of Cromwell represents a face strong and rugged, as if carved out of gnarled oak. The other portrait is of a smiling cavalier, with light hair falling over a velvet doublet. The cry of the Roundheads was, "God with us!" that of Prince Rupert's men, "Hey for cavaliers!"

Their first meeting was at Marston Moor, where five thousand of the royalists were slain; their last was at Naseby, where the royal hosts were scattered like chaff from the threshing-floor. In the royal carriage, which was captured that day, were found such proofs of the King's perfidy, that the Scotch, among whom he had taken refuge, were constrained to surrender him. He was condemned by due process and died on Tower Hill.

It could be wished that the story of Cromwell ended here; but justice requires some reference to the darker side of his life and character. One of the blots upon his memory is the record of his campaign in Ireland, where he swept the country as with a besom from Glengariffe to the Lakes of Killarney. The little children in that "Land of Sorrows" are frightened by "the curse of Cromwell" to this day.—Another was his campaign in Scotland, where he led his Roundheads in a fierce campaign against the Covenanters, his former comrades-in-arms. It was a black night when he fought old David Lesley and his ill-armed men at Dunbar, scattering them amid the growing corn and gorse. It was a darker day when he swept them through the streets of Worcester, to the fierce music of the Imprecatory Psalms. Prince Charles looked on from the cathedral spire and, seeing the rout of his partisans, betook himself in a boat to the shores of Normandy, from whence he was destined to come again in fulness of time with waving banners.

My Lord General, returning from these campaigns to London, was received with acclamations of welcome. "Praise me not," he said; "but give all glory to God!"

The Rump Parliament was then in session. Cromwell as Commander of the Army had no more right in that assemblage than the humblest yeoman; but he said, "Necessity is upon me." He entered with a guard of musketeers and pointing to the golden mace, said "Take away yon bauble!" He then commanded the legislators to retire, locked the door and took the key away with him.

That was the end of the English Commonwealth. There was no authority in England thenceforth but that of My Lord General. He ruled as a military dictator. He convened the Barebones Parliament, its members of his own appointment, and presently dissolved it. He then named a military commission, by which he was created Lord Protector of England. He declined the offer of the crown with the significant words: "I have the thing; what care I for the name? It would be no more than another feather in my hat." The land prospered under the four years of his arbitrary rule.

And then, in 1658, he died. It was a stormy Monday night in August; and amid the tumult of the winds his prayer was heard: "O Lord, I am a miserable sinner; but I am in covenant with thee, and thou wilt not leave me."

No sooner was his death announced than his work seemed to fall asunder like a house of cards. Charles came from over the sea. The body of Cromwell was taken from Westminster Abbey and his skull was affixed to the archway of Westminster Hall. But "they never fail who die" or live "in a great cause." It is easy now, looking backward over three centries, to perceive how the great Roundhead has impressed himself on history. In this brief resumé of his life and labors we have gained a somewhat comprehensive view of the conditions of his time: let us now turn to the developments of the three succeeding centuries, as they are formulated in our present civilization.

I. At the outset, we observe *a new Ideal of Character*. It is impossible to judge Cromwell with any measure of justness by the standards of to-day. If President McKinley were to enter our National Congress and dissolve it with an imperious word; if he were to take command of a troop of cavalry and sweep through Georgia to vindicate the rights of the colored people; if he were to eject from their pulpits all ministers declining to fall in with his religious convictions; if he were to usurp all the functions of the judicial, legislative and executive departments of our Government for the execution of personal plans; such measures would be regarded as high-handed. In Cromwell they can only measurably be excused by the necessity of the occasion and the customs of the time. At the close of his Scotch campaign he sent two shiploads of Covenanters over to Massachusetts to be sold into slavery. A letter of the Reverend John Cotton of Boston to Cromwell, under date July 25th, 1651, reads as follows: "The Scots, whom God delivered into your hands, have arrived hither. We have been desirous to make their yoke easy. Such as were sick of scurvy and other diseases have not wanted physic. We have not sold them into perpetual servitude, but to terms of six or seven or eight years, as the case may be." Such conduct is surely not up to the requirements of these days. We have passed on to better things. It is not for nothing that the world has for three centuries been gazing on the picture of the ideal Man.

> Ring out the old, ring in the new!
> Ring out the false, ring in the true!
> Ring out old shapes of foul disease,
> Ring in the thousand years of peace.
> *Ring in the valiant man and free,*
> *The larger heart, and kindlier hand,*
> Ring out the darkness of the land,
> Ring in the Christ that is to be!

II. *It is, moreover, a new world that we are living in.* In Cromwell's time the greatest of nations was Holland. There was the center of universal industry. There only had the controversy of civil and ecclesiastical freedom been fought to a finish. Holland alone afforded a safe refuge for all the proscribed and suffering of the earth.

Spain was her only rival; a nation of adventurous navigators going out in all directions "strange countries for to see."

As for England, it was an island about as large as the Commonwealth of New York. Its importance among the nations began with Oliver Cromwell. He was the greatest Englishman that ever lived. He was the maker of England. By a proscriptive tariff he succeeded in building up her industries at the expense of her neighbors; then, sending forth Admiral Blake with a whip at his masthead, he scourged Van Tromp from the seas, opened all avenues of commerce and invited the world to come and trade with England. And her supremacy has continued until this day.

Holland is now a fourth-rate power; Spain is no longer to be reckoned with; England is at the forefront. How long her pre-eminence will continue remains to be seen. Russia, Germany, France, Japan and America are factors of increasing importance in the problem. In any case, it is obvious that the world is a far larger world and the relations of the nations more complicated than in Cromwell's time.

III. *The Importance of the People* must be named as another of the important developments of the last three centuries. Cromwell assumed to be the defender of Popular Rights; in point of fact he was never the chosen representative of the people. He confessed as much on his return from Ireland when, marching past Temple Bar, he said: "A great multitude have come forth to greet me; but there would be a greater if I were to be hanged this day." Indeed there were no People, as we understand the term, in those days. The people were mere flies, earth-worms. Magna Charta had vindicated the barons; but the value of man as man had scarcely been discovered. There were rumblings and mutterings as of pent-up fire:

but the French Revolution was yet to come. Burns had not sung "A man's a man for a' that." True, Cromwell was ahead of his time; but there was less of promise for the cause of the People in his pretentious "Commonwealth" than in the modest cabin of the ship that sailed from Delft Haven; for there John Carver was presently made, by popular suffrage, the Governor of a new Colony, and a mighty truth was born which was destined to proclaim itself from Independence Hall in the historic words, "All men are born free and equal and with certain inalienable rights."

IV. *There is, also, a new conception of the Church to-day.* In Cromwell's time the prevailing opinion was in favor of uniformity. There was no room on earth for both Catholicism and Protestantism; one must die the death. The Pope wished all to be Catholics: Archbishop Laud was determined that all should be Episcopalians: there were some foolish folk in Scotland who were minded to have none but Presbyterians in the world: and Cromwell, setting himself against Popery, Prelacy and Presbytery alike, was resolved that all should be Independents.

There are persons now who clamor for a similar "Church-union"; but thoughtful people are for the most part convinced that denominationalism gives the best expression of religious freedom. It is needful of course that the lines of cleavage should be such that the various parts may recognize each other as members of the one body of Christ. It is a wise saying: "In essentials unity, in nonessentials diversity, in all things charity." This thought of division along rational lines, with agreement as to cardinal principles, marks a distinct advance. For there can be no freedom of conscience unless there be room for difference of opinion and for segregation. In this process of segregation there has naturally been more or less of acrid controversy; but the various branches of the Christian Church are coming closer together every day in comity and coöperation: they are seeing face to face and eye to eye; they are advancing to conquest like Israel in tribal hosts, all following the banner of the Lion of Judah.

V. *We observe, furthermore, a new view of the Relation of Church and State.* Three centuries ago, it was not supposed that the Church could exist without the protection of the secular arm, or that a nation could be other than godless without a religious "establishment." This union has been justly characterized by a famous Irishman as "That foul and adulterous connection which pollutes the purity of heaven with the abomination of earth, and hangs the tattered rags of political piety on the insulted cross of a crucified Redeemer."

The corruption of the faith of Germany is largely due to the fact that the War Lord as head of the National Church has full power of appointment to all chairs of religious instruction; so that the German Universities have been hotbeds of infidelity. The English Establishment also has been a prolific mother of abominations. This union of Church and State is against nature. It involves an obvious violation of the rights of conscience as between man and man. It fosters a spirit of fawning sycophancy which has won for the pulpit the name "Coward's Castle." There are no more shameless paupers than certain men in holy orders, with fat livings, who dare not call their souls their own, yet look down upon "dissenters" of larger piety and knowledge as an inferior order. Let us praise God that the days of disestablishment seem to be drawing nigh. Not until this age-old evil is eradicated can there be any real parity of the clergy or just distribution of rights among men.

VI. *And finally, the Field of Action has changed.* In Cromwell's time all important questions were settled by the arbitrament of the sword. The Reformation itself was a battle of a hundred years, in which the whole world was embroiled. That was the fashion of those days. Thank God, we are breaking away from it.

War is coming to be looked upon with righteous horror. Never was a more righteous conflict than ours with Spain. Yet how reluctantly we entered upon it, and with what consideration of humanity it was carried on. Where war is deemed necessary it is waged under the Code of Nations. There is a new science of International Law. The only further step is Arbitration. Then God will break the spear in sunder and cast the chariot into the fire.

In any case the Kingdom of Christ can no more be propagated by the sword. The Roundheads heard the voice of the Lord saying, "Go fight!" We hear him saying, "Go preach!" He has an army in the field to-day made up of the bravest men that ever enlisted in a noble cause. They are braver than the Roundheads, braver than the Covenanters, braver than the Huguenots, braver than the Beggars of Holland. They represent every nation in Christendom; they are at the front in the high places of the field. They are climbing the mountains, not as Napoleon's troops climbed the Alps, with great guns:

they are crossing the plains, not as the Roundheads crossed the Scottish Moors, with crossbows and culverins. "How beautiful upon the mountains are the feet of him that bringeth good tidings, that publisheth peace; that bringeth good tidings of good, that publisheth salvation; that saith unto Zion, Thy God reigneth!" The Church wants no other army. Her missionaries are gone abroad with the evangel; they are the vanguard of civilization. They are bringing in the nations as prisoners of hope: they are heralds of the coming of Christ.

Our brief and cursory retrospect has shown us some of the significant developments of three centuries of Christian Civilization. How would Cromwell stand amazed could he return to day! In his time there were a hundred millions of nominal Christians; to-day there are five hundred millions under the luminous shadow of the cross. And who shall lift the veil of the next century? For all this is a mere preparation for larger things. God is in the world; and the world grows better every day. We may not generalize amid the smoke of battle; but the backward look makes one thing clear: *Everything is going right.* The " one far-off divine event to which the whole creation moves," comes nearer every day. The future of Christ's Kingdom is assured. Let us to the watch-tower; the King's banners are waving on the distant hills; the salvation of the world draweth near.

> ' There's a fount about to stream,
> There's a light about to gleam,
> There's a midnight darkness changing into day ;
> Men of thought and men of action,
> Clear the way !"

THE FORBIDDEN FRUIT

"Now the serpent was more subtil than any beast of the field which the Lord had made. And he said unto the woman, Yea, hath God said, Ye shall not eat of every tree of the garden? And the woman said unto the serpent, We may eat of the fruit of the trees of the garden: but of the fruit of the tree which is in the midst of the garden, God hath said, Ye shall not eat of it, neither shall ye touch it, lest ye die. And the serpent said unto the woman, Ye shall not surely die: for God doth know that in the day ye eat thereof, then your eyes shall be opened, and ye shall be as gods, knowing good and evil. And when the woman saw that the tree was good for food, and that it was pleasant to the eyes, and a tree to be desired to make one wise, she took of the fruit thereof, and did eat, and gave also unto her husband with her; and he did eat."—Genesis 3, 1-6.

Of course you understand this is a mere "fable." The old Book as interpreted by advanced scholarship, is full of such folklore, legend, and artful fabrication. All its references to the supernatural must be understood in that way. Is it the fault of eminent critics if the sacred volume is thus exposed as an incongruous mixture of truth and falsehood? Certainly not! For are not these critics open and avowed lovers of Holy Writ? If they seem to be vociferous at times in impugning its truth, it is only under the extreme pressure of conscience; the same conscience which pathetically asserts their devotion to the Scriptures as the veritable Word of God.

A paper was recently read in one of our ministerial circles on "The Decline of the Revival." There was a time when God's Spirit came down upon

Churches and communities in widespread quickening; so that Christians, as with one accord, gave themselves anew to faithful service, and the unconverted being pricked to the heart cried, "Men and brethren, what shall we do?" Then the cords of the Tabernacle were lengthened, and souls sprang up like willows by the water courses. But how can such visitations of blessing be expected when not a few of God's ministers deny the authority of his Word; and the laity, in many quarters, lend their countenance to pulpit pronunciamentos which surpass the infidelity of Thomas Paine and his confrères of a hundred years ago? "For the time will come," wrote Paul to Timothy, "when they will not endure the sound doctrine; but, having itching ears, will heap to themselves teachers after their own lusts, and will turn away their ears from the truth and turn aside unto fables." God will not bless his people under such conditions. The watchword for the hour should be, Back to the Bible! We can look for no better spiritual conditions until we show ourselves loyal to the divine oracles; for both conversion and sanctification are wrought by the power of the Spirit through the Word of God.

It need scarcely be said that the Bible is in no danger of being overthrown by such assaults. The only danger is of disaster to its enemies and an utter decay of faith on the part of those who follow them. "The voice said, 'Cry!'—And he answered 'What shall I cry?'— 'All flesh is grass, and all the goodliness thereof is as the flower of the field: the grass withereth, the flower fadeth; but the Word of our God shall stand forever!'" A Spanish frigate in the

West Indies fired all night on a hostile ship which loomed through the mists in the offing. Broadside on broadside was vainly poured upon it. The sun arose and there it stood; a great, silent rock, towering out of the sea. So has the word of the Lord endured the assault of its enemies through the centuries, and so shall it abide forever.

> "Hammer away, ye rebel bands;
> Your hammers break, God's anvil stands."

As to this particular "myth," concerning the Fall of Man, there is this to be said; it rests upon data which cannot be denied. Here we are; the Race is not a myth; and by practically universal consent the Race is traced backward to a single pair. Here, also, is Sin; Sin is not a myth; and it must have had a beginning. Why may it not have begun in this way?

The Greeks trace its origin to Prometheus, who stole fire from the gods and gave it to men.—The Persians trace it to the whisper of the serpent: "All gracious things are from the Black Ahriman;" which men believed and, lo! of a hundred excellencies all but one departed from them.—The Buddhists tell of a Golden Age when the leaves never withered and sorrow was unknown; but men ate of a scum that looked like honeydew; a lie was uttered; a gray hair was seen; and "so came death into the world and all our woe." All the false religions give some account, more or less grotesque, of the origin of evil; in comparison with which the Scriptural statement, for its straightforward simplicity and reasonableness, commends itself to fair-minded men.

The First Item in the narrative is Man; that is, generic Man; Adam and Eve here standing as the complex head of the race. The end of man's creation was the glory of God. It is written that God, beholding his finished creation, pronounced it "very good"; but as yet there was no creature to look upward and say, "I thank thee!" Wherefore God created man in his own likeness and after his image, breathing into his nostrils the breath of life and making him a living soul.

(1) He was a rational being. The Greeks called him *anthropos;* that is, "the uplooker." Plato said, "He is an heavenly plant rising as from a root and blossoming toward heaven." Keppler said, "We are able to think God's thoughts after him."

(2) He was also a moral being; that is, capable of moral character. One of the philosophers defined man as "the animal that laughs;" another as "the animal that has thumbs." Benjamin Franklin called him "the tool-making animal"; and Adam Smith, "the animal that makes bargains." The one feature, however, which differentiates him from all the other orders of being is his ability to discriminate between right and wrong; or, as Socrates would say, between "the worse and better reason."

(3) He is also free; that is, possessed of a sovereign will. This is involved in his creation after the likeness of God. He was made sinless but not righteous. His innocency was that of a graven image; righteousness must be acquired by ordeal. Herein is the making of a man. A magnificent outlook is before Adam if he will choose aright; if he will avoid the evil and prefer the good. But he must determine for himself.

Not long ago "The Oregon" was launched from a shipyard at the Golden Gate, and by-and-by set out for a voyage around The Horn. It remained to be seen whether she would prove herself a staunch and trustworthy man-of-war. At length she came plowing up along the Atlantic coast and was placed in service as a tried and trusty craft; she had "rounded the Horn." Thus at man's creation he was exposed to trial; the test was temptation; the issue was character. We await the outcome; the destiny of the race depends upon it.

The Second Item in the narrative is the Tree. At this point the small scholars begin to question whether or no it was a fig-tree, an apple-tree or a grapevine. Is it not wearisome to sit by and hearken to learned disquisitions on the grain and fiber of wood, when Destiny is in the balance? Out upon the learning that expends itself on the jot and tittle! We stand among the cañons of the Yosemite, overarched by God's great conopy, with peaks and chasms of sublimity all around us, and are interrupted in our silent wonder by the tap-tapping of a hammer; a geologist in the company is chipping off specimens for a High School Museum! In point of fact it matters not what particular tree of Paradise was used for the testing of Adam; one would answer as well as another, since the question involved was obedience to divine law.

The Fall of Adam was most unjustifiable since the advantage was so greatly in his favor. He had no need of the fruit of that particular tree. The garden was full of others, laden with fruit pleasant to the eye and sweet to the taste, and God had said, "Of every tree of the garden thou mayest freely eat, but of the tree of the knowledge of good and evil, thou shalt not eat of it."—Moreover, the man had no predilection for the fruit of that tree; its taste was not yet upon his lips. Alas for us! we are handicapped by having formed the habit of sin. We have made the acquaintance of Vice, of which it is written, "Familiar with her face, we first endure, then pity, then embrace." Resistance is hard for us.—And still further, Adam had been distinctly warned: "In the day thou eatest thereof thou shalt surely die."

The Third Item in the narrative is the Serpent. At this point the small scholars wish to be heard again; but their objections are of slight consequence. If Satan is to appear at all, it might as well be in the form of a serpent as any other. He would not be permitted to come as an angel of light, for that would put the man at a disadvantage. Nor, on the other hand, would he choose to appear with hoofs and horns, for this would have been to defeat his own purpose. He would be likely to present himself in such guise as would give to temptation its most subtle and alluring form.

It is a fact of singular importance, in view of present conditions, that the temptation on this occasion was directed at Adam's faith in the divine Word. To begin with there was a suggestion of doubt as to its authenticity; "Yea, hath God said, Ye shall not eat?" The serpent intimates that the communication had really not proceeded from the Lord, but was a myth or fable, a dream perhaps, or figment of the imagination. At this point his appeal was to the inner consciousness as the ultimate authority in matters of truth. "Did God, indeed, say this? Does it sound like him?"— Next there was a suggestion of doubt as to the inerrancy of the Word; "And the serpent said unto the woman, 'Ye shall not surely die;'" that is, it could scarcely be that God meant what he said; inasmuch as the penalty was so far out of proportion to the trifling offense of tasting the fruit of a certain tree. Here again the inner consciousness is appealed to as against an *ipse dixit.*— Furthermore, there was an intimation of doubt as to the sufficiency and completeness of the Word: "For God doth know that in the day ye eat thereof, then your eyes shall be opened and ye shall be as gods knowing good and evil;" that is, revelation was good enough so far as it went, but here was a subtle scholar who, by throwing light on the divine motives, could make a substantial addition to it.

So far as appears, there is only one thing to the serpent's credit in this transaction; to wit, he made no profession of loyalty to the Word. So far forth, he was an honest serpent. He did not ask nor profess to be in holy orders. He uttered no unctuous phrases respecting his acceptance of the fallible Word as an "infallible rule of faith and practice" or his devotion to it, despite its manifest falseness, as the veritable Word of God.

The Fourth Item in the narrative is Death. The order is, Sin, shame or loss of self-respect ("they covered themselves with fig-leaves"), and then alienation from God ("the Lord called unto Adam, Where art thou? And he answered, I heard thy voice in the garden and I was afraid and hid myself"). But yesterday no sound of singing bird or murmuring brook was so sweet to Adam as the Voice; now he fears and trembles to hear it. This is death, to flee from God. This is hell, to be forever exiled from him.

"And they did eat!" How simply it is told; but what a terrific fact is here. One may hear afar off the sobs and groans of coming generations in bondage under sin; the rattle of chains and clang of prison-bolts; the voice of heated strife; the roll of chariots and clash of swords. The Reign of Terror has begun. The choice has been made between good and evil, and the race, descended from Adam as its federal and natural head, must suffer for it.

The imputation of Adam's sin may be disposed of in few words. There is a common aversion to the so-called Doctrine of "Original Sin." If the phrase is offensive let us have done with it. There is, however, a scientific fact which meets with general acceptance in our time, known as "Heredity." This will answer every purpose. There is indeed no disposition in any quarter to deny the transmission of moral evil through the veins of the children of men.

It remains to mention the sequel. No sooner had Adam sinned than God gave the prophecy of Christ: The Seed of woman shall bruise the serpent's head and it shall bruise his heel. Here is the Protevangel; the germ of all the Messianic prophecies. It shines forth like a star through a rift in the midnight clouds; it will presently be followed by another star, and yet another, until the blue dome of Revelation shall be "thick inlaid with patines of bright gold"; then the bright and morning star with healing in its beams, and then a burst of glory. The day breaks, with the angels' song, "Glory to God in the highest, peace on earth and good will toward men."

It is written that the gateway of Eden was guarded by cherubim and "a flaming sword which turned every way." But scarcely had the man and woman issued from the garden ere they built an altar, on which they offered a sacrifice, the blood of which was eloquent of the coming of this Seed of Woman, who in fulness of time should by dying expiate their sin. And from the open heavens there came a voice—the Voice which they had dreaded to hear—to be heard thenceforth all along the ages, full of lovingkindness and tender mercy, "Come! Come! Come, saith the Lord; let us reason together; though your sins be as scarlet, they shall be as white as snow!"

The practical question is not as to the origin of sin; but rather, How shall we escape from it? The man who finds himself in a burning house will not pause to analyze caloric or institute an inquiry as to the origin of the flame. He seeks the stairway, the fire-escape. Sin is a patent fact; its danger is universally felt in "a certain fearful looking-for of judgment." Is there a way out? Aye, blessed be God! "This is a faithful saying, that Christ Jesus came into the world to save sinners.—He bare our sins in his own body on the tree.—Whosoever believeth in him hath everlasting life."

As I sat in my study yesterday, a strange visitor was announced: a Syrian priest of Aleppo who, for the truth's sake, had been driven from home and obliged to seek refuge beyond the sea. He could speak scarcely a word of the English tongue, but brought a satisfactory letter of credence from the

Missionary College in Beirut. I strove in vain to converse with him. He could understand only a few simple phrases; but his eyes kindled at every mention of the name of Jesus. Finally I said, "You believe the gospel?" The word "believe" seemed to puzzle him. He knit his brows, as if trying to recollect where he had heard it; then in slow, measured tones he repeated: "God–so—loved–the—world–that–he–gave–his–only–begotten–Son-that-whosoever-believeth—in–him—should—not—perish—but—have—eternal–life." So much he knew as the ground and pillar of his faith. And, dear friends, what more can be asked of any? It is the great crucial fact of our religion. He who accepts that in sincerity will stagger at no other Scripture. All theology is here; all Christianity is here. Sin ruined the race; but God so loved the world that he gave his only-begotten Son to redeem it.

"AT THEIR WITS' END"

"And they are at their wits' end."—Psalm 107, 27.

The men who "go down to the sea in ships and do business in great waters," are proverbially superstitious. It is due, perhaps, to their living in constant touch with the supernatural: for there is but an inch of oaken plank at any moment between them and the unseen world. The horseshoe nailed to the mast is a rude tribute to this fact. The seafaring man knows that he is in the grip of an unseen power; his helplessness is ever before him.

In our context we have a vivid picture of a storm. The winds and waves are roaring: the ship mounts up to heaven and plunges again into the depths; the soul of the hardy crew is melted within them; they reel to and fro and stagger like a drunken man, *and are at their wits' end*. What then? What do men in sore extremity always do? "They cry unto the Lord in their trouble and he bringeth them out of their distresses."

Is there one of us who does not understand, from personal experience, that phrase "at their wits' end"? Are we not ever coming up against our limitations? There are times of perplexity and bewilderment when we respond instinctively to the droll words of Alexander Pope:

"You beat your pate, hoping your wits will come;
Knock as you please, there's nobody at home."

What is to be done under such circumstances? What is to be done when the night closes in and Euroclydon is upon us? We can do no better than follow the example of Paul and his companions when they were driven up and down in Adria; they "let go four anchors from the stern and wished for the day." It is vain to sit gloomily in the cabin discussing the vibratory theory of light; equally vain to go on deck and hang lanterns at peak and topmast. God alone can give the morning; he alone can relieve distress; the part of reason is to call upon him and expect the day.

It is not my purpose to generalize in this discourse, but to address seven persons in particular. I feel quite sure of their presence in this assemblage, and am equally confident that they are all at their wits' end.

The first man is one who is searching for truth. I give you credit, friend, for a sincere desire to reach a just solution of the great problems of the eternal life; but you are overwhelmed with doubt and are in danger of downright unbelief. Is it not so? You have been trusting to your own wisdom and the inevitable has come; you are at your wits' end.

In the innocent years of childhood we believe as a matter of course. The cold shadows of a cynical and materialistic world have not yet closed around us, and all verities seem near by. We reach after the stars, as for flowers growing along the way. The rainbow is just yonder; we approach it as confidently as children of larger growth pass under triumphal arches. The heavens are but the overhanging curtains of our playhouse. O, blessed childhood! Is it not wisely written, "Except ye become as little children ye shall in no wise enter the kingdom of God"?

But in the progress of the years all truths recede; the stars, the rainbow and the sky are farther and farther from us. We begin to inquire, "Is there a God?" and, "If a man die, will he live again?" We doubt and reason and apply the scientific processes of analysis to problems that can only be solved by faith. The real conflict of the soul is when the Argonauts are thus on their way to Colchis. On the open sea we are beaten about by contrary winds; we can manage the rigging, but the stress of the elements is beyond us; vain is the hope of ever finding and securing the Golden Fleece. Vain indeed unless in recognition of our infirmity we cry unto God!

Is it any wonder that we are worsted in spiritual argument when we insist on meeting the adversary on his own ground? Doubt yields to faith alone. Our unaided wits are ever at a disadvantage. But God's wisdom is infinite: there is no searching of his understanding. If we fail to appeal to that, the outcome is inevitable; doubt deepens into agnosticism and agnosticism into the black midnight of unbelief. It would have been well had we recognized our limitations long ago. The wisdom of Socrates was manifest in the remark, "I know only that I know little or nothing at all." If you have come to that conclusion, friend, you must see the reasonableness of prayer. Here is the promise for you: "If any man lack wisdom, let him ask of God, who giveth to all men liberally and upbraideth not; and it shall be given him" (James 1:5).

The second man whom I wish to address is one under conviction of sin. All are sinners. It is not my purpose to carry coals to Newcastle by trying to demonstrate a fact which is present to the inner consciousness of all. But there is a time when the consciousness of sin sweeps over the soul with the gathering force of a tempest; when a man feels the exceeding sinfulness of sin, is oppressed with a certain fearful looking-for of judgment, beats upon his breast in utter helplessness and confesses that he is at his wits' end.

It was so on the Day of Pentecost when the assembled people realized the presence of God's Spirit in the sound of a rushing mighty wind. And when one arose in the midst and pointed out their guilt as accessory to the crucifixion of the Just One, showing the red stains of murder on their hands, they were pricked to the heart and cried out, "Men and brethren, what shall we do?" It may be that you, my friend, by some visitation of adversity or extraordinary demonstration of the supernatural, have been driven to a like extremity. What, then, will you do? Penance? Nay; it is unnecessary to tell a thoughtful man that fire cannot burn out guilt or that expiation is not wrought by scourging the body for the sins of the soul. Good works, then? Nay, since every hour is but sufficient unto itself, how can future obedience blot out the record of a mislived past. What remains for you, then, but to throw up your hands and cry mightily unto God?

At a like juncture in the life of David, when he was hunted like a roe among the hills, and driven to bay, he made his appeal to a Power beyond his own, and not in vain. "This poor man cried," he says, "and the Lord heard him and saved him out of all his troubles."

The dying thief had reached the uttermost limit of despair when he cried "Lord, remember me!" Not a moment elapsed before the answer came, "To-day thou shalt be with me in Paradise." There is hope for a sinner who knows himself to be lost; and there is no hope for any other: for "the Son of Man came to seek and to save that which was lost." So long as resources of your own remain, you are likely to depend upon them; but if you have come to the end of your tether, it is obviously the part of reason to look unto the hills for help. There is hope for you, therefore, my troubled friend, in the word that is written, "The Son of Man hath power on earth to forgive sin."

The third man of whom I ask an audience is one who is confronting duty and feels he cannot discharge it. There is nothing in the world so important as this, that we should meet our responsibilities and discharge our utmost duty to ourselves and our fellowmen. Yet who is sufficient for this? Are we not all sensible of shortcoming, of avoiding our responsibilities, of shirking the burden which is laid upon us?

It is the fashion in these times to discredit the story of Jonah. In fact, however, there is nothing in Holy Writ that meets a quicker or more sympathetic response in the soul of the average man. The prophet was told to go to Nineveh at peril of his life. He pondered, questioned, and finally resolved to meet the matter half-way. He would not go to Nineveh, but he would go to Tarshish. So he paid his fare, took ship, went down into the hold and, having quieted conscience with a compromise, fell asleep. So far, my friend, the parallel is not difficult to find in personal experience. And as Jonah slept, the storm arose and down into the hold came a voice, "Arise, O sleeper, and call upon thy god!" (Have you never been awakened by a similar voice?) He appeared on deck, saying, "I fear the Lord, and I know that for my sake this great tempest is come upon you." So they cast him forth into the sea. As to what followed, let him speak for himself: "I cried by reason of mine affliction unto the Lord, and he heard me. *Out of the belly of hell cried I.* The waters compassed me about, the weeds were wrapped about my head. My soul fainted within me; I cried aloud, and he heard me. Salvation is of the Lord."

It is of infinite mercy that we are thus arrested in the avoidance of duty, and brought to realize how much easier it is to do right with the Lord's help than to have our own way. The hardest task is within the power of the weakest man who leans on an almighty arm. The word of hope is here: "I can do all things through Christ which strengtheneth me."

The fourth man whom I would particularly address is one who faces temptation. From this there is no escape. It is vain to betake oneself to a hermit's cell; the adversary will pursue us.

It may be, friend, that you have been striving to overcome an evil habit, and you have fallen once, twice, thrice. Are you discouraged? Are you quite satisfied as to your personal inability? Have you come to your wits' end? God be praised! There is hope for you.

How can a man expect to succeed in his own strength when he wrestles not only against principalities and powers, but against the prince of darkness? But if God be for us, who shall be against us? Try once more, comrade, and this time in the strength of the Omnipotent. Throw thyself on God. Put him in remembrance of his great promises. Be confident in him. Go out against thine enemy as the shepherd boy went forth to meet Goliath in the valley of Elah. The sword of Saul and armor of Saul were rejected; faith was his only panoply. As he approached his boastful foe he cried, "Thou comest to me with sword and buckler, but I come to thee in the name of the living God!" The result was, as it always is under like conditions, he came up from the valley dragging the head of Goliath by its gory hair. Victory for you, or for any man who, being at his wits' end, girds himself with divine power! Here is the word for your present stress: "God is faithful who will not suffer you to be tempted above that ye are able, but will with the temptation also make a way of escape, that ye may be able to bear it."

The fifth man is one in trouble. I know not what the trouble is, my friend; the heart knoweth its own bitterness. Is it pain perhaps? God was with the Babylonish youth in the fiery furnace. Is it poverty? He sent the ravens to feed his prophet by the brook. Is it abandonment and loneliness? No man was ever lonelier than Jacob in the heights of Bethel where he saw God's angels coming down a golden ladder to help him. Is it disappointment? Have you dreamed dreams and seen visions of success only to find your hopes thwarted and your purposes brought to naught? So did Elijah fling himself in utter desperation under the juniper tree crying, "It is enough; let me die!" But a Voice said, "Arise and eat." And he looked and, behold, a cake baken on the coals and a cruse of water; and he arose and did eat and drink, and went in the strength of that meat forty days and forty nights unto the mount of God.

Be of good courage, if in failure you have discovered the utmost limit of your strength; for at that limit ever stands the waiting God. A man's making is in his triumph over circumstances by faith in God. So wrote Paul, "We are troubled on every side, yet not distressed; we are perplexed, but not in despair; persecuted, but not forsaken; cast down, but not destroyed"; "that the excellency of the power may be of God and not of us."

The strength of God is thus made perfect in weakness. Our extremity is God's opportunity. We laugh at difficulty; we exult in the storm; we triumph when, with disjointed thigh, we stagger to the feet of the Mightiest This is the truth in the quaint words of Herrick:

> "Tumble me down, and I will sit
>   Upon my ruins, smiling yet.
> Tear me to tatters, yet I'll be
>   Patient in my necessity.
> Laugh at my scraps of clothes and shun
>   Me as a dire infection,
> Yet scarecrow-like I'll walk as one
>   Neglecting thy derision."

The sixth man is he who stands in terror of death. It is a great question, How to die? For the black camel kneels at every tent. The man who approaches alone the valley of the shadow is always at his wits' end; it is obviously the height of folly to put away preparation for the journey until the hour of setting out. To make God's acquaintance amid the busy duties of life is to know him in the hour that trieth the soul. "Yea, though I walk through the valley of the shadow of death, yet I will fear no evil, for thy rod and thy staff they comfort me."

I have heard of a lad who, being taken by his father on a long voyage, was miserably dreary and homesick. As the ship sailed homeward he brightened day by day. On the night of entering the harbor the little fellow lay asleep in his berth. He was dimly conscious of the casting of the anchor and voices of sailors above him; then of being lifted in his father's arms and carried down the rope-ladder into the little boat; then of the splashing of waves and beating of oars; then, still half asleep, of being carried in strong arms and laid in his little bed; then he awoke and it was morning, and his mother's face was bending over him. Such is death to those who are ready. It is being taken up in everlasting arms and carried through the night, to awake in the home-land and be forever with the Lord.

And my seventh auditor is the man who fears the Judgment. Nor is your fear ungrounded, my friend; since you are well aware that at the great Assize, you must plead guilty. There, if never before, you will feel yourself at your wits' end. What then? O joy unspeakable, if you can look with confidence to him who with uplifted, nail-scarred hands shall plead your case, shall offer himself as your Substitute in expiation of the penalties of broken law! I know not what a sinner can say for himself in that Great Day, if he cannot make this plea; "He bare my sins in his own body on the tree." Thus it is written: "If any man sin, we have an Advocate with the Father, even Jesus Christ the righteous."

> "Great God, when I approach Thy throne,
> And all Thy glory see,
> This is my plea, and this alone,
> That Jesus died for me."

And now, in closing, I feel reasonably sure that I have addressed not seven men, but all before me. For, are we not all truth-seekers, all sensible of sin, all under the stern obligation of duty, all facing temptations beyond our strength, all pilgrims in the Vale of Baca, all bound to pass through the little wicket-gate and stand at last in judgment? If then we are all convinced of our narrow limitations and forced to confess ourselves at our wits' end, why shall we not get down upon our knees to-night and call upon him who is ever able, ever willing, ever ready to help? Cry aloud unto God! If he spared not his own Son, but delivered him up for us all, how shall he not with him also freely give us all things? He heard David in his distress, and he will hear you. He heard Peter when the waters were closing about him, and he will hear you. He heard the dying thief in his despair, and he will hear you. O that men would praise the Lord for his goodness and for his wonderful works to the children of men!

INDIFFERENT GALLIO

"And Gallio cared for none of those things."—Acts 18, 17.

The Jews of Corinth had long been annoyed by a pestilent fellow who insisted on preaching that "Jesus is the Christ." This man had formerly been a Rabbi of high standing, a member of the Sanhedrin at Jerusalem; but he claimed to have had a supernatural vision of Jesus which changed the whole tenor of his life. He had come to Corinth two years ago; and, while working as a tentmaker for his livelihood, made a point of visiting the synagogue Sabbath by Sabbath and endeavoring to prove out of the Scriptures "that this Jesus is the Christ." On being cast out of the synagogue he had accepted the invitation of a certain Justus who lived near by, to use his home for the propagation of his views: and thus he had continued to the discomfiture of his Jewish enemies. At length, however, there seemed a prospect of relief in the appointment of Gallio as proconsul of Achaia. On his arrival at Corinth the Jews seized on the contumacious preacher and dragged him before the court, making this formal charge, "He persuadeth men to worship God contrary to the law." Paul was about to make his defense when Gallio interposed: "If this were a matter of wrong or wicked lewdness, reason would that I should bear with you; but in a question of your 'law,' look ye to it; I will be no judge of such matters." As the accusers, stung with defeat, were leaving court, they were set upon by certain Greeks who seized the ruler of the synagogue, and beat him shamefully in sight and hearing of the judgment-seat. To Gallio, however, this was mere by-play and quite beneath his notice. He looked through his fingers and winked at it. Why should he interfere in petty strife or in the quibbling of theological parties? He "cared for none of those things."

Here is a distinct and interesting type of character, not unworthy of our study. Gallio was a brother of Seneca; a skeptic like that great moralist, but a most amiable one. He was a man of broad culture, thoroughly familiar with literature and an expert in Roman jurisprudence. He is called in the records of the time, *dulcis Gallio*. He was immensely popular by reason of his complaisance and amiable disposition; but, he was wholly indifferent to many things, and among them the problems of the spiritual life. He probably regarded these as quite unsolvable; being an agnostic, after the fashion of his time. He was the product of the overwrought culture of that luxurious age, an age which has been fitly characterized by Matthew Arnold:—

> "On that hard Roman world disgust
> And sated loathing fell:
> Deap weariness and sated lust
> Made human life a hell.
> In his cool hall, with haggard eyes,
> The noble Roman lay,
> Or drove abroad in furious guise
> Along the Appian Way.

> He made a feast; drank deep and fast,
> And crowned his head with flowers.
> No easier and no swifter passed
> The impracticable hours."

I invite you to a brief contemplation of this attitude of mind; an indifference to matters of supreme importance, born of baffled research or moral weariness. It not infrequently consists with great sweetness of disposition, broad erudition and the utmost respectability. It betrays, however, a lamentable want of virility and true courage. A man can not be indifferent to great spiritual verities without being an indifferent sort of man.

I. *As to the Previous Question.* Back of all this controversy lay the proposition of Paul, "This Jesus is the Christ." And while it would appear, on the surface of the narrative, that Gallio was simply indifferent to the party quibblings of the synagogue, he was in fact turning his back on the fundamental problem of life eternal. As a man of affairs, familiar with the religious controversies of his time, he must have known about the disputed claims of Jesus. It was twenty-two years since the crucifixion, yet the dispute concerning the Man of Nazareth had gone on continuously ever since. Would his specter never be laid? Never! This question must be confronted and settled by every man.

The blame of Gallio in refusing to consider the claims of Jesus as the Christ must be measured by circumstances. He probably regarded this as a matter of mere provincial importance, not knowing that his own salvation was in the balance. He had doubtless discussed many questions in the forum and in philosophic halls, but never one so intensely personal as this: "Is Jesus the Christ?"

But what shall be said of a man who, in the Nineteenth Century, "cares nothing for this thing"? The proposition is that Jesus Christ came into the world to save sinners; and we know ourselves to be all alike concluded under sin. This proposition is sustained by the claim of Jesus himself, by the Holy Scriptures, by the eloquent events of eighteen centuries of Christian progress, and by the united testimony of some hundreds of millions of people who are prepared to certify that this Jesus has delivered them from sin's bondage and opened to them the gates of the endless life. In view of these facts we conceive it possible that a man may consider the credentials of Jesus and decide adversely; but it is incomprehensible how any can be indifferent. In a matter involving the issues of eternity, heedlessness is a sin against reason and indecision a crime against conscience. If the claim of Jesus be false, his gospel is the greatest imposture of history; if it be true, our destiny for eternity depends on our acceptance of him.

II. *As to Other Questions involved in the Messiahship of Jesus.* Had Gallio interested himself in the controversy brought before him that day for adjustment, he must have been driven to a decision *pro* or *con* as to other and affiliated matters of great importance; such as the Incarnation, the Blood-atonement, the Resurrection, the veracity of the Scriptural record and the Personality of the Spirit: These are vitally connected with the fact contended for by Paul at Antioch: "This Jesus is the Christ."

We are living in an age of controversy; and the

questions now uppermost are these very ones. What shall we do with them? Let them pass? In some quarters it is said, "If we receive Christ as our Saviour, it matters little what opinion we hold as to these controverted dogmas. Christ is everything: let the rest go." But this is impossible. As well say, "Let us keep Darwin but ignore his theory of Evolution"; or, "Let us keep Galileo but take no account of the revolution of the earth." As well say, "Let us keep life but give no heed to air, water and food." We cannot accept Christ and slight his teachings. We cannot accept Christ and spurn the essential truths which radiate from his life, character and work. Christ and Christianity are inseparable. The strength of a chain is measured by its weakest link. The credentials of the great Teacher are to be determined by the weakest truth to which he gave sanction. We cannot have Christ without believing in him.

In other quarters it is suggested that matters of theological import should be turned over for settlement to "experts." This applies particularly to the Inerrancy of Holy Scripture, but in some measure to all allied truths. As a minister of the gospel I resent the claim of any particular class of specialists to a monopoly of wisdom in this province. The presumption, indeed, is in favor rather of those who have devoted themselves to religious investigation while in close contact with affairs, as against any who pursue their researches in academic cloisters by the light of midnight oil. But justice to the gospel requires that we shall go a step further, and assert the rights of the people in these premises. There is no such thing as "esoteric Christianity." There are no "mysteries," such as are found in Pagan Religions, to be imparted only to the initiated. The glory of our religion, the historic glory of Protestantism, is that no Scripture is of such private interpretation. Scholars have their place, indeed; but the height of arrogance is reached when they call upon the people to stand aloof while they lift the curtains and pass into the *sanctum sanctorum* to solve for us the problems which concern our eternal life. Are we to waive our acceptance of the Incarnation, the Atonement, the Infallibility of the Word, until "experts" shall give us leave to accept their ultimatum? Not so have we learned the gospel. Its vital truths, clear as a crystal spring, are to be accepted by faith, buttressed by reason and resting on divine authority.

It is recorded that when the Council of Nice was engaged in heated controversy the shepherd Spiridion limped in. He had proven his devotion by suffering for the truth's sake: one eye had been pierced with a hot iron and one leg had been twisted off. "In the name of Christ," he said, "O philosophers, hear me! Our Lord came into the world and died for our salvation. He taught many things and his word is an end of controversy. To know him is to know all; to accept him is to accept all. We who are but common men challenge your right to reduce our religion to a system of wire-drawn argument. We put you in remembrance of what Jesus said, 'Except ye become as little children, ye shall in no wise see the kingdom of God.'"

III. *As to Questions of Conscience.* These also are closely related to the original question of the Messiahship of Christ. In the false religions a line is drawn between dogma and life; but there is no such distinction in Christianity. Doctrine and ethics are vitally associated: for "as a man thinketh in his heart so is he." Had Gallio been willing to face the rigid claims of Jesus as the only Saviour, he must have proceeded to a corresponding determination of all questions of conduct.

There are some things which are always right or always wrong. Here runs "the dead line." The follower of Christ must not hesitate for a moment as to those matters which are defined in the Decalogue and in the Sermon on the Mount. Impiety, dishonesty, Sabbath-breaking, murder, scandal-mongering, licentiousness, covetousness; these are always wrong, under all circumstances: and nothing can ever make them right.

But there are other things which are right or wrong according to circumstances. The idol-meats of Corinth furnish an illustration: (1 Cor. viii.). There are people who claim the right to indulge in intoxicating drink; and while certain of us see clearly the duty of abstinence for ourselves, it is not for us to impose the determinations of our conscience on others. But there must be no indifference here. Let each for himself decide, prayerfully, in the light of Biblical precept and Christian charity. "Let every man be fully persuaded in his own mind." The danger is not so much in a difference of opinion as in indecision. If you are in doubt as to the wineglass, give your conscience the benefit of the doubt, by all means. And in any case, when you have determined the right, let not a legion of devils tempt you to swerve from it; for nothing can compensate a man for a violation of his moral sense.

One thing is never right, to wit, indifference to the distinction between right and wrong. The most contemptible legend that ever was inscribed on any shield was that of the so-called "resolute Rufus," who, having the name of Jehovah on one side and of Satan on the other, wrote above them, "*In utrumque paratus*"; i.e., "Ready for either!"

IV. *As to the great Question of the Welfare of our Fellow-men.* This also is closely related to the Original Question touching the credentials of Christ. Had Gallio been concerned with reference to that matter, he must logically have proceeded to interest himself in the good of those about him; for Christ came into the world to save men with a great salvation, a salvation which should inevitably interest them profoundly in the uplifting of all. The opening word of the Lord's Prayer, "Our," has in it all the Magna Chartas and Declarations of Independence and manifestoes of civil and ecclesiastical freedom of all history. The doctrine of the Fatherhood of God, as proclaimed by his only-begotten and well-beloved Son, our Elder Brother, involves the complementary doctrine of the Brotherhood of Men.

Our Lord dwelt on the importance of being a good "neighbor." The word, however, hast lost much of its helpful significance in our modern life, and particularly in great municipal centers. We scarcely know who lives next door. The doctor comes, and we wonder who is sick; there is crape on the doorknob, and we wonder who has died. Yet the teaching of Jesus is not wholly ineffective, else why the general interest just now in the finding of a kidnapped child? There is scarcely a mother who is not praying that God will relieve the suspense of the agonized parents concerning their little one. The lost baby has become, in a sense, an inmate of every home. This sympathy is a tribute to the gospel of universal fellowship. Had not Jesus taught us to say, "Our Father," we could scarcely be thinking thus of the lost child as if it were ours. It is only in gospel light that "one touch of nature makes the whole world kin."

It is the business of Christ's people to concern themselves not only with the affairs of the neighborhood, but in the larger life of the Commonwealth. No man who has caught the genius of the Gospel can be indifferent to politics. It is by reason of our inadequate apprehension of the real principles of Christianity that we are forced to lament the present lack of public sentiment as to abuses in our municipal affairs. There are enough Christian people in New York to put an end to all prevailing corruption if only they cared about it. The power of an enlightened public sentiment has been recently shown in London, with reference to the Sunday newspaper. The *Mail* and the *Telegraph* began to print Sunday editions, only to be met by vigorous protests on every hand. I know not what measures were put in operation, what sort of sanctified boycott was instituted; it is enough that, for some reason, both papers have been constrained to withdraw their Sunday issues. Why is it that there is no corresponding outburst of Christian sentiment in our American cities? It cannot be because there is one standard as to Sabbath observance in England and another in America. It can only be on account of a lamentable indifference. We know well enough that the Sunday newspaper is an incalculable evil and a manifest violation of divine law; yet we care so little that many among us lend our patronage and become accessory to the sin.

We find another instance of culpable indifference on the part of Christian people in the matter of universal Missions. There is no divergence of opinion as to Christ's purpose respecting the conversion of the world. The Great Commission is quite clear, and equally clear is our duty concerning it. Yet we are told that the annual contribution of the Church is only about ten cents *per capita* for the conversion of the nations. Was not Doctor Duff right when he said, "We are playing at Missions?" The trouble is, many among us do not care deeply whether the world is converted or not, do not care whether Christ's commission is carried out or not, do not care whether his Kingdom is established on earth or not. "Don't care" is preventing the advent of Christ. "Don't care" is responsible for the evils that prevail in public life. "Don't care" must be held to an account for much of the crime and beggary in our streets. Indifferent Gallio blocks the wheels of progress everywhere.

In 1791 William Pitt and Edmund Burke, dining together in London, discussed the evils of the time. The dangers of the French Revolution were threatening England. Pitt said, "Never fear, my friend, you may depend upon it we shall go on as we are until the Day of Judgment." To which Burke replied, "Very likely; but it is the Day of No Judgment that I am afraid of." And, indeed, this is the ominous fact. Men look at great problems and pass no judgment. They look askance at great responsibilities and avoid them. They see the wounded traveler on the Bloody Way to Jericho and pass by on the other side. They care for none of these things. But in the light of the gospel and in prospect of the Judgment, it is the business of all earnest men, and certainly of such as profess to be Christians, to care and care profoundly for all things that have to do with the welfare of men here or hereafter. Nero has gone into history not more for his cruelty and dissoluteness than for his fiddling while Rome was burning. Gallio, with all his amiable qualities, is yet immortalized only by his culpable indifference to matters of importance occurring about him. This is the lesson, then; care for truth, care for virtue, meet the responsibilities of your life, be in earnest. There is no neutral ground for earnest men. Be fully persuaded in your own mind; and be able to give an answer to every man that asketh a reason for the hope that is in you.

THE BATTLE OF THE TWO WILLS

"Then cometh Jesus with them unto a place called Gethsemane, and saith unto the disciples, Sit ye here, while I go and pray yonder. And he took with him Peter and the two sons of Zebedee, and began to be sorrowful and very heavy. Then saith he unto them, My soul is exceeding sorrowful, even unto death: tarry ye here, and watch with me. And he went a little farther, and fell on his face, and prayed, saying, O my Father, if it be possible, let this cup pass from me: nevertheless, not as I will, but as thou wilt. And he cometh unto the disciples, and findeth them asleep, and saith unto Peter, What, could ye not watch with me one hour? Watch and pray, that ye enter not into temptation: the spirit indeed is willing but the flesh is weak. He went away again the second time, and prayed, saying, O my Father, if this cup may not pass away from me, except I drink it, thy will be done. And he came and found them asleep again; for their eyes were heavy. And he left them, and went away again, and prayed the third time, saying the same words. Then cometh he to his disciples, and saith unto them, Sleep on now, and take your rest: behold, the hour is at hand, and the Son of Man is betrayed into the hands of sinners. Rise, let us be going; behold, he is at hand that doth betray me."—Matthew 26, 36–46.

Let us begin with a syllogism. *First premise:* God's will is perfect. *Second premise:* God wills with reference to every man. *Conclusion:* The perfect man is he whose will is adjusted to the will of God.

And here is the occasion of the struggle. What we need is to have our wills brought into conformity to the divine will; but, alas! though the spirit be willing the flesh is weak. The wrestling of Jacob at the brookside "all night long till break of day" finds a sympathetic response in every earnest life. That was a stern grappling of the human and divine, each bent on winning, each refusing to let the other go. But at length omnipotence touched the thigh of human infirmity and its sinew shrank; and Jacob went limping away, triumphant in his defeat; as it is written, "When I am weak then am I strong." And indeed no man is successful in the moral province until God has grappled and thrown him; that is, until the human is brought into conformity to the divine will. He who thus succumbs is crowned "Israel," because as a prince he hath prevailed with God.

We observe a parallel also in Paul's record of the strife between the carnal and the spiritual. "I see another law in my members warring against the law of my mind"; "for to will is present with me, but how to perform that which is good, I find not.—For the good that I would, I do not: but the evil that I would not, that I do.—O wretched man that I am! Who shall deliver me from this body of death? I thank God through Jesus Christ our Lord!" He represents himself not as one loving bondage, but as a slave struggling to be free yet desperately hampered by his chains. He knows his happiness lies in his emancipation; yet he resists the magnanimous efforts of his divine antagonist to deliver him. He can triumph only in the shrinking of nis thigh. Here is the meaning of that hopeful cry, "I thank God, through Jesus Christ our Lord!"

The conflict thus outlined in the experience of Jacob and of Paul finds its consummation in Gethsemane, in Christ the representative Man, made in all points like as we are only without sin. Here is the Battle of the Two Wills at its best and fiercest. The victory of Christ is signal and glorious, finding expression in the words, "Father, thy will be done!"

> "Like him who came and conquered there,
>   In that low garden,
> So rise we victors from our prayer;
>   Christ is our warden,
> And holdeth crowns for us to wear.
> 'Thy will be done!' we bow and say;
>   What cometh after
> Is but the dawning of the day;
>   If tears or laughter,
> *God's will and ours move but one way.*"

The key of this mysterious struggle in Gethsemane is this relation of the human and divine wills. Here is the deep fountain that sent forth those piteous appeals and agonized cries. Let us follow, as we may, the line of that conflict from its beginning in the earthly life of Jesus to the bitter hour when, in the stress of battle, he sweat as it were "great drops of blood."

I. *The Advent of Christ was in pursuance of the divine will.* It was God's purpose, in which Christ himself was wholly acquiescent, that he should go into the world, in fullness of time, and suffer and die vicariously for the salvation of men.

In the sixth chapter of Isaiah we are introduced into the eternal councils of the Trinity, where a voice is heard, "Whom shall I send, and who will go for us?" The cry of the ruined race for help had come up to heaven, and there was no eye to pity and no arm to save. Should they be left to perish in their sin? Nay! "Then said I, 'Here am I, send me!'" Is it the prophet Isaiah who thus volunteers; or does he speak as the living type of One who should be wounded for the world's transgressions and bruised for its iniquities, that by his stripes the race of sinners may be healed?

If the Messianic character of that prophecy be questioned, let us interpret it by comparison with another. In the fortieth Psalm it is written, "Sacrifice and offering thou didst not desire; mine ears hast thou opened (that is, to the cry of suffering humanity and to the divine decree of salvation). Burnt offering and sin offering has thou not required. Then said I, 'Lo, I come! in the volume of the book it is written of me, I delight to do thy will, O my God! yea, thy law is within in my heart'." Here David seems to be speaking for himself; but is there not a deeper reference to David's greater Son? Is he not setting forth, out of his own experience, a sweet prophecy of what the Christ shall do in fullness of time when, in pursuance of the eternal purpose, he shall bear the world's sin in his own body on the tree?

If there be still a lingering question as to the Messianic character of these predictions, let us turn to the tenth chapter of the Epistle to the Hebrews, where the interpretation is made clear: "For the law having a shadow of good things to come, and not the very image of the things, can never with those sacrifices, which they offered year by year continually, make the comers thereunto perfect. For it is not possible that the blood of bulls and of goats should take away sins. Wherefore, *when He cometh into the world, he saith*, Sacrifice and offering thou wouldest not, but a body hast thou prepared me: in burnt offerings and sacrifices for sin thou hast had no pleasure. Then said I, Lo, I come (in the volume of the book it is written of me) to do thy will, O God. Above when he said, 'Sacrifice and offering and burnt offerings and offering for sin thou wouldest not, neither hadst pleasure therein; which are offered by the law'; then said he, 'Lo, I come to do thy will, O God!' He taketh away the first that he may establish the second. By the which will we are sanctified through the offering of the body of Jesus Christ once for all."

II. *The Life and Ministry of Jesus Christ were wholly in line with this expression of the divine will.* We have seen that he came into the world in pursuance of an eternal decree respecting his redemptive work. He girt himself with omnipotence, bound on the sandals of the preparation of the gospel, and went forth from heaven as the knight-errant of the ruined race. He next appears in the incarnation; a Child lying in a manger. Great is the mystery of godliness, God is manifest in flesh!

And from that point onward his life ran parallel to the great purpose. When his enemies called his credentials in question he defended himself in these words: "I seek not mine own will, but the will of the Father which hath sent me." (John 5, 30.)

At the age of twelve years he was found in the temple, sitting among the doctors, probably reasoning with them out of the Scriptures concerning this divine purpose of redemption. On being reproved by his parents he replied, "Wist ye not that I must be about my Father's business?" Thus it appears that from the very beginning he recognized his work, was familiar with the divine plan and was resolved to pursue it.

At the outset of his ministry he was led of the Spirit into the wilderness to be tempted. The stress of that temptation was to divert him from his intention of dying for the children of men. It closed with an offer which profoundly appealed to his natural aversion to death. The adversary, taking him up into an high mountain, showed him, as with a wave of the hand, all the kingdoms of the world and said, "I am the prince of this world. I know thy purpose: how thou comest to set up thy kingdom by the power of the cross. But why shouldst thou suffer and die? These kingdoms are mine. One act of homage and I will abdicate! Fall down and worship me and thou shalt have them all." But to that alluring suggestion the Lord made answer, "It is written!" that is, the plan has been eternally marked out and there can be no other way. He thus kept himself in line with the great purpose, even in that bitterest hour; "and, behold, angels came and ministered unto him."

He sat upon the curb of Jacob's well, near to Sychar, while his disciples went into the city to buy food. On their return they found him talking with an abandoned woman concerning the great truths of the endless life. "Master, eat," they said: he replied, "I have meat to eat that ye know not of." Seeing their look of wonder, he continued, "My meat is to do the will of him that sent me and to finish his work."

To do God's will,—that was the sole end and aim of that wonderful life. But to keep himself thus in sympathy with the divine will involved constant struggle, else he would not be a man. As a man, he had a sovereign will, the only difference between his will and ours being that his was unfettered by sin. As a man like ourselves, his will must needs be responsive to his senses. When he was an hungered and the flesh cried "Eat," he answered, "I will." At the close of a weary day in his carpenter-shop, when nerves and sinews cried "Rest," he answered, "I will," and laid himself down to sleep. And being constituted in all points as other men are, sin only excepted, he must have shared with us in the universal dread of suffering and death. This brings us to Gethsemane, where we view the strenuous shock and crisis of the battle.

III. *The thickening struggle is seen in Christ's approach to his cross.* As the end drew near he set forth on his last journey to Jerusalem. At Cæsarea-Philippi he discoursed with his disciples concerning the decease which he was presently to accomplish; he told them plainly that he must suffer and die. Chill as winter and dark as an Egyptian night fell the shadow of the cross over him. Little wonder that he was "very sorrowful." He was himself without sin, but the world's burden was upon him. On reaching Jerusalem he had much to say, through Passion Week, of his sufferings and death. His voice in the upper room had all the tender pathos of a mother's farewell to her dear ones. The night closes more and more densely about him until, at length, taking with him the three chosen, he comes to the garden of Gethsemane. "Tarry ye here," he says to them, "while I go yonder and pray."

And there under the shadow of the olive trees the great struggle was fought to a finish. The purple cup of death was pressed to his lips. He knew what it meant: the shame, the anguish, the awful gloom at noonday, the abandonment of friends, the momentary taste of hell in the hiding of his Father's face, the heartbreak of sorrow for others' sin—these were in that bitter cup. He would have been less than a man had he not shuddered; less than a man had he not cried, "O my Father, if it be possible, let this cup pass from me." He wrestled like Jacob at the brook. He struggled like Paul in the grip of Death, crying, "Who shall deliver me?" He moaned, "My soul is exceeding sorrowful." He fell upon his face in anguish. His "sweat was as it were great drops of blood." But he won! Knowing that the drinking of that cup was necessary to salvation, he drank it to its dregs, saying, "O my Father, if this cup may not pass away from me, except I drink it, thy will be done." So he became obedient unto death for us. He won the victory; and he won it as our representative. O blessed Christ, thou canst be touched with a feeling of our infirmity! Thou knowest what it is to face the King of Terrors! Thou knowest what it is to close in with a most divine and gracious purpose while the flesh shrinks and quivers. Thou hast fought even through the Valley of the Shadow for us! Thou wast "exceeding sorrowful" and "sore amazed" and "very heavy" at the visage of Death: but thou didst conquer; and conquest now is possible for us "through Christ which strengtheneth us."

All was easy after that. There could be no further resistance. The sword of Peter flashed from its scabbard to defend him from his adversaries; but he said, "Put up thy sword into the sheath": and to those who sought him he said, "I am he." He could have swept them away with a breath from his nostrils, but his path was marked out. "He was led as a lamb to the slaughter and as a sheep before her shearers is dumb, so he opened not his mouth." He ran through Via Dolorosa with willing feet, his heart singing, "In the volume of the book it is written of me; 'I rejoice to do thy will.'" They nailed him to his cross and he struggled not. His soul was saying, "Even so, Father, for so it seemeth good in thy sight." They lifted him up between heaven and earth and mocked his anguish. "Come down," they cried, "if thou be the Christ!" But he could not come down, since he was serving the divine will. He suffered on, like an unhorsed knight trudging to his destination. Legions of angels were hovering over his cross ready, at a word from those parched lips, to draw the nails and bear him to his throne; but every fevered drop of blood and every quivering nerve cried out, "O God, thy will be done!" At the end he said with a loud voice, like one who stands on the parapet, mortally wounded but victorious, "It is finished!" And thus was the world saved, by the blending of the will of Jesus with the perfect will of God.

The lesson is clear. The perfect man is he who lives the Christlike life. The crossing of the two wills is sin; the blending of the two wills is victory over sin. He who knows his own Gethsemane has found the peace that passeth understanding and can sing, whatever comes,

> I worship Thee, sweet Will of God,
>   And all Thy ways adore;
> And every day I live, I seem
>   To love Thee more and more.
> I love to kiss each print where Thou
>   Hast set Thine unseen feet:

> I cannot fear Thee, blessed Will,
>   Thine empire is so sweet.
> I have no cares, O blessed Will,
>   For all my cares are Thine;
> I live in triumph, Lord, for Thou
>   Hast made Thy triumphs mine.
> Ill that He blesses is our good,
>   And unblest good is ill;
> And all is right that seems most wrong,
>   If it be His dear will.

The best definition of a Christian is that which Christ himself has given; "Not every one that saith unto me, 'Lord, Lord,' shall enter into the kingdom of heaven, but he that doeth the will of my Father which is in heaven."

The secret of an earnest life is in the exhortation of Paul: "I beseech you, brethren, by the mercies of God, that ye present your bodies a living sacrifice, holy, acceptable unto God, which is your reasonable service. And be ye not conformed to this world: but be ye transformed by the renewing of your mind, *that ye may prove what is that good, and acceptable and perfect Will of God.*"

And the consummation of life is reached when we can pray as Christ has taught us, saying, "Our Father who art in heaven, thy will be done."

www.ingramcontent.com/pod-product-compliance
Lightning Source LLC
Chambersburg PA
CBHW030307240426
43673CB00040B/1091